W9-DHW-540

WOOD® MAGAZINE

35 great
**Outdoor
Projects**

STERLING PUBLISHING CO., INC.
NEW YORK

Edited by Peter J. Stephano

Designed by Christine Swirnoff

Library of Congress Cataloging-in-Publication Data Available

10 9 8 7 6 5 4 3 2 1

Published by Sterling Publishing Co., Inc.

387 Park Avenue South, New York, NY 10016

This edition is based on material in *WOOD*® Magazine

© 2005 by *WOOD*® Magazine

Distributed in Canada by Sterling Publishing

c/o Canadian Manda Group, 165 Dufferin Street

Toronto, Ontario, Canada M6K 3H6

Distributed in Great Britain by Chrysalis Books Group PLC

The Chrysalis Building, Bramley Road, London W10 6SP, England

Distributed in Australia by Capricorn Link (Australia) Pty. Ltd.

P.O. Box 704, Windsor, NSW 2756, Australia

Printed in China

Sterling ISBN 1-4027-1175-1

For information about custom editions, special sales, premium and

corporate purchases, please contact Sterling Special Sales

Department at 800-805-5489 or specialsales@sterlingpub.com.

Contents

This arbor/swing combo can be adapted for a number of outdoor applications. See how on page 123. If you'd like to add the swing, you'll find the step-by-step instructions on page 88.

This deck structure was created by scaling down a much larger pergola design. Learn how to build it on page 126.

1

Your Outdoor Spaces

RESIDENTIAL LANDSCAPES, as we have come to know them, are similar to homes. To want to spend time in these outdoor spaces, you need them to provide "rooms" for both private hideaways and open areas for entertaining. The outstanding ones offer places to dine, read, and nap, just like your home. How they're separated and what you decorate them with help create a sense of place that secludes you, but at the same time keeps you in touch with the world. They become spaces that you not only like to see, but desire to spend time in for relaxing, socializing, or simply enjoying the natural surroundings.

This first chapter will give you an overview of these kind of places, as well as direction in creating them using the outdoor projects set forth later in this book. This chapter, and this book, though, are not intended to be a treatise on residential landscaping.

Rather, they will help you glean new ideas on ways you can improve and personalize your outdoor spaces to make them the best they can be.

There are many ways to define spaces for different activities in your landscape. Creating sidewalks and pathways is one. Using differing textures, such as grass, brick, and cobblestone, is another. Plantings of various heights, foliage, and color work as natural dividers, too. Then, you have the option of low walls and fences to subdivide contrasting areas.

The most attractive and inviting outdoor settings combine all of the above with structures—arbors, gazebos, pergolas, and trellises. For example, the combination arbor/swing structure shown on the facing page offers not only a quiet spot for reading or conversation with its comfy seating, but a distinctive focal point as well. If the swing were removed, the pergola-like arbor could well become an entryway to another outdoor space.

Larger wooden structures also have their place in defining spaces. A roomy, unattached raised deck is the solution for many home-owners. Even a small deck at the rear of the house, shaded by a pergola (such as shown on *page 6*) works wonders. And although the pergola looks complicated, you'll be surprised how relatively easy it is to build.

Power Tool Safety

- *Always use sharp blades.*
- *Disconnect the power supply before changing blades.*
- *Make sure the switch is off before plugging in the saw.*
- *Keep fingers away from the blade, and never look away when cutting. Wear eye and ear protection.*
- *Finish cuts with a smooth motion, shutting off the switch at the end.*
- *Don't overload on a cut or let the blade bind. Cut in two passes if needed, and support the work.*
- *Never wear loose-fitting clothing.*
- *Replace a frayed cord.*

BASIC GUIDELINES FOR BUILDING OUTDOOR PROJECTS

Normally, outdoor structures aren't difficult to build because they don't require complex joinery. But you some-times need more than one pair of hands for the final assembly of some large projects (**1–1**).

Building your own outdoor projects is satisfying and a lot less expensive than buying them. For the task, normal do-it-yourself tools will do. They include a jigsaw (**1–2**), portable circular saw (**1–3**,), hammer, measuring tape and marker, level, and framing square. An exterior-quality elec-trical extension cord of sufficient gauge (#14) is a must, and so is a step ladder (wood or fiberglass is best, for safety reasons). For posts, you'll need a post-hole digger, shovel, and a container for mixing concrete (a wheelbarrow works well for this).

If you're set up for wood-working, you're also in a good position to build the projects in this book. A tablesaw (or radial-arm saw), router, drill press or drill/driver, bandsaw, or jigsaw will prove helpful. A thickness planer and a scrollsaw will help in some cases, but the work can usually be accomplished without them. (Refer to Power Tool Safety above.)

For a harmonious setting, you'll want to thoughtfully select materials for your project(s). Do you want a subdued, natural look? Then choose wood that weathers gracefully without a finish, such

An outdoor structure usually requires more than one pair of hands for the final assembly.

1–1.

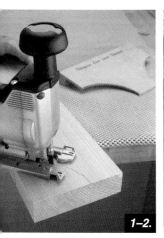

1–2. 1–3.

Left: *A portable jigsaw comes in handy for scrolling details.* **Right:** *Circular saws can produce the cuts needed on dimensional lumber.*

as cedar or pressure-treated lumber. Or maybe you'd like to paint what you build to match your house colors, or to contrast with them.

The greatest difference between crafting outdoor furniture and building other projects is the materials used. The elements of rain and sun have disastrous effects on the woods, adhesives, fasteners, and finishes typically employed for furniture. In Chapter 2, you'll get a rundown of your options when selecting exterior materials and finishes. Whatever your choices, make them consistent for visual appeal.

Remember, too, that, due to the weathering effects mentioned above, outdoor furniture normally requires finish renewal. Paints dull and wear over time, as do surface-type clear finishes, such

The Adirondack style dates back 100 years and still remains popular. Its clean, sturdy lines enhance any setting. Find plans for many such pieces in Chapter 3.

as spar varnish. Clear penetrating oils also need reapplication. You'll have to consider these realities when you decide what furniture pieces to build.

➤*Note: Before you build any large outdoor structure, check with your local government's zoning department for restrictions that may apply. If you don't, and you're found in violation of local ordinances, what you built may have to come down!*

There's no reason to spend less time choosing the furnishings for your outdoor spaces than for interior ones. Pick styles that suit the spaces available that you'll feel comfortable using.

OUTDOOR PROJECT DESIGNS

Outdoor Furniture

You'll find a myriad of styles of outdoor furniture to choose from. Adirondack-style pieces, as shown in **1–4**, conjure up images of green mountains and blue lakes. Although

1–4.

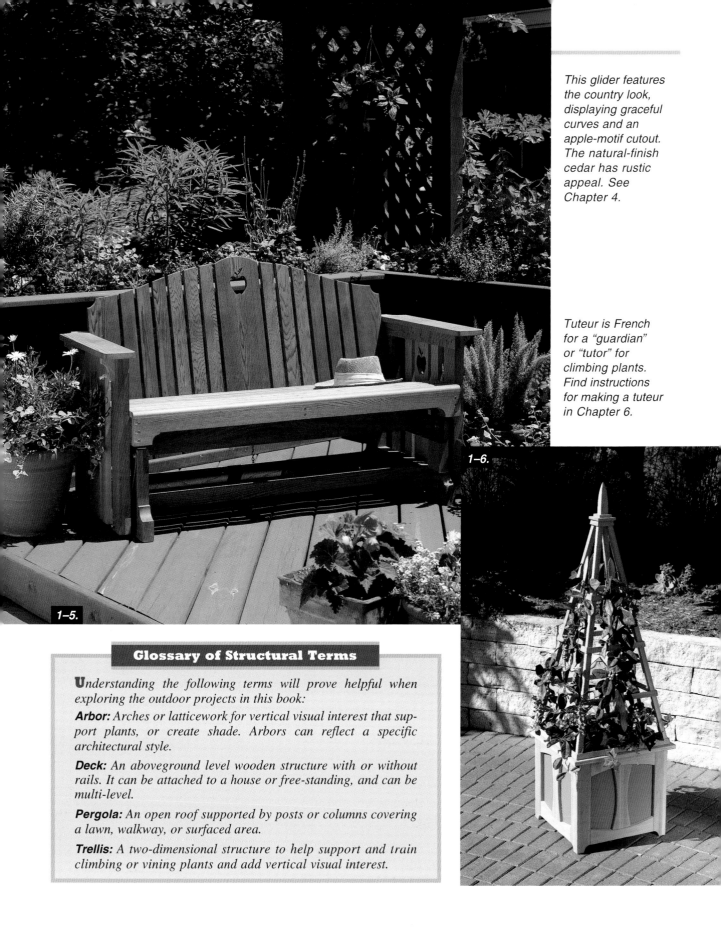

This glider features the country look, displaying graceful curves and an apple-motif cutout. The natural-finish cedar has rustic appeal. See Chapter 4.

Tuteur is French for a "guardian" or "tutor" for climbing plants. Find instructions for making a tuteur in Chapter 6.

1–6.

1–5.

Glossary of Structural Terms

Understanding the following terms will prove helpful when exploring the outdoor projects in this book:

Arbor: Arches or latticework for vertical visual interest that support plants, or create shade. Arbors can reflect a specific architectural style.

Deck: An aboveground level wooden structure with or without rails. It can be attached to a house or free-standing, and can be multi-level.

Pergola: An open roof supported by posts or columns covering a lawn, walkway, or surfaced area.

Trellis: A two-dimensional structure to help support and train climbing or vining plants and add vertical visual interest.

These lanterns with a copper iris motif will add an appealing glow to an evening gathering. Make them following the instructions given on page 171.

1–7.

thought of as "lawn" furniture, pieces in this style adapt to any setting, and look equally attractive in a natural finish, as in a painted one. In Chapter 3, you'll discover how to build an entire suite.

You might also feel at home with the country-rustic look, as evidenced in the glider shown in **1–5**. Of course, there are formal designs for outdoor furniture (as well as less formal ones). See the wide selection of building projects in Chapter 4.

Decorative Accessories

Just as within the home, the decorative accessories you choose to accent your outdoor spaces can make the difference between spectacular and ho-hum. Freestanding or hung trellises supporting

colorful vines add a bright touch, as do planters filled with blooms. Imagine the tuteur and planter shown in **1–6** on your patio.

Such details add to the enjoyment and beauty of your home as seen from outdoors. Therefore, included in the following pages are a mailbox/planter combination (*page 160*) and a great-looking house-number project that lights up the night (*page 166*). Also alluring are the candle lanterns shown in **1–7**.

Projects for Birds

There are some projects that look great, and others that do something great. That's why you'll enjoy the offerings in Chapter 7 devoted to

building for birds. Make the delightfully attractive birdbath shown in **1–8** and described on *page 174*. There's also an innovative clock birdhouse that

Birds need water, but their "watering hole" might as well be decorative.

1–8.

1–9.

Why get your knees dirty and sore? Look for this bench in Chapter 6.

of help in Chapter 6. In addition to the gardening bench and trellis shown in **1–9** and **1–10**, you'll learn how to build a heavy-duty potting bench. You'll also like the wall-hung trellis for creating a stunning display. Finally, a planter has been included that's perfect for the patio. Use it alone, or combine it with a tuteur.

And just in case you'd like to do a window treatment outside your home, you'll want to build several of the window-box design on *page 155.*

Now you'd better begin some serious reading, and then start building. Enjoy the projects!

fits perfectly on your deck or patio (*page 180*). You'll also find plans for some birdhouses designed especially for your favorite songbirds (*page 185*) and learn all you need to know about creating homes for your feathered friends.

Of course, birds have to eat, too. So build the suet feeder on *page 178* and begin the popular practice of bird feeding. Hang it from eaves near a window, and you'll soon be watching a feathered flock dining on your offerings. Build several for friends and neighbors—they're easy enough to construct.

Helpful Garden Accessories

Whether it's growing flowers for the mantel or vegetables for the table, you'll probably like to get your hands in the dirt because

gardens are a part of your landscape, too. Flower borders and planting beds not only define outdoor spaces, but give them a special beauty and mood. Whether formal or informal, flower gardens add seasonal color and texture, as do paint and wallpaper inside your home.

Even vegetable gardens add interest to a setting when structures for climbing beans or cucumbers are added. And why not think of interesting colors when building these structures, for example, dark green against light, feathery tops, and solid hues? You'll find a whole range of colors by referring to structures shown in seed catalogues or displayed in the nursery section of your local home center.

No matter what varieties you choose to grow, you'll find plenty

A traditional fan-shaped trellis is perfect for climbing roses, so why not beans? Build one from a single cedar 2 x 6. See how on page 158.

1–10.

2

Materials for Building Long-Lasting Projects

WHEN it comes to creating projects out of wood for use outdoors, remember that even the most finely crafted pieces won't hold up for long under the elements unless you have taken the materials into consideration from the very beginning. You must know which wood species to use and how to use them; what types of glues and fasteners do the best job; and which finishes will best foil the effects of weather.

In this chapter, you'll learn how different wood species react to outdoor conditions (2–1). Some require paint for longevity; others don't. And you'll discover what happens if you don't apply a finish.

Then there's the option of fasteners. Find out why they're not all created equal when it comes to durability.

The same story goes for adhesives. Choosing the right wood and the appropriate fasteners or adhesive can make the difference between projects that look good for only a season or two, and ones that last for decades.

Finishes provide the final touch. Later in this chapter is information on the finishes best suited to defy the effects of weather as well as their most suitable applications.

All of these subjects are discussed for one main purpose: To help you build projects you'll be proud to use and enjoy for years.

THE BEST WOODS FOR OUTDOOR PROJECTS

Many trees withstand the elements for centuries without a complaint. But cut one down and mill it into lumber, and it becomes vulnerable to extreme heat and cold, wind, rain, snow, ice, airborne pollutants, damaging ultraviolet rays, and more. Fortunately for us, some species hold up much better than others.

Softwood Choices

Several decades ago, almost everybody used redwood for patio furniture and other outdoor projects. Back then, the stock was widely available at a reasonable

2–1.

Common materials for outdoor projects.

Board Characteristics

How well a board resists decay depends largely on what part of the tree it came from.

Heartwood, the tree's mature interior wood, is the toughest. In many species, you can easily identify heartwood by its much deeper color.

Sapwood, which comes from the outer part of the tree, is generally lighter in color, and is a lightweight performer when it comes to strength and decay resistance. When you can, try to avoid sapwood of any species for outdoor use.

price in the higher grades that showcased the wood's warm, rich, reddish-brown heartwood.

Nowadays, many lumbermen complain about the dwindling availability of high-grade redwood. If you can find it and afford it, redwood works well for outdoor use. However, cedar costs much less than redwood, and is much more widely available. Depending on where you live, you may find your lumberyard stocked with cedar native to your region, such as western red or northern white. All cedar species are moderately soft with generally straight grain and a coarse texture.

Pressure-Treated Lumber

Pressure-treated (PT) lumber—typically southern pine saturated with chemical preservative—works especially well for fences, decks, and other outdoor structures. Prior to 2004, the most common PT preservative was chromated copper arsenate (CCA), which gave new lumber a greenish tinge. As the wood weathered, it turned gray. However, the arsenic in CCA lumber was ruled

hazardous to health by the U.S. Environmental Protection Agency and was virtually banned after 2003.

Now, more user-friendly preservatives such as amine copper quat (ACQ) and copper-azole are used instead. Both ACQ and copper-azole products are at first green. After weathering, ACQ lumber turns gray, while copper-azole becomes brownish.

When you shop for PT lumber, look for material certified by the American Wood Preservers Bureau. A stamp on each board

Safety Tips When Working with Treated Lumber

Caution: The chemicals that make wood resist decay are poisons. Observe these precautions when you work with treated lumber:

● *Wear gloves. Wash your hands thoroughly after working with PT wood.*

● *Don a dust mask. Avoid inhaling sawdust when working with treated timber.*

● *Wear eye protection when sawing and nailing.*

● *Bury waste wood or take it to a proper disposal agency. Never burn treated wood, especially indoors.*

discloses when the wood was treated, with which chemical, and where you can use the wood for best results. Either of these products can be painted or stained.

Hardwoods

Hardwoods—domestic and imported—also work well for outdoor projects. White oak, probably the most widely available exterior-grade domestic hardwood, has closed cells that make it highly resistant to decay. Don't try to substitute red oak; its open-cell structure makes it much more likely to suck up moisture that eventually will destroy your carefully crafted project.

The heartwood of white oak is a grayish brown, the sapwood nearly white. Other native exterior-use hardwoods (though not available in every region) include bald cypress, honey locust, black locust, and sassafras.

Imported hardwoods can give your outdoor project an exotic look, but at an exotic price. Heavy teak's heartwood varies from yellow brown to dark golden brown, and has an oily feel that sloughs off moisture but also inhibits gluing and finishing.

The mahogany family offers several good choices, including genuine mahogany (also called Honduran or Central American mahogany) and African mahogany (or khaya). Lauan, often incorrectly called Philippine mahogany, also works great for outdoor furniture and other projects.

Boardwalks on the East Coast pioneered the use of even more exotic hardwoods as decking material that looks good and lasts practically forever. Tropical species such as jarrah, ipe, and bangkirai are marketed under the brand name Iron Woods. Pau lope is the marketing moniker for a South American hardwood.

MISCELLANEOUS MATERIALS

Sheet Goods

When you choose sheet goods for the outdoors, make sure the glues used in their manufacture have an exterior rating. With plywood, look for the manufacturer's exterior-grade stamp.

Besides plywood, you can select siding with decorative patterns milled or embossed into its surface. For a smooth look, choose exterior-grade, medium-density fiberboard. Its nonporous surface allows you to apply a sleek, painted finish.

Screws

Many types of screws are labeled as appropriate for exterior applications, but only a few hold up to the elements (**2–2**). Among the most common options are stainless steel (which comes in different grades), silicon bronze, and steel with one of several available coatings (**2–3** and **2–4**). They are discussed on *page 16*.

TABLE 2–1	Common Materials for Outdoor Projects			
NAME		**COST**	**AVAILABILITY**	**COMMENTS**
Redwood		High	**Hard to find**	It's soft, easy to work, moderately stiff, and in some areas, dimensionally stable.
Red cedar		Moderate	**Widespread**	Lightweight, with good dimensional stability, it has relatively low structural strength.
Pressure-treated pine		Moderate	**Widespread**	Because it's not kiln-dried, treated lumber is treated pine prone to shrinkage, a factor you need to allow for in your project design.
White oak		Medium	**Widespread**	Durable and weather resistant, but not intended for structural use in contact with soil.
Mahogany		Medium	Widespread	Some types offer spectacular grain patterns that have made mahogany a furniture wood prized for centuries.
Teak		Very high	Limited	Easily worked with hand and power tools, but silica in the wood dulls cutting edges.
Plywood		Moderate	Widespread	Exterior-grade plywood is generally more stable than solid lumber; it warps, twists, and contracts very little.
Fiberboard		Moderate	Widespread	Exterior-grade, medium-density fiberboard makes an excellent base for a painted finish.
Exterior siding		Moderate	Widespread	Plywood and hardboard siding panels bring siding texture to outdoor projects.
Composites	See samples 7-10 in illustration 2–2 below.		Widespread	Practically weather/rot-proof, low maintenance, colors fade, non-loadbearing

2–2.

*All-season materials: **1.** Ipe (a tropical hardwood); **2.** 2x pressure-treated pine; **3.** 5/4 pressure-treated pine; **4.** 2x western red cedar; **5.** 5/4 western red cedar; **6.** 2x redwood; **7.** 2x Trex composite; **8.** TimberTech composite; **9.** 5/4 Trex composite; **10.** 5/4 Trex composite (brown). Be selective when choosing screws for your outdoor projects.*

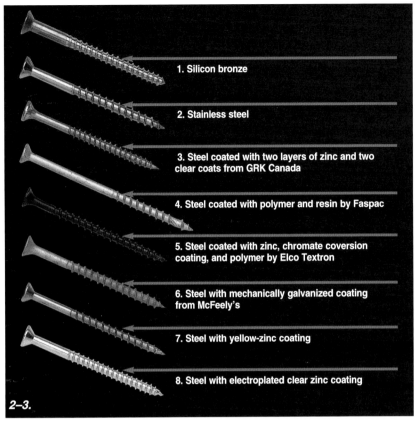

1. Silicon bronze

2. Stainless steel

3. Steel coated with two layers of zinc and two clear coats from GRK Canada

4. Steel coated with polymer and resin by Faspac

5. Steel coated with zinc, chromate coversion coating, and polymer by Elco Textron

6. Steel with mechanically galvanized coating from McFeely's

7. Steel with yellow-zinc coating

8. Steel with electroplated clear zinc coating

2–3.

Some options for screw materials and coatings.

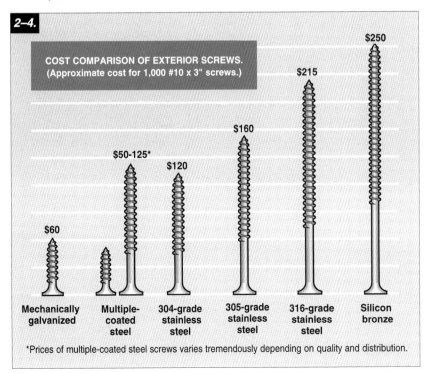

2–4.

COST COMPARISON OF EXTERIOR SCREWS.
(Approximate cost for 1,000 #10 x 3" screws.)

$60 — Mechanically galvanized
$50-125* — Multiple-coated steel
$120 — 304-grade stainless steel
$160 — 305-grade stainless steel
$215 — 316-grade stainless steel
$250 — Silicon bronze

*Prices of multiple-coated steel screws varies tremendously depending on quality and distribution.

Cost comparison of exterior screws.

Although aluminum and brass resist corrosion, they are not included here because they are too soft for most applications. Also, aluminum will corrode quickly when it comes in contact with the chemicals in treated lumber.

● *Stainless steel.* Screws made of this material may cost twice as much as coated steel fasteners, but stainless steel is well worth it if you don't want to see any rust or stain marks on your project. Whenever you invest time or expensive lumber in a clear-finished project, it doesn't make sense to use anything but stainless steel.

Most widely available stainless steel fasteners are either 304 or 305 grade. Both are appropriate for general use, although 305-grade fasteners have slightly greater corrosion resistance. For maximum corrosion resistance in extreme environments, say one where salt spray is common, spend the extra money for 316-grade stainless.

● *Silicon bronze.* This material is the standard in marine fasteners because it resists corrosion and doesn't promote rot in the surrounding wood. It costs about twice as much as 304-grade stainless steel, so reserve screws made of this material for boat-building.

● *Coated steel fasteners.* Because of the many available coatings, and different processes for applying them, this category can be confusing to say the least. Most local hardware outlets still sell the galvanized fastener as their basic exterior-grade fastener. Generally, the thicker the galvanized coating (consisting mostly of zinc), the more durable it will be. You'll find the thickest zinc coatings on hot-dipped nails, but you may have a difficult time finding hot-dipped galvanized screws. That's because the thick, globby coating tends to clog the threads and driving recess of the screw, making it difficult to drive.

Commonly available galvanized screws are either mechanically galvanized or electrogalvanized. You can quickly tell these two types apart because mechanically galvanized screws have a dull gray surface, and electrogalvanized screws have a shiny silver-color surface. Do not use electrogalvanized screws (also called clear-zinc coated) for exterior applications. They will corrode quickly when they come in contact with the elements.

Mechanically galvanized screws are generally suitable for decks and other projects made of pressure-treated lumber. Nevertheless, you should not use them with PT lumber that comes in contact with the soil, in high-moisture areas, or in areas with salt content in the air. Also keep in mind that mechanically applied zinc contains some iron that is susceptible to attack from the tannic acids that occur in redwood and cedar. The acids combine with the iron to form a dark stain around the fastener head.

shop TIP

❶ Use screws, not nails, to join your outdoor projects. Screw threads provide gripping strength to better resist inevitable wood movement that results from outdoor exposure.

❷ When driving screws into hard materials, such as PT lumber or hardwoods, opt for a screw in the largest gauge available. For example, many outlets carry 3" deck screws in No. 8 gauge, but you'll have fewer snapped screws if you spend the extra money on No. 10 screws.

If you plan to drive in deck screws near the ends of boards without predrilling, look for a fastener with an auger, serrated, or fluted point, such as the ones shown in 2–5. In tests, these screws were less likely to split the wood, and the serrated and fluted screws proved noticeably easier to drive in when using long screws in hard materials.

Square-drive and star-drive (also called Torx) recesses grip driver bits better than do Phillips-head or combination Phillips/square recesses (2–6). It is difficult to strip out a square- or star-drive recess or do serious damage to their coatings. By contrast, Phillips recesses strip out occasionally, and combination recesses, although handy, strip out excessively.

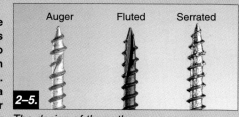

2–5. *The design of these three tips above helps prevent splits (see inset at right). Outer coatings on low-cost screws can wear off in one pass through a PT 2x board.*

2–6. Square drive | Phillips/square drive | Star (Torx) drive | Phillips drive

Screws with star- and square-drive recesses resist stripping better than those with Phillips-drive recesses, and greatly outperform screws with combination Phillips/square-drive recesses.

As you can see in **2–3**, manufacturers have improved the basic electrogalvanized fastener by adding a polymer coating (often pigmented) on top of the galvanized coating. These multiple-coated screws have several advantages. First, some of the coated screws come in colors that help the fastener blend with natural and pressure-treated wood tones. Also, the additional coatings increase corrosion resistance. For example, the outer coatings resist tannic acids, making them suitable for use with cedar and redwood.

These coatings also help prevent iron stain if the coating remains intact. This type of stain should not be confused with extractive bleed. (The latter can occur with any fastener.)

Nevertheless, any coating has the potential to wear through and expose the underlying steel to corrosion. This wear typically happens when you drive the fastener. As already shown, some low-cost coated screws lose part of the coating covering their threads after one drive through 2x PT lumber.

Virtually all fasteners show some wear in the coating covering the driving recess. If you are less than careful and leave the head of the screw slightly above the surface, foot traffic will abrade the coating, too. Therefore, it is suggested that you buy a few sample screws and test-drive them in the material you intend to use. Also, ask the manufacturer about how well the screw holds up in a salt-spray test; disregard any fastener not test-rated for a minimum of 1,000 hours.

● *Yellow-zinc coated steel.* Although fasteners with this electroplated coating are sometimes labeled as corrosion resistant, they are not appropriate for external applications.

Anchors: The Steel Solution

The old, reliable method for setting a post—dig a hole, stand the post in it, and then pour in some concrete—may be fine for installing fences. However, it's not necessarily the best way to anchor an arbor or other yard or garden structure.

For one thing, the surface of the fill around the base of the post often comes out lower than ground level. This allows water to pool around the post base, which can lead to rot. Also, the extra bury length required for the posts usually makes prebuilding a structure impractical.

Steel post bases and anchors offer a simple, effective means of mating a 4 x 4 wooden post to a concrete footing. And with one

variety, you don't even have to pour concrete, because like a metal stake, you just drive it into the ground, and tighten two bolts to clamp the post into its collar.

You'll find two kinds of bases for attaching posts to concrete footings—ones that you can fasten to concrete that's already cured and ones made to be embedded in wet concrete.

Bolt-Down Post Bases

For outdoor structures, bolt-down post bases provide solid mounting (**2–7** and **2–8**). They establish a standoff distance of about 1" between the bottom of the post and the concrete, which keeps the foot of the post above ground moisture and puddled water. The base attaches to an existing

Attach a post to existing concrete with a bolt-down base, as shown. For new work, embed an anchor bolt for the base in the concrete when you pour. You can nail these bases to wood, too. Both provide a 1" standoff height for weather exposure.

Embedded bases like the ones shown here go into the concrete as you pour your footing. Outside, use the one in the foreground, which provides 1" moisture-protection standoff when installed. The base behind it sits flush with the surface, so it's best suited for use in dry, sheltered places.

2–7.

2–8.

concrete footing with a ½" anchor bolt 5" long. To install the bolt, drill a hole for it in the concrete; then cement it into the hole with mortar or an epoxy masonry adhesive. Set the bolt so that the end extends about ¾" above the surface.

After the mortar or epoxy cures, secure the base with a nut and washer. Then, position the post, and nail or screw it in place.

Putting in a Base When Pouring Concrete

When you're pouring new concrete footings for a project, you can choose between the post bases designed to be embedded in the concrete or the bolt-down variety. Deciding which to use is largely a matter of preference or convenience.

Embedded bases offer simplicity: After pouring the concrete, you simply stick the base in place, level and align it, and then let the concrete cure.

➤*Caution: If you're anchoring a prebuilt project that has several posts, putting one base even slightly out of alignment can cause untold woe.*

For projects like these, you'll do better using the bolt-down anchors. To save the effort of drilling a hole in the footing, though, embed the bolt in the concrete when you pour it. Set the bolt in the center of each post

location; post-base designs allow some leeway for proper positioning when you bolt them down.

You also can take advantage of steel anchors when joining posts to another wooden structure, such as a deck or porch. Just nail or screw the base to the mounting surface. A U-shaped base like the one shown in **2–8** will suffice in situations where no moisture-protection standoff is necessary.

Advice on Using Anchors

When building and anchoring a structure, keep the following points in mind:

● Check local building codes for any particular requirements or limitations.

● The post bases shown here are recommended for anchoring posts that have a supporting top structure.

● Always use the number and size of fasteners specified for the base.

● Don't substitute drywall screws for nails; instead, use screws of the type and size specified by the base manufacturer.

● Outdoors, or where water may splash onto the foot of the post, install a base that stands the bottom of the post about 1" above the surface. This prevents water from puddling around the bottom of the post and wicking into the end grain.

Glues that Stick, Despite the Elements

Many adhesives make claims of being weatherproof, but no single glue can fill all your needs when building for the outdoors. Take a look at the types of joinery you'll use and the moisture your project will encounter, and then choose the glues. Here's a look at the different types of glues:

Exterior-rated yellow glue. Like regular yellow woodworking glue, this product sets up fast, giving you about 5 to 10 minutes between application and clamping. Workpieces should remain clamped for at least one hour. This type II glue (see the Shop Tip Type I and Type II Glues) is appropriate for screwed in or bolted joints on projects that will sometimes be exposed to rain, but rarely venture under water.

Epoxy. Because so many varieties exist, epoxies are tough to pin down. Some are type I waterproof, while others (mostly the fast-curing 5- and 10-minute formulations) are not. Some are thick enough to use as mixed, while others must have a thickener, such as fumed silica (shown in **2–9**), added before they can be used as an adhesive. Boatbuilders prefer epoxy because it fills gaps in joints and doesn't require clamping. Most epoxies can even join glass, plastic, or metal to wood with lasting results.

2–9.

Adding a thickener (such as the mound of silica shown) turns some epoxies from coatings into strong, paste-like adhesives.

2–10.

Resorcinol glue lines are nearly invisible in the walnut lamination on the right, but the dark lines can be a distraction in lighter-colored woods.

Polyurethane. Since coming on the U.S. market, this one-part type II glue has proven itself as versatile as epoxy but without the

shop TIP

Type I and Type II Glues

You've probably read of water-resistant glues being rated as "type I" or "type II" but wondered what that means. Is one more waterproof than the other? In fact, the U.S. government tags type I honors on an adhesive that survives strength-testing after repeated cycles of drying and dunking in boiling water.

Glues earning a type II rating were not strength-tested, but showed virtually no separation or delamination after repeated wet/dry cycles in room-temperature water.

In the real world, most of the type IIs are as weatherproof as the type Is are. However, a type I rating can give you an extra measure of confidence that your project will last.

messy mixing. Although a bead of polyurethane will expand two to three times its size to fill gaps, that foamy lattice has no strength—so joints must be tight for a strong bond. Polyurethane cures better in the presence of moisture, making it the ideal adhesive for pressure-treated lumber.

Resorcinol. Traditionally considered one of the best type I adhesives for laminating, resorcinol withstands submersion in salt water better than other glues, so it's a great candidate for projects that are constantly exposed to salty sea air. However, as you can see in **2–10**, resorcinol leaves a highly visible dark red or purple glue line that can be unattractive on projects made from light-colored wood, such as ash.

Finishes that Resist the Elements

You probably don't think of your deck, patio, or yard as a harsh environment, but nature's relentless assault takes its toll on things made of wood. You can, though, diminish the effect of this assault.

If you leave redwood, cedar, or pressure-treated wood unfinished, the weathered look soon will predominate, complete with natural checks and slight surface imperfections. In time the wood will turn gray—a color unappealing to many, and the first stage in wood deterioration. But if the rich, natural hue of new lumber appeals to you, you need to apply a product that leaves a surface film on the wood. And that presents a bit of a problem.

Outdoors, wood has two formidable foes: moisture and the ultraviolet (UV) rays in sunlight. Exterior finishes provide differing degrees of protection against those elements. Here's how to select the one that is right for your requirements (**2–11**).

Clear Finishes for Natural Color

Spar varnish, polyurethane varnish, water repellents, and penetrating oils shield wood from water while allowing all the color to show through. But clear finishes let UV rays penetrate into the grain. The wood cells react to these rays and begin to deteriorate, causing a minor commotion underneath the film. The wood

2–11.

A selection of finishes useful for outdoor projects.

Opaque Stains

Opaque stains resemble paint in that they conceal the wood's natural color, while allowing the texture to show. They're available in a variety of natural-looking colors and brighter hues, and in both oil and latex base. You also can choose either a flat opaque stain or a low-luster finish that improves washability.

Because the pigment in this type of stain is suspended in an oil or latex carrier, it's possible that all wood surfaces won't be penetrated equally. On horizontal surfaces especially, pigment that doesn't completely penetrate may collect, causing blotchy areas that wear off or blister. Also, the California Redwood Association does not recommend using stains with a latex base on redwood products.

Treated lumber, with its greenish hue, requires that you select a compatible stain color because the green tends to alter

darkens and the finish cracks, blisters, and peels.

Adding a UV filtering agent to the finish retards this reaction, but doesn't completely do away with it. If you plan to use a clear finish, be sure the one you select has UV absorbers (read the label). Even with UV protection, you'll have to renew the finish at least every two years. If you wait until it peels, you will be faced with a tedious stripping and refinishing job.

Tinting Wood with Semitransparent Stains

With their light pigmentation, semitransparent stains allow wood's natural grain and texture to show through (**2–12**). These stains are available in tones that closely match various woods. Brighter stains can either contrast with or complement your house, deck, or patio. Semitransparent

stains usually have an oil base and offer only moderate resistance to UV rays, and you'll have to recoat them every few years.

Semisolid stains have more pigment than semitransparent stains and more UV resistance as well, but they're not completely opaque.

2–12.

New, no finish | Weathered, no finish
Water repellent | Semitransparent
Solid-color stain | Spar varnish

A look at different finishing considerations.

the final appearance. With treated wood, you might want to experiment with several different stain colors until you achieve the effect you are looking for. (Some manufacturers offer special 4-ounce samples that help you take the guesswork out of selecting their products.)

Paint for Wood and Metal

Paint—from flat to glossy—isn't used often on the top grades of redwood or cedar because it completely hides grain, texture, and color. But it can be the solution to covering the greenish hue of treated wood. And for protecting metal parts, you have no other choice.

If you decide to paint a wooden outdoor project, no matter what wood you've selected, be sure to apply an oil- or alkyd-based primer first, and then sand slightly before finishing for better adhesion. On metal, use a primer or topcoat containing rust inhibitor.

You can expect painted furniture's horizontal surfaces to undergo much more wear and tear than do vertical surfaces, such as fences or house siding, so avoid the need for early renewal by selecting the highest-quality exterior-grade enamel available.

And finally, while all of these products retard or prevent wood deterioration, none of them succeed completely (or for very long) without recoating. The chart on *page 23* compares exterior finishes with their longevities.

Elements of a Long-Lasting Paint Job

How long your paint job lasts depends on the first decision you made when you started your project—which wood to use. Some woods simply hold paint better than others. For instance, softwood with narrow bands of summerwood (the dark portion of the grain) and fine-grained hardwoods hold paint better.

Preparation is key, too. Paint will not stick well to the hard, glossy, planed surface most lumber has when it comes from the mill: You have to roughen the wood to give it some tooth. Sanding the bare wood before painting extends paint life, as does applying a paintable water repellent or water-repellent preservative.

Next, apply an alkyd (oil-based) exterior primer (**2–13**). (Generally, oil-based primers hold up better than water-based latex primers.) Prime all exposed surfaces and any parts that will come in contact with the ground. Cover the alkyd primer with two topcoats, either latex or oil-based. And, don't lay on extra-heavy coats expecting better protection; thick coats probably will crack, resulting in less protection for your handiwork. Ideally, the dried coating—primer and both topcoats—should be about as thick as a sheet of newspaper.

Final Coat

First Top-coat

Brushed-On Alkyd Exterior Primer

2–13.
Elements of a long-lasting paint job.

Lightening Wood with Bleach

Stains put color into wood. Bleaches take it out, letting you lighten almost any wood to a nearly white color. The trick with bleaches is to use the right one for the right job. Two-part bleach—sodium hydroxide and hydrogen peroxide—removes the natural color from wood. Chlorine bleach removes dye from wood, just as it removes color from laundry. Oxalic acid removes rust and water stains. Whichever type you use, neutralize it afterward as directed by the maker, sand lightly, then apply a clear finish.

Laying the Finish On

After you've decided on a finish for your outdoor project, you need to figure out how you're going to get it from the can onto the wood (**2–14**). The applicator that's right

TABLE 2–2	Outdoor Finishes at a Glance				
FINISH TYPE	**APPEARANCE**	**APPLICATION**	**COATS**	**RENEW**	**COMMENTS**
Spar varnish	Gloss	Brush, spray	2 to 3	1 to 2 years	When spar varnish fails, its finish cracks and peels; removing an old finish is tough.
Polyurethane	Gloss	Brush, spray	2 to 3	1 to 2 years	Sunlight causes the finish semigloss to darken and crack; hard to remove.
Water repellent	Dull sheen	Brush, roll on	1 to 2	1 year	Wood eventually darkens repellent and must be lightly sanded before renewal.
Penetrating oil	Dull or flat	Wipe on/off	1 to 2	6 months	Wood weathers and the surface darkens. Frequent renewal is a hassle.
Bleach	Lightens a clear finish.	Brush, wipe on/off	NA	NA	Gives wood a pale, weathered wood's natural look that must be protected with color.
Semitransparent stain	Flat	Brush, roll on	1	2 years	Transparency lets the wood grain stain show through; eventually the color fades and the wood weathers.
Opaque stain	Flat	Brush, roll on	1	2 years	Conceals wood's grain but not its texture. Pigments can blotch and wear off.
Paint (oil, acrylic, latex bases)	Flat to high gloss	Brush, roll, spray	2	2 to 3 years	Conceals both grain and texture in wood. Prime first. Special paints for metal include rust inhibitor.

for this job depends partly on the finish you've chosen, partly on the amount of surface you have to cover, and partly on the look you want. Here's what's available for applicator options.

Brushes

These trusty tools get the nod for most finishing chores. Just be sure to purchase brushes with synthetic bristles (nylon, polyester, or a nylon/polyester blend) for water-based finishes and latex paints or natural (animal hair) bristles for oil-based finishes and paints. The reason: Because of their pores, natural bristles absorb loads of water, making them puffy and hard to control. And oil-based finishes will attack and break down synthetic bristles, which means you'll end up with bristles sticking to the surface. Disposable foam brushes work fine with either type of finish, and do an especially good job with stains.

Methods for applying a finish include brushes, rollers, pads, and mittens.

2–14.

Rollers

Rollers make short work of large, flat surfaces, and you can also buy smaller trim rollers for getting into tight spots. Both types have a plastic or wood handle (often machined to accept an extension handle) and a metal frame on which the roller cover is installed.

The type of finish—water- or oil-based—determines the type of cover your roller needs. Luckily, most covers, which are manufactured from mohair, lamb's wool, acetate, or polyurethane foam, are labeled with the finish for which the roller was designed.

You'll also notice on the package that roller covers vary in nap depth—from $\frac{1}{16}$" to $1\frac{1}{2}$". Use long naps for rough surfaces, short ones for smooth work. The nap in turn is fastened to a cardboard or plastic sleeve. If you're using water-based finish, buy a roller with a plastic sleeve. For oil-based finish, your best bet is a cardboard sleeve.

Pads and Mittens

Pad painters may consist of a carpet-like material or plastic foam inserted in a plastic mop-like applicator or a paint brush handle.

Though excellent for applying paint to almost any surface, they really earn their keep with irregular ones, such as shakes, railings, spindles, fencing, screening, and shutters.

A painting mitten makes short work of coating railings, spindles, and similar items. You simply put on a thin, disposable plastic glove to keep your hand clean, stick it into the thick-nap mitten, and dip the mitten into the finish. You can coat a railing or spindle quickly by grasping it and sliding the mitten along its length. And you can poke finish into narrow or cramped places where a brush would only create spatters.

Sprayers

For a smooth, rich finish that goes on in a hurry, consider spraying the finish onto your project with an aerosol can or pressurized spray gun (**2–15**). Spraying can be messy, of course, but now you can find equipment that shoots finishes through a pad like the one on a pad painter.

Pressurized painting has gotten neater, too, thanks to high-volume, low-pressure (HVLP) equipment. Unlike conventional spray guns, which blast out air at up to 40 pounds per square inch, HVLP units need only 4 to 10 psi to do the job. The result: Up to 85 percent of the finish lands on the workpiece compared with 36 percent for ordinary sprayers. You waste less finish and you don't get overspray on everything in sight.

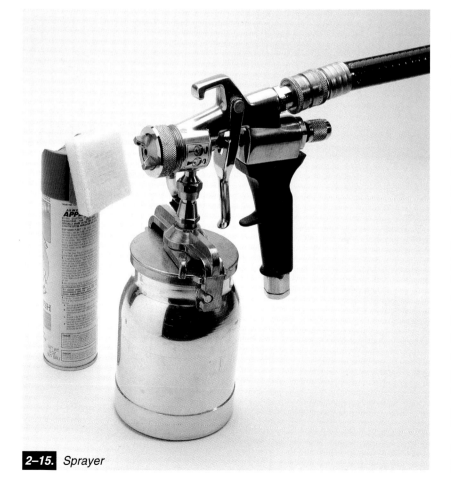

2–15. *Sprayer*

3

Traditional Adirondack Furniture

DURING the late 1800s and early 1900s great lodges in New York's Adirondack Mountains beckoned families to come and spend their summer vacations there. The mountains were appealing, with their sparkling lakes and cool breezes blowing through the tree tops. Furniture was placed on the long porches, green lawns, and lake fronts for guests to gather, relax, and enjoy the setting.

The furniture favored back then featured wide boards, simple lines, and sturdy construction. Yet, it was designed for comfort, and proved irresistible for lazy times. At some point, that style came to be called "Adirondack," and its popularity has never dwindled.

This chapter includes seven pieces of furniture designed in the Adirondack style. The first four—a chair, footstool, table, and rocker—are meant as a set for eye-catching placement in your outdoor setting. The next three pieces—a chair, footrest, and double settee—display more of a Northwoods or lakeland look. You'll quickly discover how easy all are to build and may want to make several while you're at it. When you're finished, take a load off your feet and lounge around, Adirondack style.

ADIRONDACK LAWN CHAIR

Cut the Chair Pieces

1 To form the chair-back splats, rip and crosscut a piece of 1" pine (¾" actual thickness) to 7 x 33" (A), a second piece to 5 x 29", and a third to $5\frac{7}{8}$ x $26\frac{1}{2}$".

2 Mark a $3\frac{1}{2}$" radius on one end of A, and a $2\frac{15}{16}$" radius on one end of the other two boards. Using a bandsaw or portable jigsaw, cut the radii on the three boards, and then finish-sand edges and surfaces. (A palm sander can be used.) Rip the two $5\frac{7}{8}$"-wide boards in half to make two splat B's and two splat C's.

3 Rip and crosscut the three back support pieces (D, E, F) to the sizes listed in the Materials List. The parts are shown in **3–3** and **3–4** (*page 28*). Then, cut a piece of

Adirondack lawn chair

Materials List for Adirondack Lawn Chair

PART	FINISHED SIZE			MATL.	QTY.
	T	W	L		
A center splat	¾"	7"	33"	P	1
B* inside splats	¾"	2⅞"	29"	P	2
C* outside splats	¾"	2⅞"	26½"	P	2
D lower support	¾"	3½"	19½"	P	1
E top support	¾"	1½"	18½"	P	1
F mdl. support	¾"	3¼"	25"	P	1
G seat supports	¾"	4⅞"	37½"	P	2
H slats	¾"	1½"	21"	P	13
I front legs	¾"	5½"	19¾"	P	2
J* supports	¾"	3¼"	3¼"	P	2
K armrests	¾"	6¼"	28"	P	2

*Initially cut parts marked with an * oversized. Then, trim each to finished size according to the instructions.
Material Key: P = Pine.
Supplies: ⅜" dowel, double-faced tape; #8 x 1" flathead wood screws; #8 x 2" flathead wood screws; exterior primer; and paint.

scrap the same size as D for use later.

4 To form leg/seat supports (G), use double-faced tape to tape together (face-to-face) two pieces of 1 x 6 measuring at least 37½" in length. Transfer the Leg/Seat Support pattern (**3–5** on *page 29*) onto the top piece, and then cut both pieces to shape (a bandsaw can be used for this). Sand the cut edges to remove the saw marks. Separate the pieces and, referring to the pattern again, mark the seat slat starting point and screw hole centerpoints on both of the leg/seat supports.

5 Rip and crosscut 13 seat slats (H) to size. Rip bevels on four of the slats as detailed on the leg/seat pattern *(3–5)*. Also, rip a 25° bevel along one edge of the middle back support (F) where shown on the Screw Hole Detail in **3–2**.

6 To form the front legs (I), crosscut two 1 x 6 pieces to 19¾" in length. Designate one end the top, and place a mark 5½" in from the edge. At the opposite end, mark in 2¼" from the same edge. Draw a line connecting the two marks. Tape the two pieces together and cut them to shape. Next, plane or sand to the line. (The pieces can be cut on a bandsaw, and the cut edge can be planed flat on a jointer.)

7 To shape the arm supports (J), cut two 4 x 4" squares of ¾"-thick scrap material. From

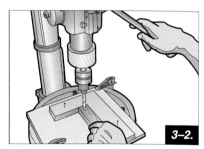

SCREW HOLE DETAIL

$3/8$" plug $3/8$" long — Sand plug flush after assembly.

#8 x 1" F.H. wood screw

$3/4$"

$3/8$" hole $1/4$" deep

(H)

$7/64$" pilot hole $1/2$" deep

$5/32$" hole, countersunk

#8 x 1" F.H. wood screws

(A) (B) (C)

(C) (B)

$1 \frac{7}{16}$"

$2 \frac{3}{4}$" half lap $3/8$" deep

(F)

$1 \frac{7}{16}$"

$3/8$" hole $1/4$" deep with a $5/32$" hole centered inside

$7/64$" pilot hole $1/2$" deep

(H)

(D)

$3/8$" plug $3/8$" long

(K)

(J)

$5 \frac{1}{2}$"

$2 \frac{1}{2}$"

$3/4$"

R=$3 \frac{1}{4}$"

$1 \frac{3}{4}$"

$19 \frac{3}{4}$"

$13 \frac{1}{2}$"

$1/4$"

$2 \frac{1}{4}$"

(I)

(H)

$3 \frac{1}{4}$" half lap $3/8$" deep

#8 x 2" F.H. wood screw

(G)

(J)

(K)

(I)

2"

1"

1"

10"

3–1.

EXPLODED VIEW OF LAWN CHAIR

#8 x 1" F.H. wood screws

one corner, use a compass to draw a $3 \frac{1}{4}$" radius. Then, cut and sand the two pie-shaped arm supports to shape.

8 Rip and crosscut two pieces of stock to $6 \frac{1}{4}$ x 28" for the armrests (K). Tape the two pieces together face-to-face. Then, enlarge and transfer the Armrest pattern (**3–5** on *page 29*) to the top piece of stock. Cut the armrests to shape. Sand the cut edges, then separate the two. Transfer the screw centerpoints from the pattern onto both of the armrests.

9 Cut a $3 \frac{1}{4}$" half lap $3/8$" deep across the bottom side of each armrest where shown on **3–1** and the Armrest pattern in **3–5**. Cut a mating half lap.

Counterbore the Screw Holes

1 Chuck a $3/8$" drill bit into your drill press and adjust the stop so it drills $1/4$" deep in $3/4$"-thick stock. (A brad-point bit can be used.)

2 Lay the backrest splats (A, B, C) good face up on a flat

surface and in the order shown in **3–1**. Align the bottom ends of the boards. On both C's, mark points $3/8$", $14 \frac{7}{8}$", and $22 \frac{3}{8}$" from the bottom ends. With a straightedge, lightly draw lines across all splats connecting those marks.

3–2.

Counterboring holes in the seat slats with a drill press.

$R=3\frac{1}{2}$"

$R=2\frac{15}{16}$"

$\frac{3}{8}$" plug
$\frac{3}{8}$" long

#8 x 1" F.H.
wood screw

$\frac{1}{2}$"

$\frac{3}{8}$" hole
$\frac{1}{4}$" deep

$\frac{5}{32}$" hole
countersunk

$\frac{7}{64}$" pilot hole
$\frac{1}{2}$" deep

$\frac{3}{8}$"

25° bevel

SCREW HOLE DETAIL

(E)

$23\frac{1}{2}$"

(C)

(B)   (A)

$\frac{1}{4}$"

$19\frac{1}{2}$"

(D)

$\frac{7}{64}$" pilot hole
$\frac{1}{2}$" deep

3–3.

CHAIR BACK

$\frac{3}{8}$" plug
$\frac{3}{8}$" long

#8 x 1" F.H.
wood screw

(A)

(E)

(C)

(B)

(D)

(K)

(K)

(F)

(I)

(G)

3–4.

**ATTACHING THE
CHAIR BACK**

$\frac{3}{8}$" plug
$\frac{3}{8}$" long

(G)

#8 x 2" F.H. wood screw

the jig on the drill-press table and clamp it in place. Drill the holes.

5 Counterbore the holes in the outside faces of both leg/seat supports (G) where indicated in **3–5**. Next, mark centerpoints on the front legs for the three screw holes located on the outside face and the two on the inside face (see **3–1** for reference). Counterbore those holes in both front legs.

6 Counterbore the holes in the top surface of both armrests, using the dimensions on the armrest grid for centerpoint locations.

7 Drill $\frac{5}{32}$" holes through all of the $\frac{3}{8}$" counterbored holes. (The parts can be backed with a piece of scrap stock to prevent chip-out.)

Assemble the Lawn Chair

1 Place part D and the same-sized scrap piece you cut earlier on edge about 18" apart on a flat surface. Referring to **3–3**, lay the backrest splats (A, B, C) across part D. Space the five splats flush with the edge and ends of D. Space the five splats so the back measures $19\frac{1}{2}$" wide. Using a $\frac{7}{64}$" bit and your portable drill, drill a pilot hole through the $\frac{3}{8}$" counterbored holes at the bottom of each splat and $\frac{1}{2}$" deep into part D. (See the Screw-Hole Detail in **3–1** on *page 27* for details on how all holes are drilled and plugged.) Glue and screw the backrest splats to part D.

3 Clamp a fence to your drill-press table $1\frac{7}{16}$" from the center of the bit. Place either edge of pieces B and C and both edges of piece A against the fence, and drill $\frac{3}{8}$" holes $\frac{1}{4}$" deep centered on the pencil marks. Lay the splats aside for now.

4 To counterbore the seat slats (H), find the center at the end of a slat scrap and drill a $\frac{3}{8}$" hole $\frac{1}{4}$" deep $\frac{3}{8}$" in from the end. See the Screw-Hole Detail in **3–1** for reference. Next, make the right-angle jig shown in **3–2**. Using the scrap piece as a guide, position

3–5. **LEG/SEAT AND ARMREST GRIDDED PATTERNS**

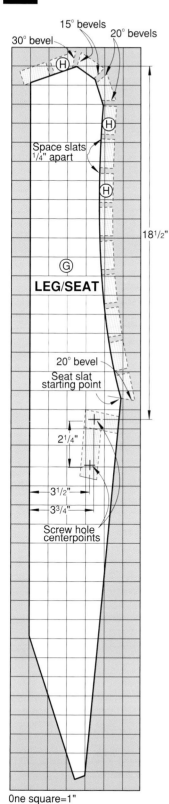

LEG/SEAT

15° bevels
30° bevel
20° bevels
Space slats 1/4" apart
18 1/2"
G
20° bevel
Seat slat starting point
2 1/4"
3 1/2"
3 3/4"
Screw hole centerpoints

One square=1"

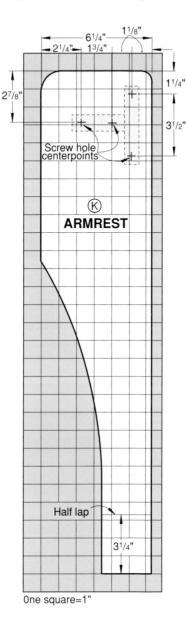

ARMREST

6 1/4"
1 1/8"
2 1/4"
1 3/4"
2 7/8"
1 1/4"
3 1/2"
Screw hole centerpoints
K
Half lap
3 1/4"

One square=1"

2 Draw a line across the back of the backrest 23½" up from the bottom, and make a mark ½" in from both edges. Position the top edge of part E on the line, then check splat spacing and total back width (19½"). Drill the pilot holes into E, apply glue, and drive the screws.

➤ *Note: For joints that have to stand up to the extremes of Mother Nature, use water-resistant glue, or resorcinol glue.*

3 Assemble the seat by standing both part G's on their bottom edge and parallel to one another 19½" (inside measurement) apart (countersunk holes to the outside). Now, place the rear beveled seat slat on top of both part G's, aligning it with the start point marks. Drill the pilot holes. Then, apply glue to the ends on the underside of the slat, reposition it, and drive the two screws. Next, position the 15° beveled slat at the nose of the seat, and attach it the same way. Now, square the seat and attach the remaining slats, spacing them about ¼" apart.

4 Using a ⅜" plug cutter, cut seventy ⅜"-long plugs. Next, glue and insert the plugs in the counterbored holes in the seat slats and backrest, aligning the grain of the plug with the piece being plugged. Let the glue dry, then sand the plugs flush.

5 Clamp the front legs (I) to part G using the dimensions in **3–1** on *page 27,* (13½" to top of

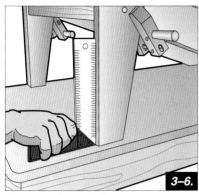

Squaring the front legs. **3–6.**

seat, and ¼" back from the front edge of the leg). Square each leg as shown in **3–6**. Adjust, if necessary. Drill the pilot holes and drive the three screws in each leg.

6 Spread an even coat of glue on the mating half-lap joints on the two armrests (K) and the back support (F). Checking the inside corners for square, glue and clamp the pieces together.

7 Apply an even coat of glue to the top of the right front leg. Then, referring to the Armrest pattern in **3–5**, position the armrest assembly (F, K), lapping the armrests over the legs ¾" on the inside and ½" on the front edge. Holding the armrest steady (this can be achieved with a couple of bar clamps), drill the pilot holes and drive the screws into each.

8 Attach the armrest supports (see **3–1**), driving the four screws into each.

9 Position and clamp the backrest assembly between the armrests and leg/seat supports,

checking that the mating surfaces are flush. With the pieces correctly positioned, drill the pilot holes into both parts D and F, and drive the screws where shown on **3–4**, *page 28.*

10 Glue and install the remaining plugs, aligning the grain of the plug with the surrounding wood. Let the glue dry, then sand the plugs flush with the surrounding wood surface.

11 Finish-sand the entire chair, and apply an exterior finish. (An enamel primer and semigloss enamel white paint can be used.)

ADIRONDACK FOOTSTOOL

Cut and Shape the Parts

1 From ¾"-thick pine stock, rip and crosscut two pieces to 3⅝ x 14½" for the feet (A), two pieces to 2 x 14" for the rails (B), two pieces to 4 ½ x 11" for the legs (C), and one piece to 2½ x 14½" for the stretcher (D). (Letter each part after cutting for easy identification while building the project.)

2 Stack the two feet (A) and rails (B) face-to-face using double-faced carpet tape. Enlarge the Foot and Rail half-pattern

grids (**3–8**, *page 32*) to full-size half patterns, and make two copies of each. Flip one copy of each over, and trace the pattern through onto the back of the paper. Then attach the halves at the centerlines to make a full-sized pattern of each. Now, adhere each pattern to one face of its respective stack.

3 Band saw the feet and rails to shape, keeping your blade outside the line. Then, sand to the line. Using your combination square, transfer the screw-hole centerpoints shown on the leg pattern to the face of the bottom leg in the stack. Separate the pieces, and drill four ⅜" counterbores ¼" deep in each foot. Repeat this procedure for the two rails. Now, drill a ⁵/₃₂" shank hole centered in each counterbore on both feet and rails.

4 Lay out and cut a ¾ x 2½" notch in one end of each leg (C) where shown in **3–9**, *page 33.* Work carefully; you want accurate cuts so that the legs will fit snugly around the stretcher. Then, set your tablesaw miter gauge at 8°, and miter-cut the other end of both legs where shown in **3–9**. (For uniformity, attach a scrap wood extension and stop block to the miter gauge and miter both legs at the same time.) Now, sand all footstool parts smooth using 100-grit sandpaper.

Adirondack
footstool

PART	FINISHED SIZE			MATL.	QTY.
	T	W	L		
A feet	3/4"	3 5/8"	14 1/2"	P	2
B rails	3/4"	2"	13 3/4"	P	2
C legs	3/4"	4 1/2"	11"	P	2
D stretcher	3/4"	2 1/2"	14 1/2"	P	1
E slats	3/4"	1 1/2"	16"	P	5
F slats	3/4"	1 1/2"	16"	P	4

Materials List for Adirondack Footstool

Material Key: P = Pine.
Supplies: Double-faced tape; #8 x 1" flathead wood screws; #8 x 1 1/2" flathead wood screws; #8 x 2" flathead wood screws; exterior primer and paint.

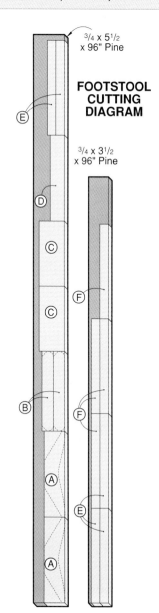

3/4 x 5 1/2 x 96" Pine

FOOTSTOOL CUTTING DIAGRAM

3/4 x 3 1/2 x 96" Pine

Assemble the Footstool

1 Assemble and dry-clamp the feet (A), stretcher (D), and legs (C) to check the fit. Then, disassemble the parts, apply water-resistant glue to the mating surfaces, and reclamp.

2 Use the shank holes in the feet as guides to drill 7/64" pilot holes in the legs and stretcher. (For dimensions, see the Footstool Exploded View and Screw Hole Detail in 3–7.) Then, drive #8 x 1 1/4" flathead screws into the feet and legs, and use #8 x 2" screws to attach the legs to the stretcher. Now, remove the clamps.

3 Glue and clamp the rails (B) to the top outside edges of the legs where shown in the Footstool Section View (3–9, on *page 33*). To do this, center both rails along the top ends of the legs, and align their top edges flush with the leg ends. Using the rail shank holes for guides as before, drill pilot holes in each leg. Now, drive #8 x 1" flathead wood screws, and remove the clamps.

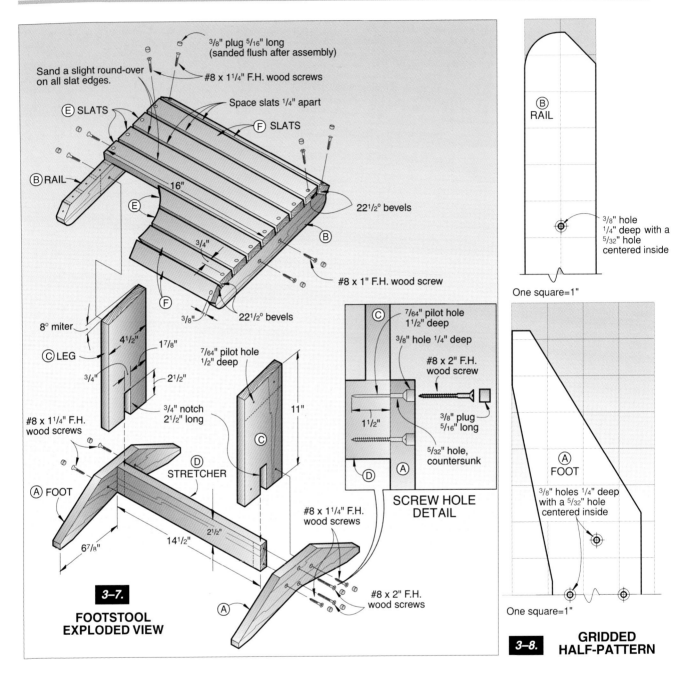

3/8" plug 5/16" long (sanded flush after assembly)

Sand a slight round-over on all slat edges.

#8 x 1 1/4" F.H. wood screws

(E) SLATS

Space slats 1/4" apart

(F) SLATS

(B) RAIL

16"

(E)

22 1/2° bevels

(B)

3/4"

(F)

#8 x 1" F.H. wood screw

8° miter

(C) LEG

4 1/2"

1 7/8"

3/4"

2 1/2"

7/64" pilot hole 1/2" deep

22 1/2° bevels

3/8"

3/4" notch 2 1/2" long

#8 x 1 1/4" F.H. wood screws

(D) STRETCHER

11"

(C)

(A) FOOT

6 7/8"

14 1/2"

2 1/2"

#8 x 1 1/4" F.H. wood screws

#8 x 2" F.H. wood screws

(A)

3–7.

FOOTSTOOL EXPLODED VIEW

SCREW HOLE DETAIL

(C) 7/64" pilot hole 1 1/2" deep

3/8" hole 1/4" deep

#8 x 2" F.H. wood screw

3/8" plug 5/16" long

1 1/2"

5/32" hole, countersunk

(D) (A)

(B) RAIL

3/8" hole 1/4" deep with a 5/32" hole centered inside

One square=1"

(A) FOOT

3/8" holes 1/4" deep with a 5/32" hole centered inside

One square=1"

3–8.

GRIDDED HALF-PATTERN

4 Measure the distance between the outside edges of the two rails. (The distance on the rails of the footstool displayed here was 16".) Cut five 1½"-wide slats (E) to this length from ¾" stock. Cut four more slats (F) to these same dimensions, but tilt your blade to 22½°, and bevel-rip one edge of each. (See the Footstool Section View [**3–9**, on *page 33*] for reference.)

5 Lay out, counterbore, and drill a shank hole at both ends of all nine slats where dimensioned on the Footstool Exploded View (**3–7**) and Footstool Section View (**3–9**). (Clamp a fence and stop block to the drill-press table to ensure uniform hole placement.) Now, sand a slight roundover on all slat edges, then sand the slats themselves smooth.

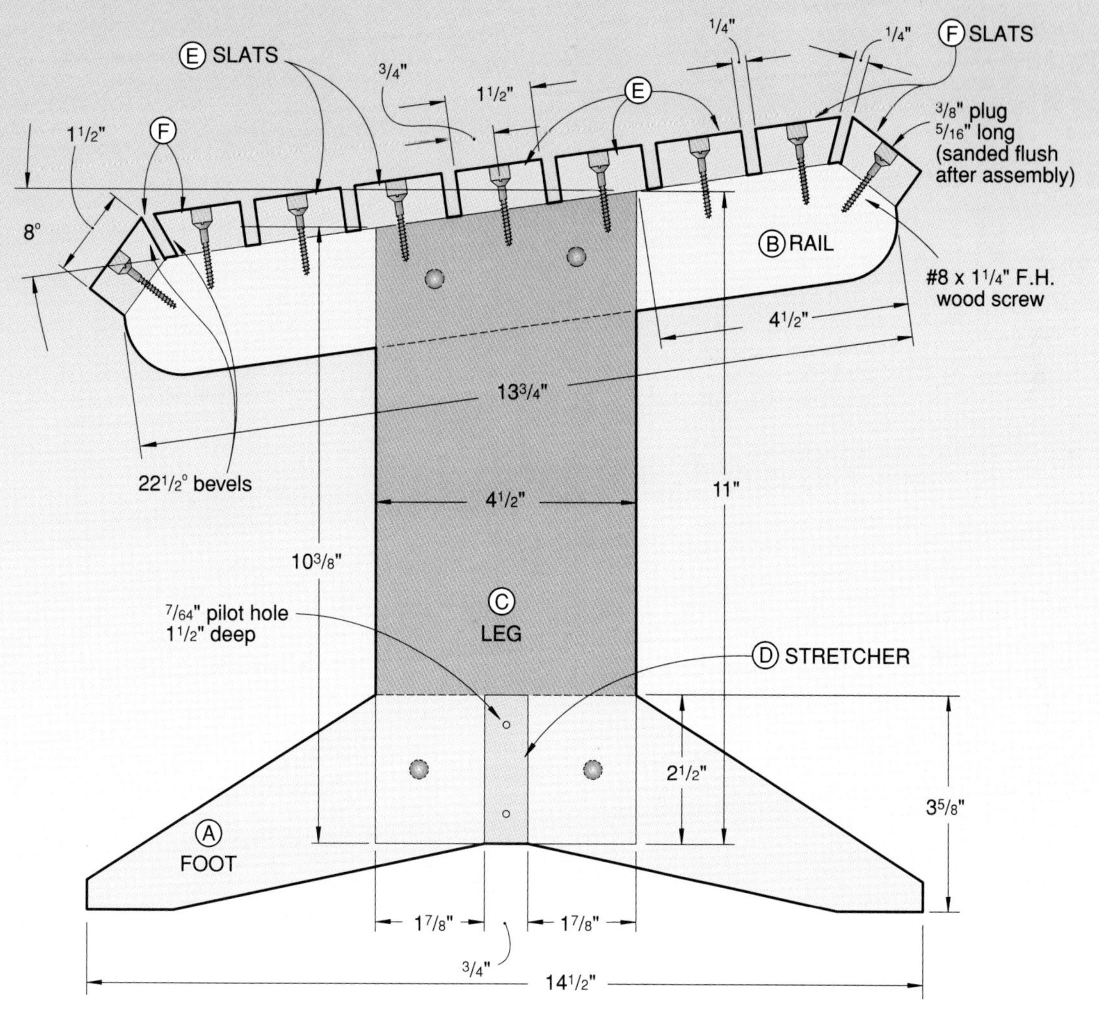

3–9.

**FOOTSTOOL
SECTION VIEW**

6 Starting with one of the beveled slats (F) on the angled flat surface at one end of the rails, attach each slat in succession using glue and screws. (For positioning, see the Footstool Section View.) After attaching the first slat, use a ¼"-thick strip of scrap to space the slats consistently.

7 To plug the counterbores, follow the same approach described for the Adirondack chair to cut, glue, align, and sand 30 plugs. Finish-sand and paint your footstool as you did the chair.

ADIRONDACK TABLE

Cut and Assemble the Table Frame

1 To make the tapered legs (A), rip and crosscut four pieces of ¾"-thick stock to 5 x 17½". Next, lay out and cut the tapered inside edge of each leg on these four pieces where shown on the Table Exploded View in **3–10**. (A tablesaw and an adjustable tapering jig were used for the table shown, but you can also use your bandsaw.)

2 Rip and crosscut two side rails (B) and two end rails (C) to the dimensions listed in the Materials List. Use a compass to mark the 2 ¼"-radius pattern shown in **3–11** onto both ends of each end rail. Next, band-saw the ends of the end rails to shape, keeping your blade outside the marked line. Then, sand to the line to complete the shaping.

3 Lay out the screw-hole center-points on the side and end rails where shown and dimensioned on

Adirondack table

the Table Exploded View (**3–10**). Then, drill and countersink 5/32" shank holes through the four rails. Now, sand the rails smooth.

4 Glue and clamp the legs (A) to the side rails (B), making sure that each leg aligns flush with the side-rail edges and ends. (➤ *Note: To withstand the elements, especially moisture, construct your table using water-resistant glue, slow-set epoxy, or resorcinol glue.*)

Next, using the shank holes you drilled in the side rails as guides, drill 7/64" pilot holes ½" deep in the legs. Attach the side rails to the legs using #8 x 1¼" flathead wood screws. Then, unclamp.

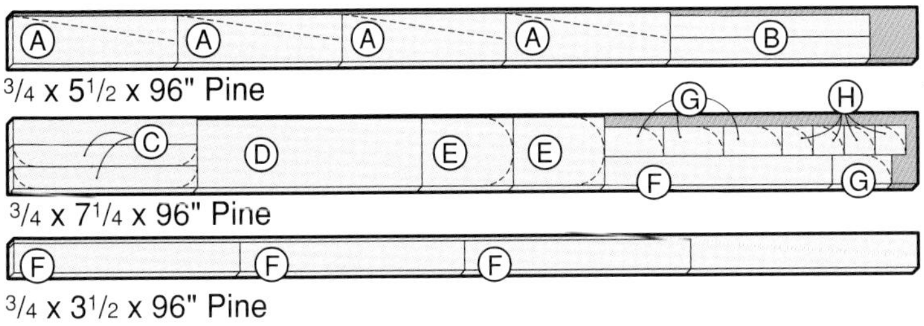

Materials List for Adirondack Table

PART	FINISHED SIZE			MATL.	QTY.
	T	W	L		
A legs	¾"	5"	17½"	P	4
B side rails	¾"	2¼"	21"	P	2
C end rails	¾"	2¼"	19½"	P	2
D top	¾"	7"	24"	P	1
E* ends	¾"	7"	9"	P	2
F top	¾"	3"	24"	P	4
G* ends	¾"	3"	5½"	P	4
H* ends	¾"	3"	2½"	P	4

*Cut parts to final size during construction. Please read all instructions before cutting.
Material Key: P = Pine.
Supplies: Double-faced tape; #8 x 1" flathead wood screws; #8 x1¼" flathead wood screws; #8 x 1½" flathead wood screws; exterior primer and paint.

TABLE CUTTING DIAGRAM

Ⓐ   Ⓐ   Ⓐ   Ⓐ   Ⓑ
³/₄ x 5¹/₂ x 96" Pine

Ⓒ   Ⓓ   Ⓔ   Ⓔ   Ⓖ   Ⓗ   Ⓕ   Ⓖ
³/₄ x 7¹/₄ x 96" Pine

Ⓕ   Ⓕ   Ⓕ
³/₄ x 3¹/₂ x 96" Pine

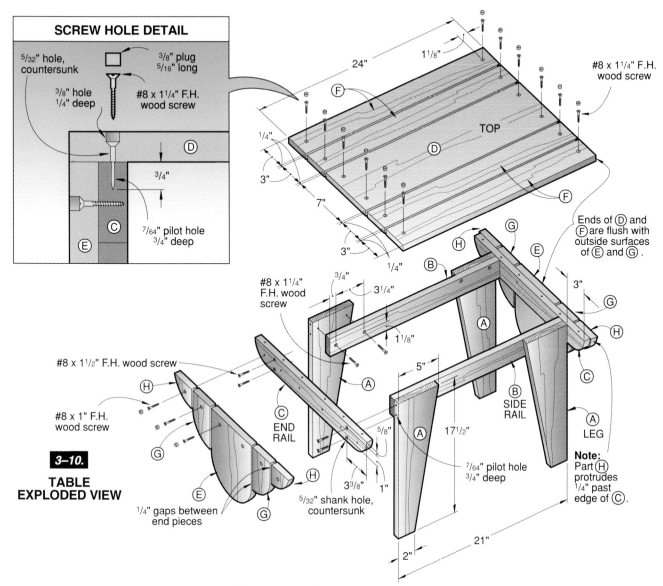

SCREW HOLE DETAIL

5/32" hole, countersunk

3/8" plug 5/16" long

3/8" hole 1/4" deep

#8 x 1 1/4" F.H. wood screw

7/64" pilot hole 3/4" deep

3/4"

24"

1 1/8"

#8 x 1 1/4" F.H. wood screw

TOP

1/4"

3"

7"

3"

1/4"

Ends of D and F are flush with outside surfaces of E and G.

3"

#8 x 1 1/4" F.H. wood screw

3/4"

3 1/4"

1 1/8"

5"

#8 x 1 1/2" F.H. wood screw

#8 x 1" F.H. wood screw

5/8"

17 1/2"

7/64" pilot hole 3/4" deep

END RAIL

SIDE RAIL

LEG

Note: Part H protrudes 1/4" past edge of C.

3–10.

TABLE EXPLODED VIEW

3 3/8"   1"

5/32" shank hole, countersunk

1/4" gaps between end pieces

2"

21"

5 Glue and screw the end rails (C) to the leg/side rail assemblies, making sure that the top edges of all parts are flush. (See the Table End View in **3–11** for reference.) Next, stand the table frame on a flat surface, and check for wobble. If the frame wobbles, identify the longest leg(s), and sand the bottom end(s) until the table sits flat. (A stationary disc sander can be used for the sanding.)

Prepare the Tabletop and End Pieces

1 From 3/4"-thick stock, rip and crosscut a piece to 7 x 24" for the tabletop center (D) and two pieces to 7 x 10" for the mating ends (E). Next, cut the four remaining tabletop pieces (F) to size. The tabletop pieces (D, F) should measure 1 1/2" longer than the distance from one end-rail face to the other. In other words,

the top pieces need to extend 3/4" beyond the outside end-rail face at each end. See the Screw Hole Detail accompanying the Table Exploded View (**3–10**).

2 Cut eight remaining end pieces (G, H) to 1" longer than the lengths listed in the Materials List.

3 Transfer the 3 1/2" radius shown in **3–11** onto one end of one E part. With the edges and ends flush, stack this part E on top of the other part E, using double-faced tape. Band-saw the radius to shape, keeping your blade just outside the marked line. Sand to the marked line. Then, crosscut the two parts E to length, separate the pieces, and remove the tape.

4 Transfer the 3"-radius pattern onto the ends of parts G and H. Then, repeat the stacking and band-sawing procedures described in the previous step. Sand all radii smooth as before. Finally, crosscut the parts to the length listed in the Materials List.

5 Lay out screw-hole center-points on the five tabletop pieces (D, F) where shown on the Table Exploded View in **3–10**.

Next, drill and counterbore shank holes as dimensioned on the Screw Hole Detail. (Clamp a fence and stop block to your drill-press table to ensure accuracy.) Using **3–11** for reference, lay out, counterbore, and drill shank holes in the ten end pieces (E, G, H). Finally, sand the tabletop and end pieces smooth.

Finish and Assemble the Table

1 Position the tabletop pieces (D, F) on the table frame where shown on the Table Exploded View in **3–10**. Center them end-to-end and side-to-side. Next, check for square, and also check to make sure you have a ¾" overhang at each end. (You can cut ¼"-thick scrap spacers

and place them between the parts to ensure even spacing.)

2 After positioning parts D and F, clamp them to the end rails (C). Using the shank holes as guides, drill $\frac{7}{64}$" pilot holes ¾" deep in the end rails. Then, screw the top pieces to the end rails using #8 x 1¼" flathead wood screws.

3 Using the same technique, attach the 10 end pieces (E, G, H) to the end rails. To do this, align each part with its mating tabletop piece, and butt it snugly against that piece. After attaching the parts, sand the ends of the top pieces flush with the outside faces of the end pieces.

4 To plug the counterbores, first cut twenty-four $\frac{3}{8}$ x $\frac{5}{16}$"

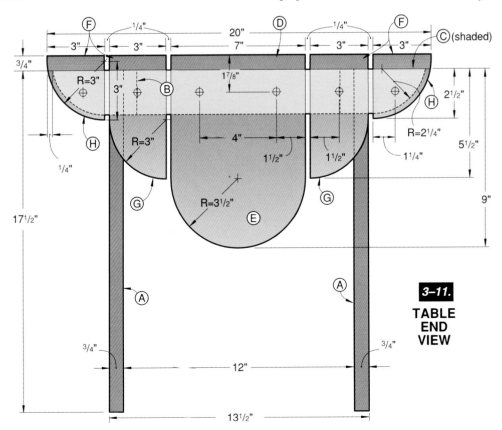

3–11.
TABLE END VIEW

plugs. (You can resaw scrap pine stock to a thickness of $5/16"$, and then cut the plugs from it with a $3/8"$ plug cutter.) Next, glue a plug into each counterbore. (Align the plug so its grain is aligned with that of the surrounding stock.) After the glue dries, sand the plugs flush.

5 Sand all surfaces that still need it. Then, prime and paint your table. (For all-weather resistance and durability, first apply an oil-based primer and, after it dries, follow with two coats of oil-based acrylic enamel paint.)

ADIRONDACK ROCKER

Cut the Back, Seat, and Support Parts

1 To make the chair-back splats, rip and crosscut two pieces of 1" clear pine ($3/4"$ actual thickness) to $7 \times 34"$ (A), two pieces to $5\frac{7}{8} \times 30"$ (B), two pieces to $5\frac{7}{8} \times 27"$ (C), and one $7 \times 28"$ piece for (D). (See the Cutting Diagram on *page 38* on how to lay out your stock.) The parts are initially cut oversized to help make cutting of the radii easier.

2 Using a compass, mark a $3\frac{1}{2}"$ radius on one end of the three 7"-wide pieces (A, D), and a $2^{15}/16"$ radius on one end of the

Adirondack rocker

four remaining pieces (B, C). (See **3–16**, *page 41,* for reference.) Next, using a bandsaw or portable jigsaw, cut the marked radii on all seven boards and sand the edges. (Saw outside the line, and sand to the line.) Rip the four $5\frac{7}{8}"$-wide boards in half (lengthwise) to make four B and four C pieces. (See Exploded View 1 in **3–12**, *page 39,* for reference.)

3 Rip and crosscut the back support pieces (E, F, G) to the sizes listed in the Materials List. Next, cut the middle back support pieces (H, I) to size. Set your tablesaw blade 25° from perpendicular, and bevel-

Materials List for Adirondack Rocker

PARTS	FINISHED SIZE			MATL.	QTY.
	T	W	L		
A splats	$3/4"$	7"	33"	P	2
B* splats	$3/4"$	$2\frac{7}{8}"$	29"	P	4
C* splats	$3/4"$	$2\frac{7}{8}"$	$26\frac{1}{2}"$	P	4
D* splat	$3/4"$	7"	27"	P	1
E support	$3/4"$	$3\frac{1}{2}"$	47"	P	1
F support	$3/4"$	4"	47"	P	1
G support	$3/4"$	$1\frac{1}{2}"$	$46\frac{1}{4}"$	P	1
H support	$3/4"$	3"	51"	P	1
I support	$3/4"$	$3\frac{1}{4}"$	$52\frac{1}{2}"$	P	1
J spreader	$3/4"$	$2\frac{5}{8}"$	47"	P	1
K seat slats	$3/4"$	$1\frac{1}{2}"$	$48\frac{1}{2}"$	P	13
L* seat supports	$3/4"$	$4^{15}/16"$	$34\frac{1}{2}"$	P	2
M* seat support	$3/4"$	$4^{15}/16"$	18"	P	1
N* legs	$3/4"$	$5\frac{1}{2}"$	$19\frac{3}{4}"$	P	2
O* rockers	$3/4"$	$4\frac{5}{8}"$	$37\frac{1}{4}"$	P	4
P armrests	$3/4"$	$6\frac{1}{4}"$	28"	P	2
Q* brackets	$3/4"$	$3\frac{1}{4}"$	$3\frac{1}{4}"$	P	2

*Initially cut parts oversized. Then, trim each to finished size according to the instructions.
Material Key: P = Pine.
Supplies: Water-resistant glue; 8d finish nails; #5 common nails; #8 x 1" flathead wood screws; #8 x 2" deck screws; #8 x 3" deck screws; exterior primer and paint.

ROCKER CUTTING DIAGRAM

$3/4$ x $7^1/4$ x 96" Pine (1 x 8)

$3/4$ x $9^1/4$ x 96" Pine (1 x 10)

$3/4$ x $7^1/4$ x 96" Pine (1 x 8)

$3/4$ x $9^1/4$ x 96" Pine (1 x 10)

$3/4$ x $9^1/4$ x 96" Pine (1 x 10)

$3/4$ x $9^1/4$ x 96" Pine (1 x 10)

$3/4$ x $5^1/2$ x 96" Pine (1 x 6)

$3/4$ x $9^1/4$ x 96" Pine (1 x 10)

$3/4$ x $9^1/4$ x 96" Pine (1 x 10)

$3/4$ x $5^1/2$ x 96" Pine (1 x 6)

$3/4$ x $5^1/2$ x 96" Pine (1 x 6)

rip one edge on H. Using the same saw-blade setting, rip a $3/8$" bevel along one edge of the second middle back support piece (I) where shown on the Screw Hole Detail in **3–14**.

4 Cut the front seat spreader piece (J) to size. Put it aside until later.

5 Cut nine seat slats (K) to the size listed in the Materials List. Saw four more seat slats (K), but bevel-rip their edges where shown on the Seat Support pattern in **3–22** on *page 43*. (Also refer to **3–17**.)

Make the Legs and Seat Supports

1 To form the seat supports (L), cut two 1 x 6 x 36" pine pieces and tape them face-to-face with double-faced (carpet) tape. Next, enlarge and transfer the Seat Support pattern (shown in **3–22**) to the top piece. Mark the hole centerpoints onto the top piece. (You can use carbon paper to transfer these lines onto the face of the top piece.) Saw the seat supports to shape. Sand the cut edges to remove the saw marks.

2 Designate the left and right supports, and mark their outside faces. While the supports are still taped together, drill the seven $5/32$" shank holes through both supports where marked. Next, drill the $3/8$" counterbores (centered over the shank holes) $1/4$" deep into the outside surfaces of both supports. (Turn the piece over in order to counterbore the holes into the outside face of the second support.) Now, separate the seat supports. If necessary, use a splash of lacquer thinner or acetone to weaken the double-faced tape's bond. Counterbore the remaining three shank holes on the inside faces of both supports. Again using the Seat Support pattern in **3–22** (*page 43*) mark the seat slat starting points on the inside face of both supports. Remove the pattern.

3 For the center seat support (M), cut a piece of 1" pine

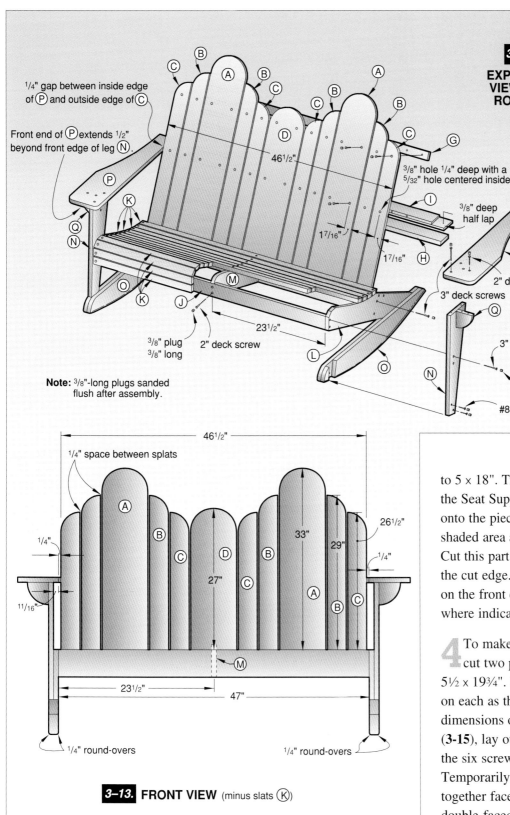

3–12.

EXPLODED VIEW 1 OF ROCKER

1/4" gap between inside edge of (P) and outside edge of (C)

Front end of (P) extends 1/2" beyond front edge of leg (N).

46 1/2"

3/8" hole 1/4" deep with a 5/32" hole centered inside

17/16"

17/16"

3/8" plug 3/8" long

#8 x 1" F.H. wood screw

3/8" deep half lap

3/8" deep half lap

2" deck screw

3" deck screws

3" deck screw

3/8" plug 3/8" long

#8 x 1" F.H. wood screw

23 1/2"

3/8" plug 3/8" long

2" deck screw

Note: 3/8"-long plugs sanded flush after assembly.

46 1/2"

1/4" space between splats

26 1/2"

1/4"

33"

29"

1/4"

27"

1/4"

11/16"

23 1/2"

47"

1/4" round-overs

1/4" round-overs

3–13. **FRONT VIEW** (minus slats (K))

to 5 x 18". Trace the front half of the Seat Support pattern (**3–22**) onto the piece (identified by the shaded area and dashed lines). Cut this part to shape and sand the cut edge. Now, cut the notch on the front edge (for part J) where indicated on the pattern.

4 To make the front legs (N), cut two pieces of pine to 5½ x 19¾". Designate one end on each as the top, and, using the dimensions on the Leg drawing (**3-15**), lay out the taper and the six screw-hole centerpoints. Temporarily tape the two pieces together face-to-face with double-faced (carpet) tape.

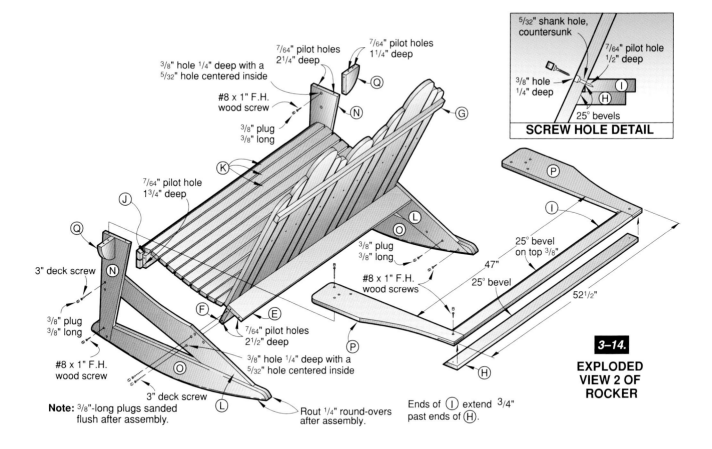

3/8" hole 1/4" deep with a 5/32" hole centered inside

7/64" pilot holes 2 1/4" deep

7/64" pilot holes 1 1/4" deep

Q

#8 x 1" F.H. wood screw

N

3/8" plug 3/8" long

K

G

J

7/64" pilot hole 1 3/4" deep

Q

5/32" shank hole, countersunk

7/64" pilot hole 1/2" deep

3/8" hole 1/4" deep

I

H

25° bevels

SCREW HOLE DETAIL

P

I

3" deck screw

N

3/8" plug 3/8" long

#8 x 1" F.H. wood screw

O

3" deck screw

L

Note: 3/8"-long plugs sanded flush after assembly.

F

E

7/64" pilot holes 2 1/2" deep

3/8" hole 1/4" deep with a 5/32" hole centered inside

Rout 1/4" round-overs after assembly.

O

L

P

3/8" plug 3/8" long

#8 x 1" F.H. wood screws

O

L

25° bevel on top 3/8"

47"

25° bevel

52 1/2"

3–14.

EXPLODED VIEW 2 OF ROCKER

H

Ends of (I) extend 3/4" past ends of (H).

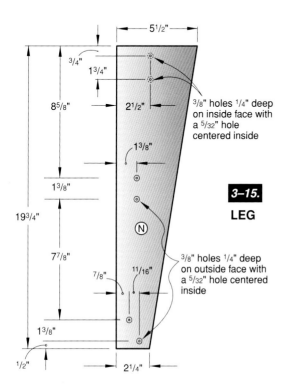

5 1/2"

3/4"

1 3/4"

8 5/8"

2 1/2"

3/8" holes 1/4" deep on inside face with a 5/32" hole centered inside

1 3/8"

1 3/8"

19 3/4"

N

7 7/8"

7/8"

11/16"

3/8" holes 1/4" deep on outside face with a 5/32" hole centered inside

1 3/8"

1/2"

2 1/4"

3–15.

LEG

5 Cut the leg taper where marked. (One way is to make the cut on your bandsaw, and plane the cut edge straight.) Designate a left and right leg, and mark their outside faces. Drill the 5/32" shank holes through both pieces. Separate the pieces, and counterbore the screw holes on the inside and outside faces where directed in **3–16**.

Make the Rockers and Armrests

1 To form the two rockers (O), cut four pieces of 1" pine to 5 x 38". Using double-faced tape, stack these pieces together in two pairs. Designate one pair as the left rocker, and one pair as the right rocker, and mark their outside faces. Enlarge and transfer the Rocker pattern (**3–22**, *page 43*) onto the top piece of each pair of rocker blanks.

2 Saw and sand the rocker pieces to shape. Separate the rocker pieces and remove the tape, but keep the paired parts together.

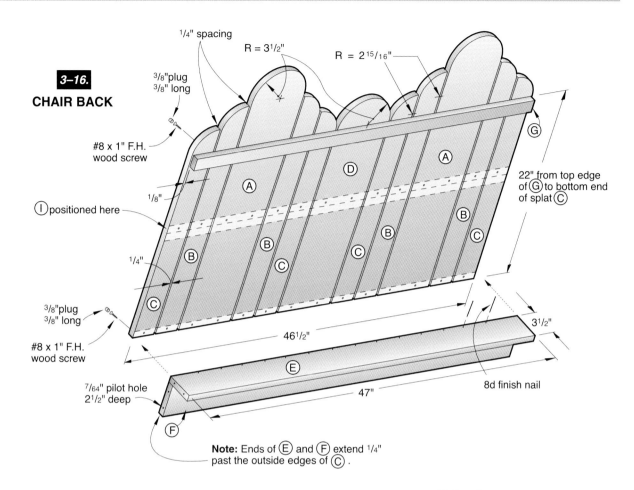

3–16.
CHAIR BACK

¹/₄" spacing

R = 3¹/₂"

R = 2¹⁵/₁₆"

³/₈"plug
³/₈" long

#8 x 1" F.H.
wood screw

¹/₈"

Ⓘ positioned here

¹/₄"

³/₈"plug
³/₈" long

#8 x 1" F.H.
wood screw

⁷/₆₄" pilot hole
2¹/₂" deep

22" from top edge
of Ⓖ to bottom end
of splat Ⓒ

46¹/₂"

3¹/₂"

47"

8d finish nail

Note: Ends of Ⓔ and Ⓕ extend ¹/₄"
past the outside edges of Ⓒ.

3–17.

ANGLE FINDER
UNDERSTANDING
OUR ANGLES

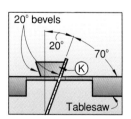
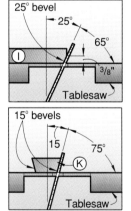
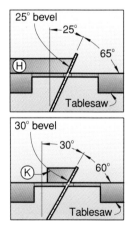

3 Using the enlarged Rocker pattern again, mark the front leg cutaway (shaded area near the front of the pattern) on the outside piece of each rocker pair. Next, mark the cutaway for the seat

support piece (L) near the back on the inside rocker piece on each pair. Now, cut each rocker piece where marked. Set these parts aside for now.

4 For the armrests (P), rip and crosscut two pieces of 1" stock to 6¹/₄ x 28". Stack the pieces together face-to-face using double-faced tape. Trace the Armrest pattern outline (**3–25**, on *page 45*) onto the top piece, and mark the screw-hole centerpoints. Make the top piece the left armrest and the bottom piece the right armrest.

5 Saw the armrests to shape, and sand the cut edges. Drill the ⁵/₃₂" shank holes through both pieces where marked. Now, separate the pieces. Counterbore the shank holes into the top of each armrest.

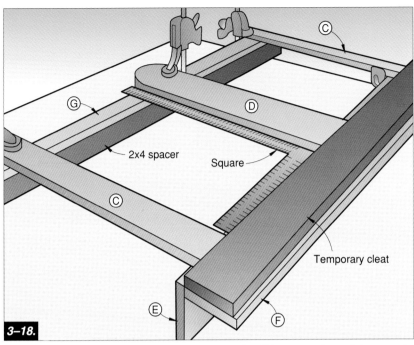

3–18.

Lay out the back parts, position the middle splat (D), square it, and then work outward in both directions, clamping the parts temporarily to keep them from moving.

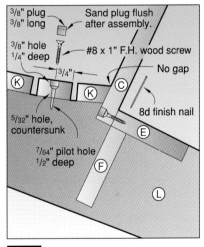

3–19. **ASSEMBLY STEP 1**

Start the Subassemblies

1 Glue and clamp the lower back supports (E, F) at a right angle where shown on the Assembly Step 1 drawing (**3–19**). (Construct your rocker using water-resistant glues, slow-set epoxy, or resorcinol so the rocker will hold its own against the elements.) Drive 8d finish nails through E and into F. Set the nails, fill the holes with putty, let the putty dry, and sand smooth.

2 Cut two 2¾"-wide by 48"-long pieces of 2 x 4 stock for temporary supports. Position the lower back supports (E, F), the top back support (G), and also the back splats (A, B, C, D) where shown on the Assembly Step 2 drawing (**3–20**). Mark the lengthwise center on the edge of parts E and G, and center the middle back splat (D) on these two marks. Square the center splat to part E where shown in **3–18**, and clamp the parts temporarily to keep them from moving. (It is also helpful to clamp a cleat to the top of part F to aid in aligning the bottom edges of the splats.)

3 Mark the centerpoints for two screw holes ⅜" up from the bottom edge of the center splat (D). Drill a ⅜" hole ¼" deep with a $5/32$" shank hole centered inside. (To drill these holes, use a combination bit that forms the shank hole, counterbore, and pilot hole in one operation.) Glue and

6 Cut a ⅜"-deep half lap across the underside of each armrest where shown on the Exploded View 1 (**3–12**, *page 39*) and the Armrest pattern (**3–25**, on *page 45*). Mark and cut a mating half lap ⅜" deep across each end of the middle back support (I).

7 To make the armrest brackets (Q), cut two 4" squares from 1" scrap. With a compass, draw a 3¼" radius on each. Cut both pieces to shape, and sand these edges.

3–20. **ASSEMBLY STEP 2**

3–21.

Temporary support

Position for E-F subassembly

Scrap supports nailed to inside face

L

O

Nail temporary supports to the inside face of the rocker/seat support to position the lower back support during assembly. Use #5 common nails so you can easily remove them later.

screw the center back splat (D) to the edge of E, using #8 × 1" flathead wood screws.

4 Working outward from the center back splat (D), square and attach the remaining back splats to the support (F) where shown in **3–16** (*page 40*). Space the splats ¼" apart. Note that the ends of the E-F assembly extend ¼" beyond the outside edges of the two end splats (C). Note from looking at the Front View

drawing (**3–13**), that the back splats, when assembled, measure 46½" wide.

5 Position the top edge of the upper back support (G) 22" from the bottom edge of the back splats. Clamp it in place. Note that the edges of the outside splats extend ⅛" beyond the ends of the upper back support.

6 To attach the upper back support to the back splats,

measure up 21¼" from the bottom on the two outside back splats and mark. Next, using a long straightedge or chalk line, make a line across the front of the back splats, connecting these two marks. Temporarily remove the back support (G), apply glue to the mating surfaces, and reclamp it in position. Next, use the line you just made as a centerline to help locate and drill the counter-bored, shank, and pilot holes. Drive the screws.

7 Plane a piece of pine stock to ⁷⁄₁₆" thick. Use a plug cutter to cut one hundred and twenty five ⅜"-diameter plugs from it. Glue a plug into each hole to cover the screws along the bottom of the back splats. Align the grain of the plugs with the grain of the wood being plugged. Sand the plugs flush with the splats. Set the remaining plugs aside for now.

8 Dry-fit the pieces to check the fit. Then, glue, assemble, and clamp the legs, seat supports, and

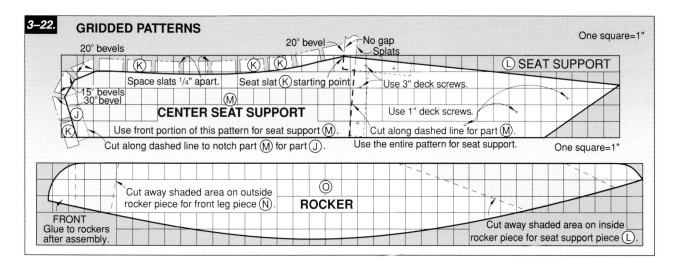

3–22. **GRIDDED PATTERNS**

One square=1"

20° bevels

20° bevel — No gap — Splats

K K K L SEAT SUPPORT

Space slats ¼" apart. Seat slat K starting point Use 3" deck screws.

15° bevels 30° bevel

M

CENTER SEAT SUPPORT Use 1" deck screws.

J

K Use front portion of this pattern for seat support M. Cut along dashed line for part M.

Cut along dashed line to notch part M for part J. Use the entire pattern for seat support. One square=1"

Cut away shaded area on outside rocker piece for front leg piece N.

O

ROCKER

FRONT Glue to rockers after assembly.

Cut away shaded area on inside rocker piece for seat support piece L.

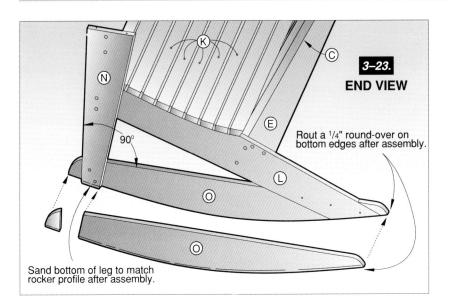

3–23.
END VIEW

90°

Rout a ¼" round-over on bottom edges after assembly.

Sand bottom of leg to match rocker profile after assembly.

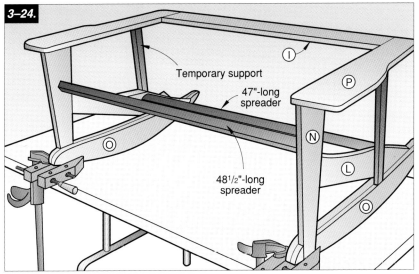

3–24.

Temporary support

47"-long spreader

48½"-long spreader

This view shows the leg seat/support rocker assemblies with spacers and the armrest/back support in position.

rockers. (See **3–23** for reference.) When assembling, square (90°) the front edge of the legs with the top edge of the rockers. Drive the two screws attaching each leg and the three screws attaching each seat support to the rockers. Glue a plug in these counterbored holes, and sand them flush. Remove the clamps. Glue and clamp the small

end pieces to the rockers. Sand the protruding leg tips to match the rocker profile.

9 Rout a ¼" roundover along the bottom edges of each rocker. Then finish-sand all rockers.

10 Using the Seat Support pattern (**3–22**) for refer-

ence, mark on the inside face of the seat supports where the lower back support assembly (E, F) joins them. Cut scrap pieces, and, as shown in **3–21** (*page 43*), nail the scrap pieces to the seat support to position the lower back support during assembly. (Use #5 common nails so you can remove the supports later.)

11 Apply glue to the half laps on the armrests (P) and the back support piece (I). On a flat surface, assemble and clamp these pieces. Square each armrest to the back support. Drill the counter-bored, shank, and pilot holes through the parts where shown on the Exploded View drawings 1 and 2 (**3–12** and **3–14**, *pages 39 and 40*). Drive the #8 x 1" flat-head wood screws.

12 Rip and crosscut two 1½ x 47½" temporary spreaders. As shown in **3–24**, clamp your two leg/rocker assemblies to a flat surface. (Place a sheet of plywood on top of a pair of sawhorses.) Now, position the spacers between the leg/rocker assemblies and clamp them.

Put the Subassemblies Together

1 To support the rocker armrest/back support assembly (I, P) during assembly, temporarily nail 16¾"-long temporary supports to the sides of the seat supports where shown in **3–24**. (Position these supports to hold the armrests

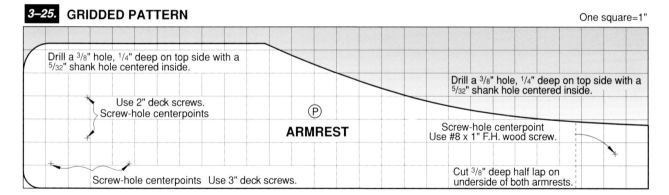

3–25. GRIDDED PATTERN — One square=1"

Drill a $3/8$" hole, $1/4$" deep on top side with a $5/32$" shank hole centered inside.

Use 2" deck screws.
Screw-hole centerpoints

ⓟ

ARMREST

Drill a $3/8$" hole, $1/4$" deep on top side with a $5/32$" shank hole centered inside.

Screw-hole centerpoint
Use #8 x 1" F.H. wood screw.

Screw-hole centerpoints Use 3" deck screws.

Cut $3/8$" deep half lap on underside of both armrests.

level or parallel with the top edge of the laminated rockers. Also, level the tops of the rockers with the work surface when clamping. This makes it easy to level the armrests.) Now, using a pencil and combination square, mark a centerline lengthwise along the top edge of each leg (N).

2 Place the armrests/back support assembly (I, P) on the legs and temporary supports. See the Front View drawing (**3–13**, *page 39*) and **3–24** for reference when positioning the parts. Then, clamp this assembly to temporarily hold the parts in place.

3 Apply glue to the ends of the front spreader/support (J), and position it between the legs where shown on the Exploded View 1 drawing (**3–12**, *page 39*). Clamp the assembly to hold the part in place. Then, drive #8 x 3" deck screws through the legs/seat supports, and into both ends of the spreader/support.

4 With an assistant's help, lower the back assembly between the armrests/back support assembly

until the ends of the lower back supports (E, F) sit on the scrap guides you tacked to the inside faces of the leg/seat support/rocker assemblies earlier. Clamp the two assemblies together. (Apply long pipe clamps lengthwise to hold the entire assembly together.)

5 If necessary, move the armrest/back support assembly forward or back until the middle back support fits snugly against the rocker back. Sight through the two shank holes in each armrest, align them with the centerline on the top of each leg, and drive #8 x 3" deck screws through these armrest holes and into the leg. (On the rocker shown on *page 37*, the armrests extend $1\frac{1}{16}$" beyond the inside face of the legs and $\frac{1}{2}$" beyond the front edge of each leg.) With a $\frac{7}{64}$" bit, drill through the four remaining holes in the seat supports (L) sides to form pilot holes in the ends of the bottom back supports (E, F). Drive #8 x 3" deck screws through these holes and into the support ends.

6 Glue, clamp, and screw the armrest brackets in position using 2" deck screws.

7 To add back strength and rigidity, center (lengthwise) and glue the second back support (H) to the underside of the middle support (I). (See Exploded View 2 [**3–14**, *page 40*] for reference.) Clamp the supports.

8 Drill the counterbored holes, and screw the back splats to the middle back support (I) where dimensioned on the Screw Hole Detail accompanying the Exploded View 2 drawing in **3–14**. Remove the temporary spreaders and supports nailed to the rocker during assembly.

Add the Seat Slats

1 To position the center seat support (M), mark the rocker's centerpoint on the front spreader (J) and the bottom of the center splat (D). Next, center the middle seat support on these lines, and glue and screw it in position. Then, glue the plugs in the screw holes, and sand them flush with the surface.

2 Glue and screw the seat slats (K) to the seat supports (L) and the middle seat support (M) where shown on the Exploded View 1 drawing (**3–12**, *page 39*), the Seat Support pattern (**3–22**, *page 43*), and the Assembly Step 1 drawing (**3–19**, *page 42*). (Start at the back, placing the seat slat with one 20° bevel tightly against the back splats. After centering a slat on the seat supports, drill the counterbore, shank, and pilot holes, and drive the screws. To get uniform slat spacing, use ¼"-thick spacers between the slats while attaching them.)

3 Glue a 7/16"-long plug in the counterbored screw holes that have not been plugged yet. Sand the plugs flush with the surfaces.

4 Finish-sand the entire chair with 100- and 150-grit sandpaper. Next, apply the exterior finish of your choice. (One suggestion is to apply a coat of an oil-based exterior primer, wait until it thoroughly dries, and then recoat all the end grain to ensure a good seal. After the primer coat dries, follow with two coats of semigloss white enamel paint, sanding lightly between coats with 320-grit sandpaper.)

LAKELAND LAWN CHAIR AND FOOTREST

Assemble the Chair Frame

1 Cut the rear legs (A) to the size listed in the Materials List. Enlarge each half of the Chair Rail-Leg Half-Pattern in **3–42** (*page 55*) to full size and make two copies of each. Adhere them to the legs with spray adhesive, mating the halves where shown on the small-scale drawing on the pattern. Band-saw and sand the rear legs to shape. Rout the chamfers.

2 Cut the rear rail (B) and front rails (C) to the size listed. Lay out the centerpoints of the shank holes and the endpoints and midpoints of the arcs, where shown in the Rails drawing in **3–28**. Use a fairing stick to draw the arcs, as shown in **3–26**. To make the fairing stick shown, use cord and a narrow piece of tempered hardboard.) Drill the counter-sunk shank holes, and band-saw and sand the rails to shape. Set aside one front rail for the footrest.

Lawn chair and footrest

Materials List for Lakeland Lawn Chair and Footrest

PART		FINISHED SIZE			MATL.	QTY.
		T	W	L		
Chair						
A	rear legs	1½"	5¼"	30⅞"	C	2
B	rear rail	1½"	5¼"	22"	C	1
C*	front rails	1½"	5¼"	22"	C	2
D	cleat	¾"	¾"	17½"	C	1
E	front legs	1½"	3½"	19¾"	C	2
F	brackets	1½"	3"	5"	C	2
G	splat rail	1½"	5¼"	26¾"	C	1
H	wedges	1½"	3¼"	2⅜"	C	2
I	arms	1"	5½"	28"	C	2
J	back splat blanks	¾"	4⅜"	27"	C	6
K	rear slat	¾"	5¼"	22"	C	1
L	nose blank	1½"	3½"	22"	C	1
M*	slats	¾"	2½"	22"	C	10
Footrest						
N	side rails	1½"	4¼"	16⅛"	C	2
O	front legs	1½"	3½"	12½"	C	2
P	rear legs	1½"	3½"	9⅞"	C	2

*One front rail and six slats required for the footrest.
Material Key: C = Cedar.
Supplies: Water-resistant glue; spray adhesive; 1⅝",
2½", and 3" deck screws; ⅜" carriage bolts 3½" long;
⅜" flat washers; ⅜" nuts.
Bits: 1⅛" Forstner bit; ⅜" brad-point drill bit;
⅛" roundover router bit; chamfer router bit.

3 Glue and clamp the rear and front rails (B, C) to the rear legs (A), where shown in the Exploded View drawing in **3–27**, *page 48*. (The front edge of the rear rail aligns with the end of the seat's curve, where noted on the pattern.) Use a water-resistant glue. With the rails' shank holes as guides, drill pilot holes into the rear legs, and drive in the screws.

4 Cut the cleat (D) to the size listed. Glue and clamp it to the back of the front rail (C), flush with its top edge and centered side-to-side. Drill pilot and counter-sunk shank holes through the cleat into the rail. Drive in the screws.

5 Cut the front legs (E) to size. Drill the carriage bolt holes and countersunk shank holes, where shown on the Exploded View drawing in **3-27**. Make sure you have a mirrored pair. Rout the chamfers.
➤*Note: Chamfers at the bottoms of the front and rear legs prevent their edges from splintering as the chair is moved around on your patio, porch, or deck.*

6 Make two copies of the brackets (F) in **3–41** (*page 54*). Adhere them to 1½"-thick stock, and band-saw and sand them to shape. Drill countersunk shank holes, where shown. Glue and clamp the brackets to the legs'

LAWN CHAIR AND FOOTREST CUTTING DIAGRAM

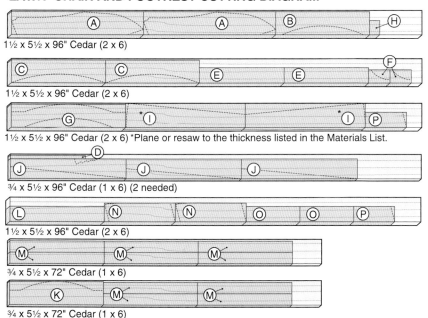

1½ x 5½ x 96" Cedar (2 x 6)

1½ x 5½ x 96" Cedar (2 x 6)

1½ x 5½ x 96" Cedar (2 x 6) *Plane or resaw to the thickness listed in the Materials List.

¾ x 5½ x 96" Cedar (1 x 6) (2 needed)

1½ x 5½ x 96" Cedar (2 x 6)

¾ x 5½ x 72" Cedar (1 x 6)

¾ x 5½ x 72" Cedar (1 x 6)

3–26.

To draw the rail's arc, bend a narrow strip of hardboard to connect the marked endpoints and midpoint.

3–27.

EXPLODED VIEW OF LAWN CHAIR AND FOOTREST

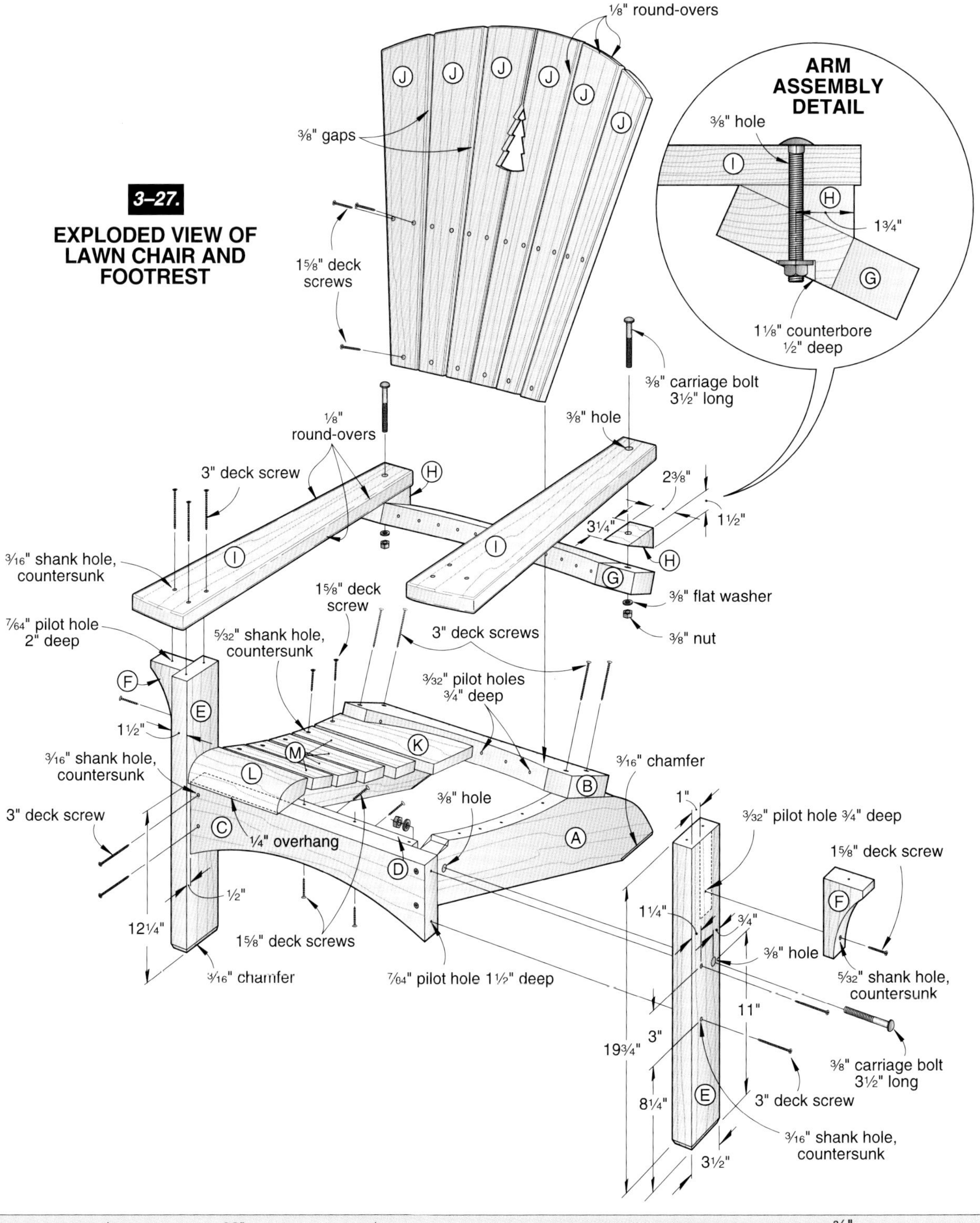
1/8" round-overs
J
3/8" gaps
1 5/8" deck screws
ARM ASSEMBLY DETAIL
3/8" hole
I
H
1 3/4"
G
1 1/8" counterbore
1/2" deep
3/8" carriage bolt
3 1/2" long
1/8"
round-overs
3/8" hole
3" deck screw
2 3/8"
1 1/2"
3 1/4"
3/16" shank hole,
countersunk
3/8" flat washer
3/8" nut
7/64" pilot hole
2" deep
1 5/8" deck
screw
5/32" shank hole,
countersunk
3" deck screws
3/32" pilot holes
3/4" deep
F
E
K
L
M
3/16" chamfer
B
3/8" hole
C
1/4" overhang
A
D
1"
3/32" pilot hole 3/4" deep
1 5/8" deck screw
1/2"
12 1/4"
1 5/8" deck screws
3/16" chamfer
7/64" pilot hole 1 1/2" deep
1 1/4"
3/4"
3/8" hole
5/32" shank hole,
countersunk
11"
3"
19 3/4"
8 1/4"
3" deck screw
3/16" shank hole,
countersunk
3 1/2"

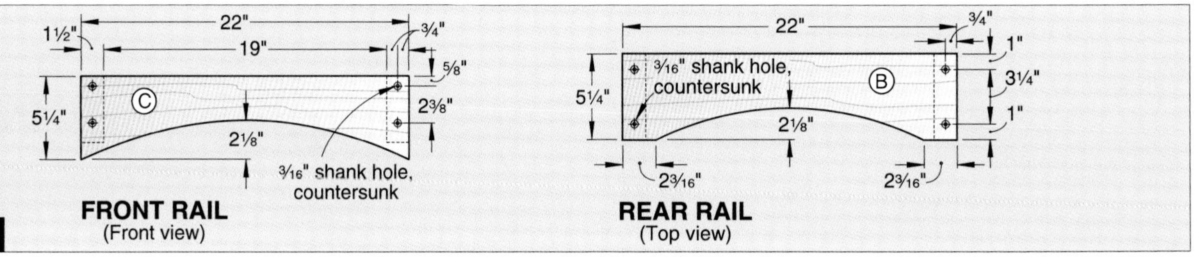
22"
1 1/2"
19"
3/4"
5/8"
5 1/4"
C
2 3/8"
2 1/8"
3/16" shank hole,
countersunk
FRONT RAIL
(Front view)
22"
3/4"
1"
3/16" shank hole,
countersunk
B
3 1/4"
5 1/4"
2 1/8"
1"
2 3/16"
2 3/16"
REAR RAIL
(Top view)

3–28.

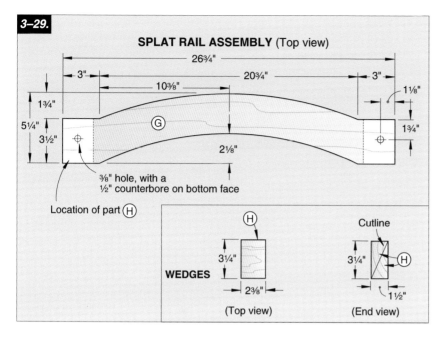

3–29.

SPLAT RAIL ASSEMBLY (Top view)

26¾"

3" 20¾" 3"

10⅜" 1⅛"

1¾"

5¼" 1¾"

3½" G 2⅛"

⅜" hole, with a
½" counterbore on bottom face

Location of part H

WEDGES

H

3¼" 2⅜" (Top view)

Cutline

3¼" H
1½"

(End view)

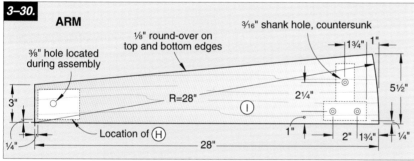

3–30.

ARM

⅛" round-over on
top and bottom edges

³⁄₁₆" shank hole, countersunk

⅜" hole located
during assembly

1¾" 1"

R=28" I 2¼" 5½"

3"

Location of H 1" 2" 1¾" ¼"

¼" 28"

outside faces, flush at the top and centered side-to-side. Using the shank holes in the brackets as guides, drill pilot holes into the legs, and drive in the screws.

7 Measure up 12¼" from the bottom of each front leg (E), and make a mark on its inside face. Working on a flat surface, glue and clamp the front legs to the rear legs and rails assembly (A/B/C/D). Position the face of the front rail (C) ½" back from the front legs' front edges, and align the top of the front rail with your marks, where shown on the Exploded View drawing in **3–27**. Using the shank holes in the front legs as guides, drill pilot holes into the front rail, and drive in the screws. Using the ⅜" holes as guides, drill ⅜" holes through the rear legs. Insert carriage bolts, and fasten them with washers and nuts.

3–31.

3–32.

Far left: *Position your drill-press fence 1¾" from the bit's center. With assembly G/H supported on a scrap board, drill the ½"-deep counterbores.*

Near left *Clamp a scrap stock straight-edge to your workbench. Apply double-faced tape to the back of one center splat, and stick it to the bench so it is square to the scrap.*

8 Cut the splat rail (G) to the size listed. Once again using your fairing stick, lay out the curves where shown in **3–29**, *on page 40*. Band-saw and sand the splat rail to shape.

9 Cut a $1\frac{1}{2}$ x $3\frac{1}{4}$ x $2\frac{3}{8}$" piece of stock for the two wedges (H). Draw the diagonal on one end, where shown in the End View in **3–29**. Band-saw on the line to separate the two wedges, and sand the sawn faces smooth. Apply glue to the wedges' sawn faces, and clamp them to the splat rail (G), where shown on the Exploded View drawing in **3–27** and in **3–29** (*pages 48* and *49*).

10 Chuck a $1\frac{1}{8}$" Forstner bit in your drill press, and drill counterbores in the splat rail for the bolts that hold the splat rail and wedges assembly to the arms (I), where shown on the Exploded View drawing in **3–27** and in **3–29**, and as shown in **3–31**. Switch to a $\frac{3}{8}$" brad-point bit and drill holes centered in the counterbores.

3–33.

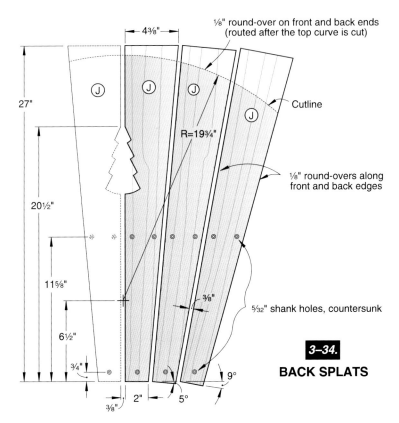

3–34.
BACK SPLATS

Make the Arms, Back, and Seat

1 Plane $1\frac{1}{2}$"-thick lumber to 1" thick, and cut the arms (I) to the size listed. Using a beam compass, mark the front radii, and then mark the tapered outside edges, where shown on **3–30**, on *page 49*. Band-saw, joint, and sand the arms to shape. Lay out the centerpoints of the counter-sunk shank holes. Make sure you have a mirrored pair of arms, and then drill the holes. Rout $\frac{1}{8}$" roundovers along the top and bottom edges.

Inserting $\frac{3}{8}$" spacers, position the other splats. Adhere the tree patterns with spray adhesive. Apply masking tape, and mark the hole locations. Draw the radius.

2 Cut the back splat blanks (J) to the size listed. Draw the $4\frac{3}{8}$" to 2" taper along one edge of each of the six blanks, where shown on **3–34**. Band-saw and joint the splat blanks to shape. Make 5° cuts on two blanks and 9° cuts on two blanks, where shown on **3–34**.

3 Make a copy of the Tree Cutout pattern (**3–41**, *page 54*). To locate the cutout and shank hole centerpoints, and draw the seat back's top radius, lay out the splat blanks on your workbench, as shown in **3–32** and **3–33**.

4 Band-saw and sand the ends of the splats and the tree cutouts. Drill the countersunk

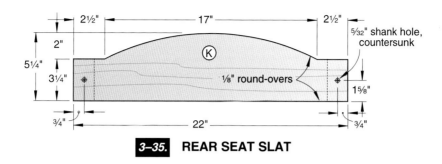

3–35. **REAR SEAT SLAT**

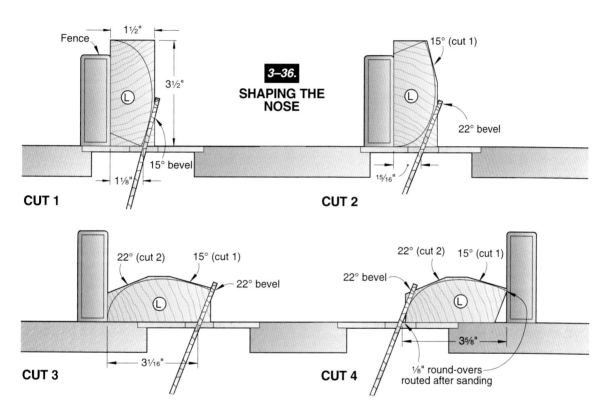

3–36. **SHAPING THE NOSE**

CUT 1

CUT 2

CUT 3

CUT 4

holes. Rout ⅛" roundovers on the splats' front and back edges, including the cutouts and their top ends.

5 Cut the rear slat (K) to the size listed. Lay out its shape where shown on **3–35**. Band-saw and sand the slat to shape. Rout ⅛" roundovers on the top edges. Drill the countersunk shank holes.

6 Cut the nose blank (L) to the size listed. Make a copy of the two Nose patterns shown in **3-41** (*page 54*), and adhere them to the ends of the blank. Rough out the profile on your tablesaw by making the four cuts shown in **3–30**. Refine the shape with a block plane and sandpaper. Rout the ⅛" roundovers, where shown.

7 Cut the slats (M) to the size listed. Rout ⅛" roundovers on the top edges. Drill countersunk shank holes where shown on the Exploded View drawing (**3–27**, *page 48*).

➤ *Note: Six of the slats (M) will be used on the footrest.*

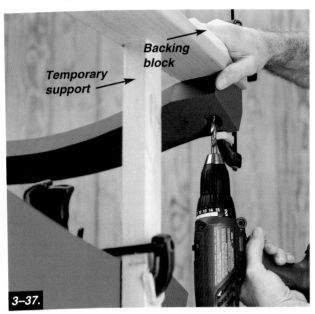

3–37.

Using the holes in the splat-rail assembly (G/H) as guides, drill ⅜" holes through the arms. Backing blocks prevent splintering.

3–38.

With a center splat in place, insert ⅜" spacers and add the rest of the splats, one at a time, drilling pilot holes and driving in the screws.

Apply an Outdoor Finish

1 Ease the edges of all the parts with a sanding block, and sand all surfaces to 120 grit. Apply an exterior water-repellent oil finish. (For the lawn chair and footrest shown on *page 46*, a water repellent with cedar toner was used, and all the surfaces were fully saturated.) Wherever possible, dip exposed end grain in the finish, especially the bottoms of the legs and the tops of the back splats. Let the parts dry for 48 hours.

2 Apply a color to the frame assembly (A/B/C/D/E/F), splat rail assembly (G/H), and the tree cutouts on the back splats. (An acrylic latex solid-color deck stain was used for the lawn chair

and footrest shown on *page 46*. Wipe away any finish that gets on the rounded-over edges of the tree cutouts. Set the parts aside to dry.

Assemble the Chair

1 To support the arms (I) during assembly, cut two 19¾"-long temporary supports from scrap. Clamp them vertically to the rear legs just forward of the rear rail (B). With their ends resting on the supports, position the arms on the

front legs where shown on **3–30** (*page 49*). Using the shank holes in the arms as guides, drill pilot holes into the legs and brackets, and drive in the screws.

2 Inserting scrap blocks between the clamps and the arms, clamp the splat rail assembly (G/H) to the arms. The arms overhang the back and inside edges of the wedges (H) by ¼". The distance between the arms is 21½". Drill ⅜" holes

3–39. FOOTREST SIDE RAIL

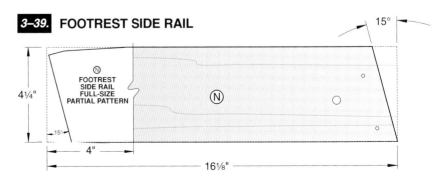

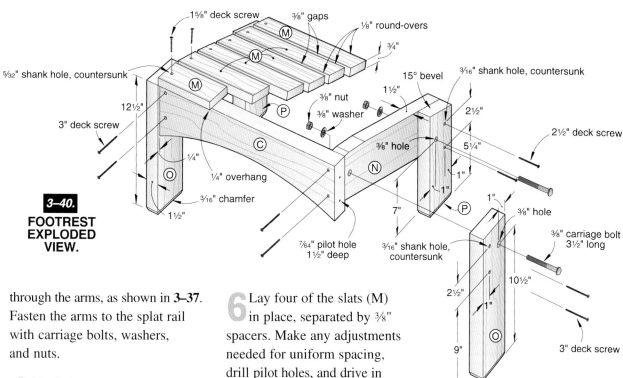

3–40.
FOOTREST
EXPLODED
VIEW.

through the arms, as shown in **3–37**. Fasten the arms to the splat rail with carriage bolts, washers, and nuts.

3 Mark the centerlines of the rear rail (B) and the splat rail (G). Position one center splat $\frac{3}{16}$" from the marks with its bottom end flush with the bottom of the rear rail, and clamp it in place. Using the shank holes in the splat as guides, drill pilot holes into the rear rail and splat rail, and drive in the screws. Add the rest of the splats, as shown in **3–38**.

4 Insert $\frac{3}{8}$" spacers between the back splats and the rear slat (K). Drill pilot holes into the rear legs (A), and drive in the screws.

5 Clamp the nose (L) in place, overhanging the front rail (C) by $\frac{1}{4}$", where shown on the Exploded View drawing in **3–27**, *page 48*. Drill pilot and counter-sunk shank holes through the cleat (D) into the nose. Drive in the screws.

6 Lay four of the slats (M) in place, separated by $\frac{3}{8}$" spacers. Make any adjustments needed for uniform spacing, drill pilot holes, and drive in the screws.

Assemble and Finish the Footrest

1 Cut the side rails (N) to the size listed. Make two copies of the Footrest Side Rail partial pattern (**3–43**, *page 56*), and adhere them to the rails with spray adhesive, where shown on **3–39**. Make the 15° angle cuts on the ends. With your disc or belt sander, form the two angled flats where the two top slats (M) will rest.

2 Retrieve the previously cut front rail (C). Glue and clamp the side rails (N) to the front rail, flush at the sides and top, where shown on **3–40**. Using the shank holes in the front rail as guides, drill pilot holes into the side rails. Drive in the screws.

3 Cut the front legs (O) and rear legs (P) to the sizes listed. Make the 15° angle cuts at the top ends of the rear legs, where shown on **3–40**. Drill the countersunk shank holes and $\frac{3}{8}$" bolt holes. Rout the chamfers. Glue and clamp the legs to the front and side rails assembly. Using the holes in the legs as guides, drill pilot holes into the front and side rails, and bolt holes through the side rails. Drive in the screws, and fasten the bolts with washers and nuts.

4 Finish the footrest frame assembly (C/N/O/P) the same as you did the chair parts. After 48 hours, give the frame assembly its color coat.

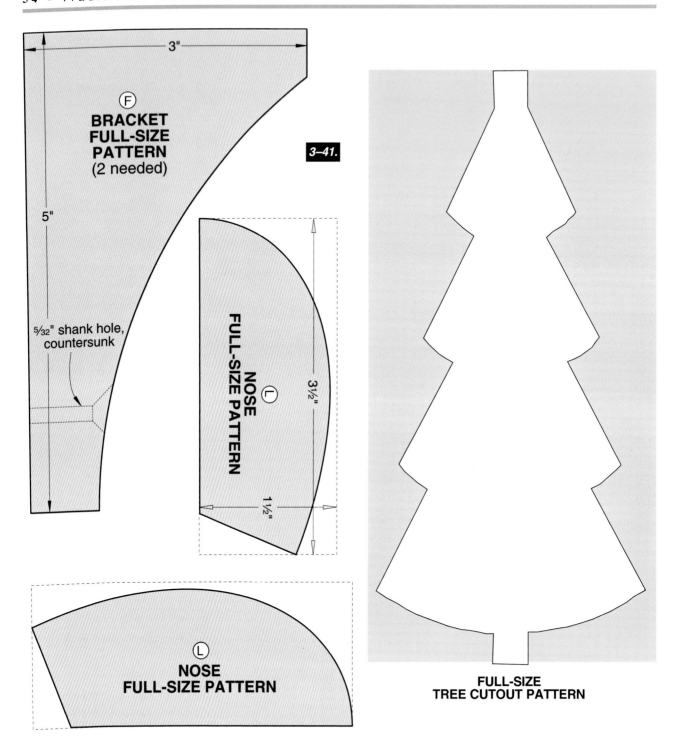

(F) BRACKET FULL-SIZE PATTERN (2 needed)

3"

5"

3–41.

5/32" shank hole, countersunk

(L) NOSE FULL-SIZE PATTERN

3½"

1½"

(L) NOSE FULL-SIZE PATTERN

FULL-SIZE TREE CUTOUT PATTERN

With the finish dry, retrieve the six slats (M). Position one slat flush with the front edges of the front legs, and another flush with the rear edges of the rear legs. Drill pilot holes, and drive in the screws. Position the rest of the slats, inserting ⅜" spacers between them. Make any adjustments needed for uniform spacing, drill pilot holes, and drive in the screws.

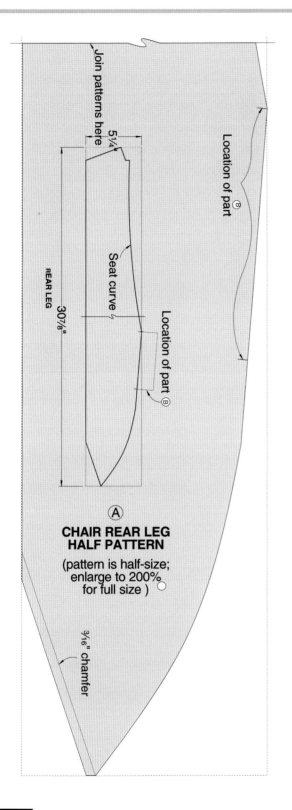

Join patterns here

5¼

Location of part Ⓑ

Seat curve

REAR LEG

30⅞"

Location of part Ⓑ

Ⓐ

CHAIR REAR LEG HALF PATTERN

(pattern is half-size; enlarge to 200% for full size)

³⁄₁₆" chamfer

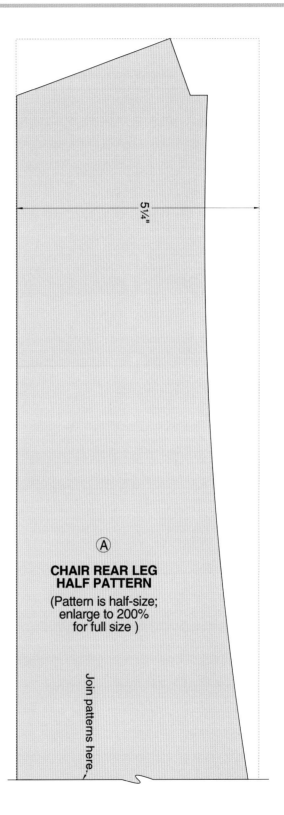

5¼"

Ⓐ

CHAIR REAR LEG HALF PATTERN

(Pattern is half-size; enlarge to 200% for full size)

Join patterns here.

3–42.

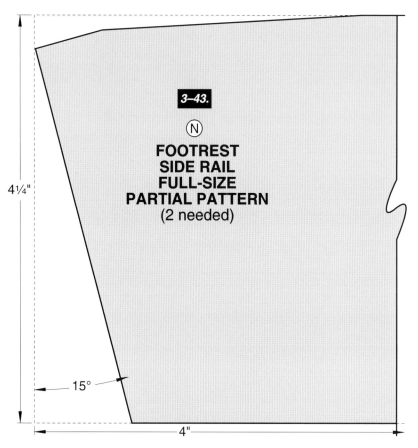

3–43.

Ⓝ

**FOOTREST
SIDE RAIL
FULL-SIZE
PARTIAL PATTERN**
(2 needed)

4¼"

15°

4"

DECK SETTEE FOR TWO

You'll want to mate this piece with the lawn chair and footrest on the preceding pages. You can use the same pattern for the legs, but you'll have to copy the pattern for the center supports in **3–54** *(page 63)*.

Make the Rear Legs

1 Start by making full-size copies of the gridded patterns for the rear legs (A) and the center supports (B) (**3–54** and **3–55**, on *pages 63* and *64*). Use spray adhesive to attach them to appropriate lengths of 1½"-thick cedar.

Deck settee for two

2 Parts A and B both share the same curved top profile and nose shape. Make the cuts for the front seat slat notch before you saw the curved contours on these pieces. To do this, stand each piece on end and use a miter gauge and backing board to make the initial cut, as shown in **3–45** and **3–46** *(page 59)*. Use the rip fence to help guide this cut. Move the rip fence for the second cut and adjust the blade to 90°.

3 Next, use a bandsaw or jigsaw to cut the curved contours in parts A and B. Cut in the waste area, then sand to the outline on each piece. Finally, drill the 3/8" holes for the carriage bolts.

Cut the Other Frame Members

1 Cut the front legs (C) to size, and drill the required bolt and screw holes in each. (See the Parts View drawings in **3–53**, on *page 62*.) Also cut the armrest supports (D); these attach to the front legs. Then glue and screw the supports in place.

Materials List for Deck Settee for Two

PART		FINISHED SIZE			MATL.	QTY.
		T	W	L		
A*	rear legs	1½"	5½"	30⅞"	C	2
B*	center supports	1½"	5⅛"	23"	C	2
C*	front legs	1½"	3½"	19¾"	C	2
D*	armrest supports	1½"	3"	5"	C	2
E*	front rail	1½"	5"	55"	C	1
F*	rear cross-member	1½"	5½"	55"	C	1
G*	seat back support	1½"	5½"	61½"	C	1
H*	end wedges	1½"	3½"	3½"	C	2
I*	center wedge	1½"	3½"	11⅜"	C	1
J*	table frame upright	1½"	3½"	12½"	C	2
K*	table frame cross rails	1½"	2¾"	8"	C	2
L	cleats	⅞"	⅞"	19"	C	2
M	armrests	1¹/₁₆"	5½"	28"	C	2
N	table front slats	¾"	3⅝"	9¼"	C	2
O	tabletop slat	1¹/₁₆"	3⅝"	27"	C	1
P	tabletop slats	1¹/₁₆"	3⅝"	26⅞"	C	2
Q	seat back splats	¾"	4⁷/₁₆"	26¼"	C	4
R	seat back splats	¾"	4⁵/₁₆"	25¹¹/₁₆"	C	4
S	seat back splats	¾"	4"	24⅛"	C	4
T	front seat slat	1½"	3½"	55"	C	1
U	center seat slats	¾"	2½"	22"	C	8
V	rear seat slats	¾"	5¼"	22"	C	2
W	loon blank	½"	4"	8"	C	1

*Parts labeled with an * get painted.
Material Key: C = Cedar.
Supplies: 1" brass flathead wood screws (2); 1½" deck screws(62); 2" deck screws (32); 3" deck screws (24); ⅜ x 3½" carriage bolts with nuts and flat washers (6); ⅜ x 4" carriage bolts with nuts and flat washers (2); paint; water-repellent finish.

DECK SETTEE FOR TWO CUTTING DIAGRAM

*Plane or resaw to thickness listed in the Materials List

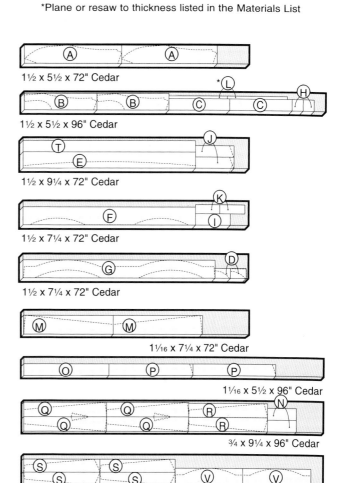

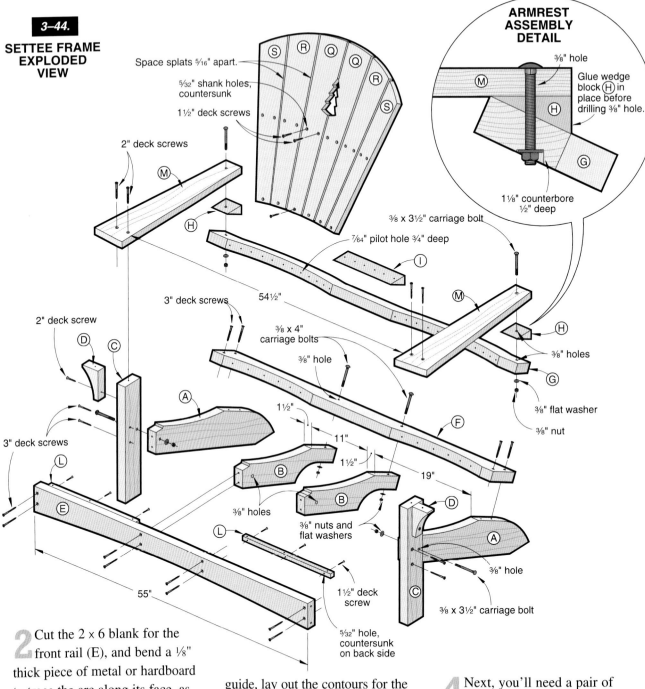

3–44.

SETTEE FRAME EXPLODED VIEW

Space splats 5/16" apart.

5/32" shank holes, countersunk

1½" deck screws

2" deck screws

ARMREST ASSEMBLY DETAIL

3/8" hole

Glue wedge block (H) in place before drilling 3/8" hole.

1⅛" counterbore ½" deep

3/8 x 3½" carriage bolt

7/64" pilot hole ¾" deep

3" deck screws

54½"

2" deck screw

3/8 x 4" carriage bolts

3/8" hole

1½"

11"

1½"

19"

3/8" holes

3/8" flat washer

3/8" nut

3" deck screws

3/8" holes

3/8" nuts and flat washers

3/8" hole

55"

1½" deck screw

5/32" hole, countersunk on back side

3/8 x 3½" carriage bolt

2 Cut the 2 x 6 blank for the front rail (E), and bend a ⅛" thick piece of metal or hardboard to trace the arc along its face, as shown in **3–49** and **3–50**, on *page 60*. Band-saw and sand to the line. Finally, drill countersunk holes for the eight mounting screws.

3 Again using the Parts View drawing (**3–53**, *page 62*) as a guide, lay out the contours for the rear cross member (F) and the seat back support (G) on 2 x 6 stock. Then cut and sand the curves. Drill holes for the carriage bolts and wood screws in the rear cross member, but leave the seat back support intact.

4 Next, you'll need a pair of end wedges (H) and one center wedge (I) that mount on the seat back support. (See **3–55**, on *page 64*.) Use a bandsaw to cut the wedges to shape, then glue them in place.

5 To locate and drill the bolt holes in the seat back support, use a simple guide block that hooks over the end wedges. (See the Drilling the Armrest Hole Detail and Guide Block drawings in **3–56**, on *page 64*.)

6 Cut the table frame uprights (J) and table frame cross rails (K) for the center table; drill the bolt and screw holes. (See **3–47** on *page 60* and the Parts View drawings in **3–53**, on *page 62*.)

7 Cut the two cleats (L), and drill the screw holes. (See **3–53** on *page 62* for reference.)

➤ *Note: Before proceeding any further, apply whatever paint, stain, or finish you've chosen for the frame components. (See the Materials List for information on which parts get painted.) For the deck settee shown on page 56, two coats of a solid-color latex stain was used. This stain is designed for use on decks, so it will be quite durable for this furniture project.*

Make the Slats and Splats

1 While the finish on the frame components is drying, start cutting the other parts—armrests (M); table front slats (N); the tabletop slats (O, P); the seat back splats (Q, R, S); and the front, center, and rear seat slats (T, U, V). (See the Parts View drawing in **3–53** *(page 62)* and the dimensions in the Materials List.)

2 The profile of the front seat slat (T) requires some creative work on the tablesaw. (See **3–48**, *page 60*.) Then, use a block plane to round over the ridges, followed by sandpaper to smooth the final surface to shape.

3 Apply finish to all of the unpainted parts after they are cut to size, sanded, and drilled for screws.

➤ *Note: Use a water repellent (in cedar tone) for added protection for these parts. It mimics a clear finish, but actually adds a more uniform color.*

Assemble the Lower Frame

1 Start the settee frame assembly by bolting the rear legs (A) to the front legs (C).

2 Use 3" deck screws to fasten the front rail (E) and the rear cross member (F) to the leg assemblies.

3 Bolt and screw the center supports (B) in place, as shown in **3–44**.

4 Attach the cleats (L) to the inside face of the front rail, flush with the top edge. (See **3–52**, on *page 61*.)

5 Assemble the center table frame (J, K), and make sure it fits in between the center supports (B). Then, fasten the table front slats (N), and bolt the unit in place. Use galvanized $\frac{3}{8} \times 3\frac{1}{2}$" carriage bolts.

6 Cut a pair of temporary support legs (each 19¾" long) from a 2 × 6, and two short spacer blocks each 3¼" wide. Clamp the spacer blocks and support legs to

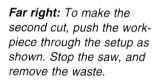

Near right: *With the pattern adhered to the leg blanks, cut the notched ends first. Note the support fence and clamp used.*

Far right: *To make the second cut, push the work-piece through the setup as shown. Stop the saw, and remove the waste.*

3–45.

3–46.

3–47.

CENTER TABLE EXPLODED VIEW

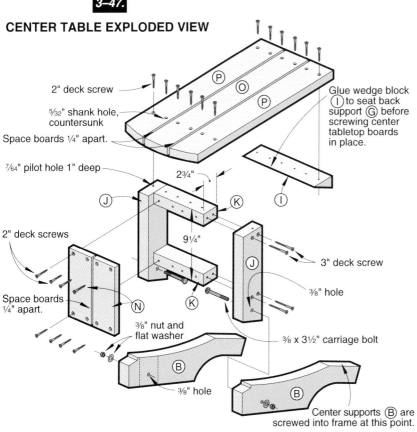

2" deck screw

$5/32$" shank hole, countersunk

Space boards $1/4$" apart.

$7/64$" pilot hole 1" deep

$2 3/4$"

Glue wedge block (I) to seat back support (G) before screwing center tabletop boards in place.

2" deck screws

$9 1/4$"

Space boards $1/4$" apart.

3" deck screw

$3/8$" hole

$3/8$" nut and flat washer

$3/8$ x $3 1/2$" carriage bolt

$3/8$" hole

Center supports (B) are screwed into frame at this point.

3–48. **FRONT SEAT SLAT PROFILE-CUTTING SEQUENCE**

Fence

CUT 1

15° bevel

$1 1/8$" Tablesaw

CUT 2

22° bevel

$15/16$" Tablesaw

CUT 3

22° bevel

$3 1/16$" Tablesaw

CUT 4

22° bevel

$3 5/8$" Tablesaw

Cutting the front rail. With the end and center blocks temporarily fastened to the front rail with screws, bend a thin metal or hardboard strip to trace the arc.

Below: *Gluing the leg. Clamp temporary support legs to each end of the frame to position the seat-back support and connecting chair.*

3–49.

3–50.

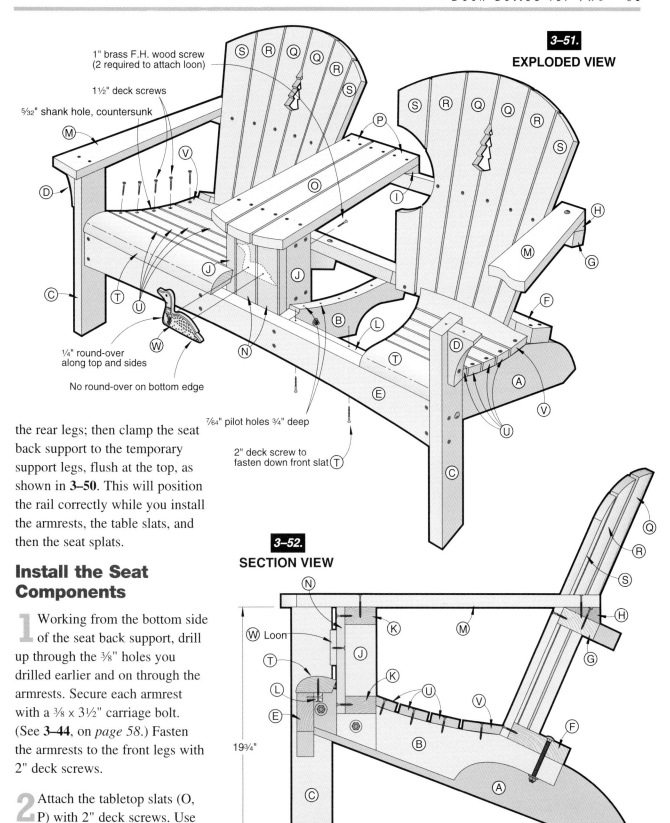

3–51.
EXPLODED VIEW

1" brass F.H. wood screw
(2 required to attach loon)

1½" deck screws

5/32" shank hole, countersunk

¼" round-over
along top and sides

No round-over on bottom edge

7/64" pilot holes ¾" deep

2" deck screw to
fasten down front slat (T)

3–52.
SECTION VIEW

19¾"

the rear legs; then clamp the seat back support to the temporary support legs, flush at the top, as shown in **3–50**. This will position the rail correctly while you install the armrests, the table slats, and then the seat splats.

Install the Seat Components

1 Working from the bottom side of the seat back support, drill up through the ⅜" holes you drilled earlier and on through the armrests. Secure each armrest with a ⅜ x 3½" carriage bolt. (See **3–44**, on *page 58*.) Fasten the armrests to the front legs with 2" deck screws.

2 Attach the tabletop slats (O, P) with 2" deck screws. Use ¼" shims to space these boards.

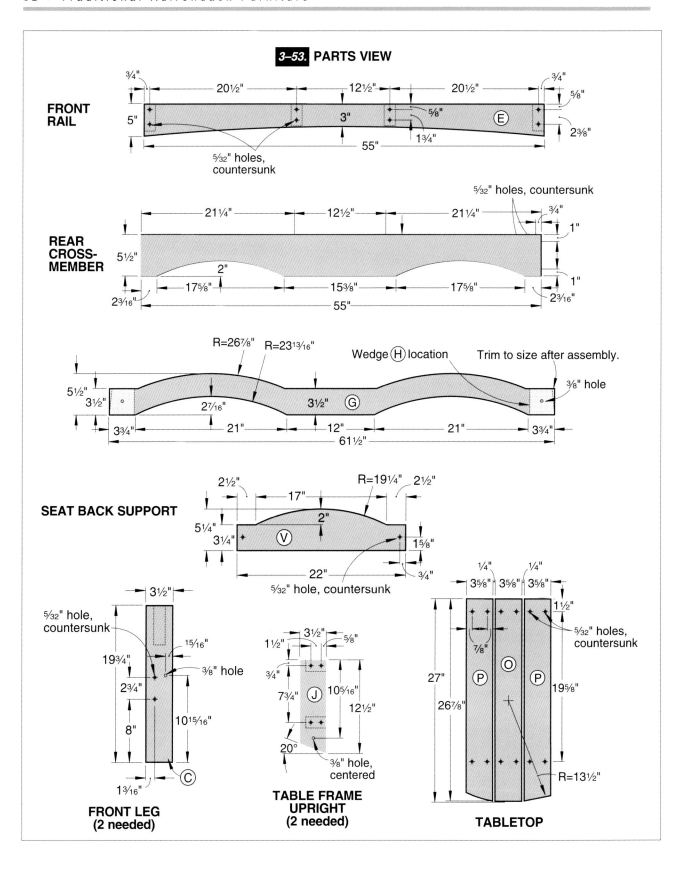

3–53. PARTS VIEW

FRONT RAIL

REAR CROSS-MEMBER

SEAT BACK SUPPORT

FRONT LEG
(2 needed)

TABLE FRAME UPRIGHT
(2 needed)

TABLETOP

3–54. **SETTEE FOR TWO GRIDDED PATTERNS**   **One square = 1"**

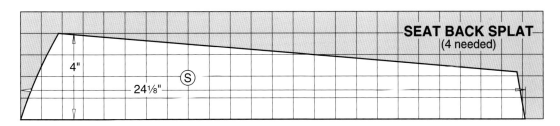

SEAT BACK SPLAT
(4 needed)

4"

$24\frac{1}{8}$" — S

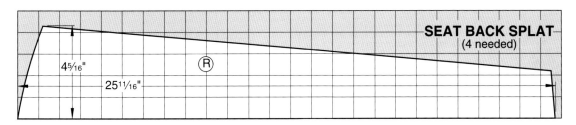

SEAT BACK SPLAT
(4 needed)

$4\frac{5}{16}$"

$25\frac{11}{16}$" — R

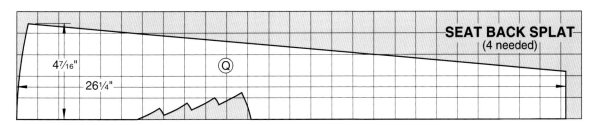

SEAT BACK SPLAT
(4 needed)

$4\frac{7}{16}$"

$26\frac{1}{4}$" — Q

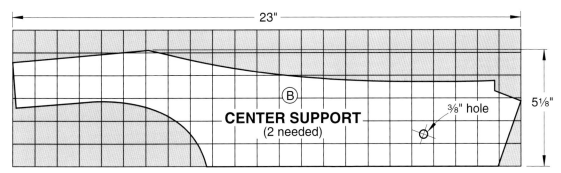

23"

B

CENTER SUPPORT
(2 needed)

$\frac{3}{8}$" hole

$5\frac{1}{8}$"

3 Next, clamp a scrap board to the underside of the rear cross member (F), and arrange the seat back splats (Q, R, S) in place, working from the center out. Place $\frac{5}{16}$" shims in between the splats, and fasten the splats with $1\frac{1}{2}$" deck screws. When they're secured, you can remove the clamps and support boards, including the temporary support legs.

4 Fasten the front (full-length) seat slat (T), driving 2" screws up through the cleats (L).

5 Next, arrange the center seat slats (U) and the rear seat slats (V) on the rear legs and center supports. After positioning the slats for uniform spacing between them (about $\frac{3}{8}$"), fasten them with $1\frac{1}{2}$" deck screws. Now, do one final check to make

sure all the bolts are tight, and the settee will be ready for your patio or deck.

If you'd like to add the loon to the front face of the center table, see the full-size pattern in **3–57**, on *page 65*. Center and fasten the loon to the center table front $\frac{1}{2}$" above (T) with 1" brass flathead wood screws driven from behind.

3–55.

**SETTEE FOR TWO
GRIDDED PATTERN**
One square =1"

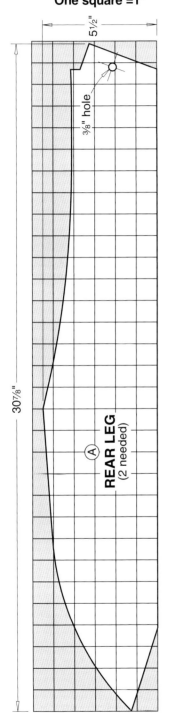

5½"

$30\frac{7}{8}$"

⅜" hole

Ⓐ

REAR LEG
(2 needed)

3–56. **PARTS VIEW CONTINUED**

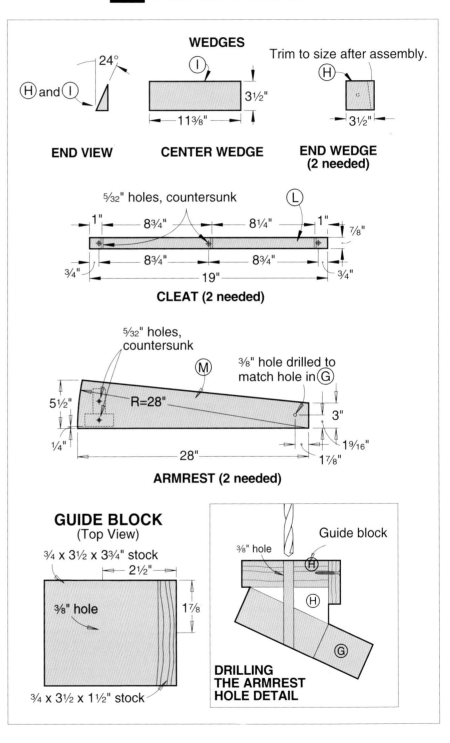

WEDGES

Trim to size after assembly.

24°

Ⓗ and Ⓘ

Ⓘ

$3\frac{1}{2}$"

$11\frac{3}{8}$"

Ⓗ

$3\frac{1}{2}$"

END VIEW   **CENTER WEDGE**   **END WEDGE**
(2 needed)

$\frac{5}{32}$" holes, countersunk

1" $8\frac{3}{4}$" $8\frac{1}{4}$"   1"

Ⓛ

$\frac{7}{8}$"

$\frac{3}{4}$" $8\frac{3}{4}$" $8\frac{3}{4}$" $\frac{3}{4}$"

19"

CLEAT (2 needed)

$\frac{5}{32}$" holes,
countersunk

Ⓜ

⅜" hole drilled to
match hole in Ⓖ

$5\frac{1}{2}$"   R=28"

3"

$\frac{1}{4}$"

28"

$1\frac{9}{16}$"

$1\frac{7}{8}$"

ARMREST (2 needed)

GUIDE BLOCK
(Top View)

¾ x 3½ x 3¾" stock

2½"

⅜" hole

$1\frac{7}{8}$

¾ x 3½ x 1½" stock

⅜" hole

Guide block

Ⓗ

Ⓗ

Ⓖ

**DRILLING
THE ARMREST
HOLE DETAIL**

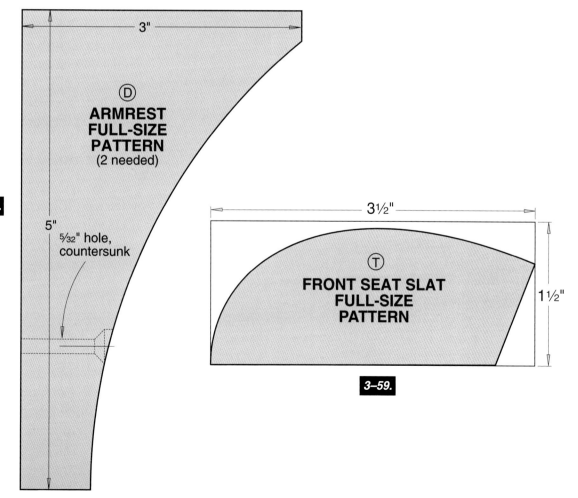

Paint center of eye red.

Paint entire cutout black.

Paint all markings white.

$\frac{1}{4}$" round-over

No round-over

3–57. **LOON FULL-SIZE PATTERN**

3–58.

3"

Ⓓ
ARMREST FULL-SIZE PATTERN
(2 needed)

5"

$\frac{5}{32}$" hole, countersunk

$3\frac{1}{2}$"

Ⓣ
FRONT SEAT SLAT FULL-SIZE PATTERN

$1\frac{1}{2}$"

3–59.

4

Seasonal Seating Surprises

Whether you like to spend your relaxing time on the deck, patio, porch, or lawn, this chapter holds something for you. It contains a mix of seating styles (and accessories) that look great and feel just right in many a setting. To start off, imagine the glider shown on the next page residing on your patio. What a place to spend some time with a good book and a cool drink! Its straightforward construction won't overly challenge you.

On *pages 75* to *81*, you'll be charmed by the traditional design of the rocker for two. You'll like it so much that you'll build the accompanying chair and table, too. The white oak and mahogany components are stunning in a natural finish, and they're sure to last for a generation or more. And, you might even want to add the nostalgic porch swing on *page 88* to complement the rocker, chair, and table. It's also made of oak.

The settee on *page 93* adds a more formal touch to your outdoor setting. Reminiscent of English garden furniture, its elegant lines would look good indoors, too.

Finally, the picnic suite presented on *page 99* is sure to please your family and friends when you want to dine outdoors. The angular style offers a contemporary touch, but the all-cedar construction ensures decades of use.

What are you waiting for? Why not get started on some seasonal seating now.

PATIO GLIDER

Built of western red cedar, this project only requires some strap iron and inexpensive bronze bushings for smooth-action swing arms that support the seat (refer to photo on facing page). Colorful cutouts in the back and ends make it the apple of everyone's eye.

Make a Solid Base

1 Cut the uprights (A), base end tops (B), feet (C), and the top and bottom cross members (D, E) to the sizes listed in the Materials List (*page 68*).

2 Mark the locations, and cut half-lap joints across both ends of the uprights (A) and base end tops (B). (See **4–1** on *page 69* for reference.) This can be done on a tablesaw using a dado blade. To support the pieces while cutting, attach a wooden extension and stop to the miter

Patio Glider

gauge. Cut scrap stock first to verify the depth of cut and location of the stop.

3 Mark the location, and cut a 1½" dado ¾" deep centered from end-to-end in the base end top (B).

4 Using the dimensions on the Foot Detail in **4–1**, mark the outline and dado locations on both feet (C). Cut a pair of dadoes on the inside and then the outside surfaces of each foot where marked. Now, cut the feet to shape.

5 Using the gridded pattern in **4–2**, mark the bottom edge of the lower cross members (E), and cut them to shape.

6 Use a drum sander to sand the radii on parts C and E.

➤ *Note: The tannic acid in western red cedar is notoriously hard on galvanized and other coated screws. To avoid the unsightly black streaks that appear over time as the project weathers, use stainless steel screws. Also, construct your glider using a water-resistant glue so that it will stand up to the weather.*

7 Glue and screw the base ends (A, B, C) in the configuration shown in **4–1**.

8 To facilitate adding the metal swing arms later, mark the centerpoints on the top corners of each assembled base end where

shown in **4–1**. Using a ¼" brad-point bit mounted in your drill press, drill the holes.

9 Drill ⁵⁄₃₂" countersunk shank holes in the base ends where shown in **4–1**. Dry fit, then glue and clamp the cross members (D, E) in place between the end assemblies. When the glue dries, drive 2½" deck screws to secure the cross members in place. Sand the base smooth.

Make the End-Frame Assemblies

1 Cut the end-frame slats (F, G, H) and rails (I) to size. Note that parts F, G, and I are cut from ¾" stock, and part H is from 1½"-thick stock.

Materials List for Patio Glider

Part	FINISHED SIZE			MATL.	QTY.
	T	W	L		
BASE					
A uprights	1½"	3"	11"	C	4
B frame tops	1½"	3"	21"	C	2
C feet	1½"	4⅛"	25"	C	2
D top cross-member	1½"	3"	44½"	C	1
E bottom cross-member	1½"	3⅛"	44½"	C	2
END PANELS					
F slats	¾"	4"	22"	C	2
G slats	¾"	2"	22"	C	4
H slats	1½"	3"	22"	C	4
I rails	¾"	2"	21"	C	4
SEAT FRAME					
J cross-member	1½"	3½"	48"	C	1
K cross-member	1½"	1¾"	48"	C	1
L supports	1½"	3½"	20"	C	3
SEAT SLATS AND CLEAT					
M slats	¾"	1⅜"	48"	C	12
N cleat	¾"	1½"	48"	C	1
BACKREST ASSEMBLY					
O* splats	¾"	4½"	16"	C	2
P* splats	¾"	2"	**	C	12
Q* splat	¾"	7"	21"	C	1
R top cleat	¾"	1"	46"	C	1
S armrests	¾"	4¼"	24⅛"	C	2
T supports	¾"	2"	3"	C	4
U brace	¾"	2"	56½"	C	1
V cleat	¾"	1"	47"	C	1

*Initially cut parts oversized. Trim to finished size according to the instructions.
See the patterns in **4–5 for exact lengths of splats O, P, and Q.
Material Key: C = Cedar.
Supplies: 1¼", 1½", 2½" deck screws; eight ¼ x 2¼" roundhead stainless steel machine screws with ¼" locknuts and flat washers; #6 x ⅝" brass flathead wood screws; ⅛ x 1 x 48" flat steel, 8½" of 2/0 open link coil chain and two ½" screw eyes; exterior finish.

PATIO GLIDER CUTTING DIAGRAM

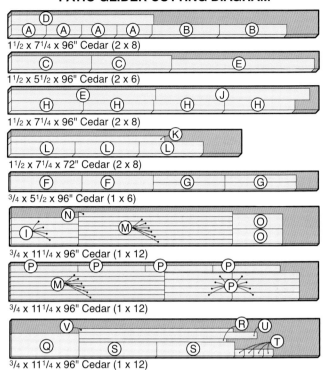

1½ x 7¼ x 96" Cedar (2 x 8)

1½ x 5½ x 96" Cedar (2 x 6)

1½ x 7¼ x 96" Cedar (2 x 8)

1½ x 7¼ x 72" Cedar (2 x 8)

¾ x 5½ x 96" Cedar (1 x 6)

¾ x 11¼ x 96" Cedar (1 x 12)

¾ x 11¼ x 96" Cedar (1 x 12)

¾ x 11¼ x 96" Cedar (1 x 12)

2 Using your tablesaw fitted with a dado blade, cut a 2"-wide rabbet ¾" deep across both ends of each outside slat (H).

3 Transfer the apple pattern in **4–7** *(page 71)* to the center slats (F), 3" from the top end of each, where shown on the End-Frame View in **4–3**, *page 70*. Drill a blade-start hole, and scroll-saw the patterns to shape.

4 Glue and screw each end frame together in the configuration shown in **4–3**.

5 For attaching the swing arms later, mark the centerpoints near the bottom corners of each assembled end frame where shown on the end frame view. Using a ¼" brad-point bit mounted in your drill press, drill the holes where marked. Sand the end frames.

shop TIP

● **You can apply considerable pressure with handscrews, but some woodworkers have difficulty twisting the smooth handles. Inserting them in sections of old bicycle inner tubes provides an easy solution to this gripping problem. Use talcum powder to help ease the inner tube onto the handles.**

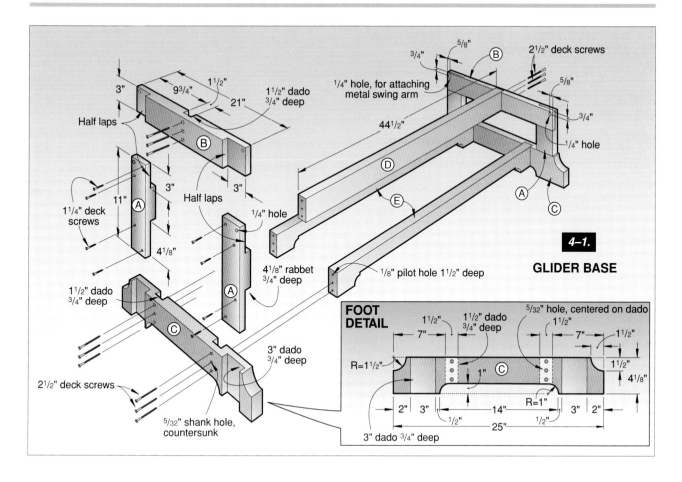

4-1.

GLIDER BASE

Construct the Seat Frame and Add the Slats

1 Cut the seat-frame cross members (J, K) and supports (L) to size.

2 Mark the locations, and cut rabbets and dadoes in the cross members (J, K) where dimensioned on the Seat-Frame drawing (4-4).

3 Transfer the gridded patterns in 4-2 and 4-5 *(pages 70 and 71)*, and cut the bottom edge of the front cross member (J) and supports (L) to shape. Sand the cut edges.

4 Glue and screw the seat frame together, checking for square.

5 Cut the seat slats (M) and rear cleat (N) to size, bevel-ripping the front edge of N at 15° where shown on the Section View drawing in (4-13, on *page 74*).

6 Nail or clamp stops to your wooden drill-press auxiliary table. Now, drill a countersunk mounting hole, centered from front to back and ¾" from the ends of each seat slat.

7 Rout a ½" roundover along the front edge of the front slat (M). Rout a ⅛" roundover along the back edge of the front slat and along the front and back edges (not ends) of all the remaining slats (M). (See the Exploded View [4-8, on *page 72*] and Section View drawing [4-13, on *page 74*] for reference.)

8 Starting at the front and working toward the back, screw the slats, but not the rear cleat (N), in place. (To check the spacing, use spring clamps to hold the last five slats and cleat N in place before attaching. It's important that N attaches to the seat frame where shown on the Section View drawing in 4-13, on *page 74*). Set aside the rear cleat (N) for now to be added later.

Construct the Backrest Assembly

1 Cut the backrest splats (O, P, Q) and the top cleat (R) to the sizes listed in the Materials List.

2 Transfer the gridded pattern shown in **4–5** to the top of the splats, and cut them to shape. Then crosscut the opposite end to cut the splats to the finished length stated on the splats pattern. Rout ⅛ " roundovers along the top front edge of each splat. Sand the splats smooth.

3 Enlarge, then transfer the Apple pattern shown in **4–7** to the center splat (Q), 1½" from the top end of the splat. Drill a blade-start hole, and use a scroll-saw to cut the apple shape.

4 Keeping the bottom edges flush and the good face down, position the backrest splats (O, P, Q) on a flat work surface. Place

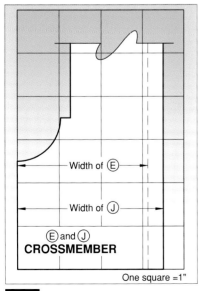

Width of (E)

Width of (J)

(E) and (J)
CROSSMEMBER

One square =1"

4–2. **GRIDDED PATTERN**

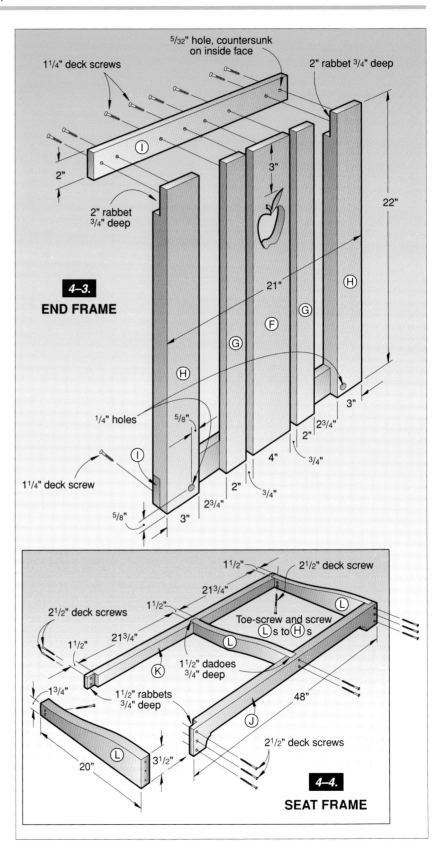

4–3.
END FRAME

4–4.
SEAT FRAME

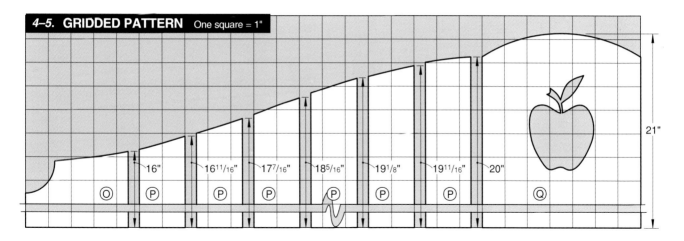

4–5. GRIDDED PATTERN One square = 1"

16" 16¹¹/₁₆" 17⁷/₁₆" 18⁵/₁₆" 19¹/₈" 19¹¹/₁₆" 20"

21"

Ⓞ Ⓟ Ⓟ Ⓟ Ⓟ Ⓟ Ⓟ Ⓠ

½" spacers between the splats, starting with the center splat, and work toward the ends. Now, position the rear cleat (N) and top cleat (R) on the splats where dimensioned on the Section view drawing in **4–13**, on *page 74*. The ends of the rear cleat (N) should protrude ½" beyond the outside edge of each end splat (O). Drill countersunk mounting holes, and screw the splats to the cleats. Keep the bottom ends of the

splats flush with the bottom cleat (N). Use a framing square to keep the pieces square to each other.

5 Set the seat frame assembly on your workbench.

6 As shown in **4–6**, clamp the backrest assembly to the seat frame, drill countersunk mounting holes, and screw the backrest bottom cleat (N) to the seat-frame rear cross member (K) at 6" intervals.

Assemble the Patio Glider

1 Place one end-frame assembly (F, G, H, I), outside face down, on your workbench. Use a framing square to mark a reference line on the inside face of the end frame 10⅞" from the top end. With the aid of a helper, position the seat assembly on the end frame so that the bottom edge of the seat support (L) aligns with the marked reference line. (See the Section View [**4–13**] for positioning help.) Drill mounting holes, and drive four screws

4–6.

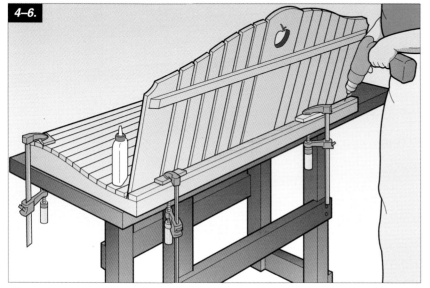

Clamp the backrest assembly to the seat frame, drill countersunk mounting holes, and screw the backrest bottom cleat to the seat-frame crossmember.

4–7.

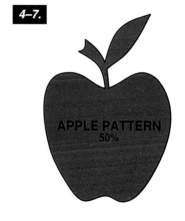

APPLE PATTERN
50%

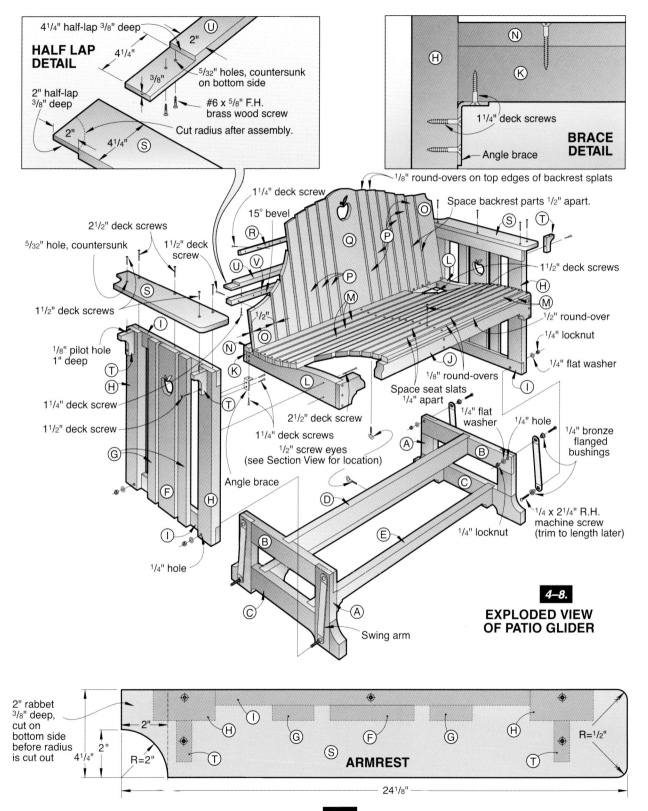

HALF LAP DETAIL

$4^{1}/4$" half-lap $^3/8$" deep
$4^{1}/4$"
2"
$^3/8$"
$^5/32$" holes, countersunk on bottom side
#6 x $^5/8$" F.H. brass wood screw
2" half-lap $^3/8$" deep
2"
$4^{1}/4$"
Cut radius after assembly.

BRACE DETAIL
$1^{1}/4$" deck screws
Angle brace

$1^{1}/4$" deck screw
15° bevel
$2^{1}/2$" deck screws
$^5/32$" hole, countersunk
$1^{1}/2$" deck screw
$^1/8$" round-overs on top edges of backrest splats
Space backrest parts $^1/2$" apart.
$1^{1}/2$" deck screws
$1^{1}/2$" deck screws
$^1/8$" pilot hole 1" deep
$1^{1}/4$" deck screw
$1^{1}/2$" deck screw
$^1/2$"
$^1/2$" round-over
$^1/4$" locknut
$^1/4$" flat washer
$^1/8$" round-overs
Space seat slats $^1/4$" apart
$2^{1}/2$" deck screw
$1^{1}/4$" deck screws
$^1/2$" screw eyes (see Section View for location)
Angle brace
$^1/4$" hole
$^1/4$" flat washer
$^1/4$" hole
$^1/4$" bronze flanged bushings
$1/4$ x $2^{1}/4$" R.H. machine screw (trim to length later)
$^1/4$" locknut
Swing arm

4–8.
EXPLODED VIEW OF PATIO GLIDER

2" rabbet $^3/8$" deep, cut on bottom side before radius is cut out
2"
2"
$4^{1}/4$"
R=2"
R=$^1/2$"
ARMREST
$24^{1}/8$"

4–9.

through the seat support (L) and into the inside face of the end-frame slats (H). Repeat the process to attach the opposite end frame.

2 Cut the armrests (S), supports (T), and armrest brace (U) to the sizes listed in the Materials List. (See **4–12**, the gridded pattern for the supports [T].) Cut the brace cleat (V) to size, bevel-ripping the front edge at a 15° angle.

3 Cut mating half-lap joints on the ends of the armrests and brace to the size shown on the Half-Lap Detail in **4–8**. Checking for square, glue and screw the armrests to the brace.

4 Transfer the shape from the Armrest drawing in **4–9**, and cut the armrest front corners and outside back corners to shape. Using the pattern at right, cut the supports (T) to shape.

5 Position and clamp the armrest assembly (S, U) on top of the end frames and against the back face of the backrest assembly. Drill the mounting holes, and screw the assembly in place.

6 Glue and screw the brace cleat (V) to the bottom side of the backrest brace (U). Now, drill countersunk mounting holes through the brace cleat and into the back of the splats. Drive screws through each of these holes.

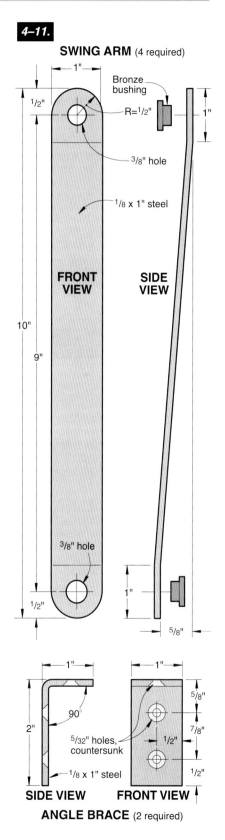

Connect the steel swing arms from the rear holes in the base to the rear holes in the seat assembly. Form the swing arms as shown at right.

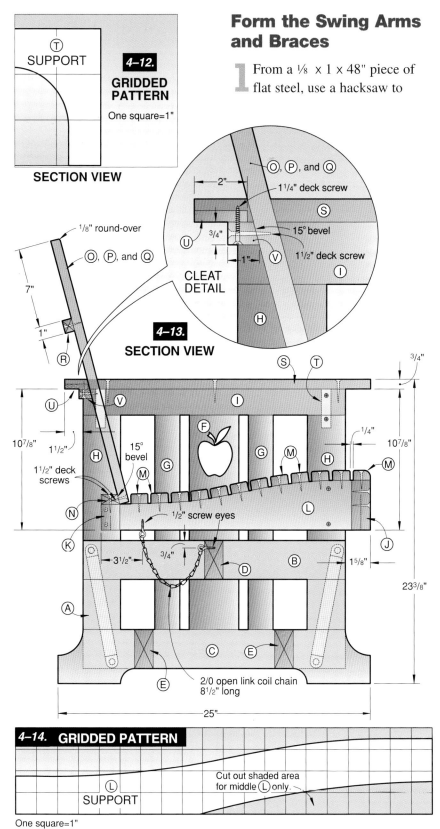

4–12. GRIDDED PATTERN
SUPPORT
One square=1"
SECTION VIEW

4–13. SECTION VIEW
CLEAT DETAIL

4–14. GRIDDED PATTERN
SUPPORT
Cut out shaded area for middle L only.
One square=1"

Form the Swing Arms and Braces

1 From a 1/8 x 1 x 48" piece of flat steel, use a hacksaw to cut four pieces measuring 10" long each. Drill a 3/8" hole in each end of each swing arm where shown on the pattern in **4–11**. Grind the corners round.

2 Clamp each end of each swing arm in your wood-worker's vise, and bend to the angle shown on **4–11**.

3 To form a pair of angle braces, cut two 3"-long pieces from the remaining flat steel stock. Bend them to the shape shown on the pattern. Drill mounting holes, and screw the braces in the corner where parts K and H meet. The braces strengthen the joint.

4 Press a bronze bushing into each 3/8" hole in each swing arm where shown on the pattern in **4–11**.

5 As shown in **4–10** *(page 73)*, position the seat assembly, back face down, on either your workbench or the floor. Position the base in front of it, and connect the two swing arms from the rear top holes in the base to the rear holes in the seat assembly. Repeat the process to attach the front swing arms. Use a hacksaw and file to trim the protruding ends of the bolts flush with the outside ends of the locknuts.

6 To keep the glider from swinging too far back, attach a pair of screw eyes and an 8½" length of 2/0 open-link coil chain to parts D and the middle L where shown on the Section View drawing (**4–13**).

7 Finish-sand the entire assembly, and add an exterior finish. The patio glider shown on *page 67* was finished with a penetrating clear wood finish with water repellent. It's critical to get a good seal on the bottom of the base (those parts that come in direct contact with the ground or patio). Recoat the chair annually. For an added touch, paint the inside edges of the apples red and the stems and leaves green. Be sure to select durable acrylic enamels that are recommended for outdoor applications.

Rocker for two

ROCKER FOR TWO

Here's a classically styled love seat just meant for dreaming. Its slatted and contoured seat and back provide plenty of casual comfort. It's easy to build, so you may want to add the slatted chair and side table on *page 81*.

Build the Rocker

1 Cut four pieces of ¾" white oak to 6¼" width x 32" length for the rocker blanks (A). Plane or resaw each piece to ⅝" thick.

2 Using the dimensions in **4–17** *(page 77)*, mark the dado locations on each rocker blank. Cut the dadoes. (It is suggested that you clamp an

shop TIP

● The porch rocker shown here was built of weather-resistant white oak and Honduras mahogany so it can be used outdoors. Don't substitute Philippine mahogany (which isn't really mahogany at all) or red oak; neither will stand up to weather.

Materials List for Rocker for Two

PART	FINISHED SIZE			MATL.	QTY.
	T	W	L		
Rocker Assembly					
A* rocker blanks	⅝"	6¼"	32"	WO	4
B* back legs	1¹⁄₁₆"	2"	24¹⁄₁₆"	HM	2
C* front legs	1¹⁄₁₆"	2"	23⅜"	HM	2
D rails	¾"	1¾"	17"	HM	2
E armrests	¾"	3¼"	21¼"	WO	2
F stretchers	1¹⁄₁₆"	2"	50⅛"	HM	2
Seat Assembly					
G* seat supports	1¹⁄₁₆"	4¾"	21"	HM	3
H* back supports	1¹⁄₁₆"	3"	23"	HM	3
I* slats	⁵⁄₁₆"	1½"	48"	WO	20
J top slat	¾"	1¹⁵⁄₁₆"	48"	WO	1

*Initial dimensions shown.
Materials Key: WO = White oak; HM = Honduras mahogany.
Supplies: double-faced tape; spray adhesive; ¼ x 2½" flathead brass machine screws with brass washers and cap nuts; #8 x ¾" flathead brass wood screws; #8 x 1½" flathead brass wood screws; #12 x 2" flathead brass wood screws; clear exterior finish.

CUTTING DIAGRAM

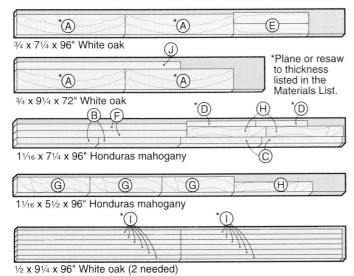

¾ x 7¼ x 96" White oak

¾ x 9¼ x 72" White oak

*Plane or resaw to thickness listed in the Materials List.

1¹⁄₁₆ x 7¼ x 96" Honduras mahogany

1¹⁄₁₆ x 5½ x 96" Honduras mahogany

½ x 9¼ x 96" White oak (2 needed)

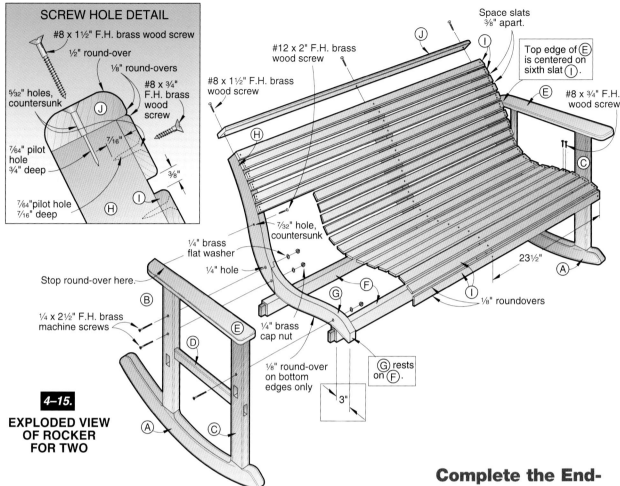

SCREW HOLE DETAIL

#8 x 1½" F.H. brass wood screw

½" round-over

⅛" round-overs

#8 x ¾" F.H. brass wood screw

$\frac{5}{32}$" holes, countersunk

$\frac{7}{64}$" pilot hole ¾" deep

$\frac{7}{16}$"

$\frac{7}{64}$" pilot hole $\frac{7}{16}$" deep

⅜"

#12 x 2" F.H. brass wood screw

#8 x 1½" F.H. brass wood screw

Space slats ⅜" apart.

Top edge of (E) is centered on sixth slat (I).

#8 x ¾" F.H. wood screw

$\frac{7}{32}$" hole, countersunk

¼" brass flat washer

¼" hole

Stop round-over here.

¼ x 2½" F.H. brass machine screws

¼" brass cap nut

⅛" round-over on bottom edges only

(G) rests on (F).

3"

23½"

⅛" roundovers

3"

4–15.

EXPLODED VIEW OF ROCKER FOR TWO

auxiliary fence to your miter gauge, and clamp a stop to the fence to ensure that the dadoes are consistently positioned from blank to blank.)

➤ *Note: So that your porch rocker can stand up to the elements, construct the rocker using water-resistant glue, slow-set epoxy, or resorcinol glue.*

3 Glue the mating rocker blanks (A) face to face, with the dadoes aligned and the ends and edges flush. Clamp, and immediately remove glue squeeze-out from the mortises.

4 Using double-faced tape, stick the two rocker blanks together face to face, with the edges and ends flush.

5 Enlarge the Gridded Rocker patterns (on *page 80*) onto a 6 x 31" piece of paper. Using spray adhesive, adhere the pattern to one of the rocker laminations, aligning the dadoes on the pattern with those cut in the wood.

6 Band-saw the taped-together rocker laminations to shape. Sand the rocker edges flush. Separate the rockers, and remove the tape.

Complete the End-Frame Assemblies

1 From 1$\frac{1}{16}$"-thick Honduras mahogany, cut the legs (B, C) to size. From ¾" mahogany, cut the rails (D) to size.

2 Using the dimensions on the End-Frame Assembly drawing (**4–16**), and **4–19** and **4–20** *(page 78)*, carefully mark the mortise, tenon, and hole locations on each leg. Mark the tenon locations on each end of the rails.

3 Following the four-step procedure in **4–20**, form the mortises. Then, cut tenons on the legs and rails.

4–16.
END FRAME ASSEMBLY

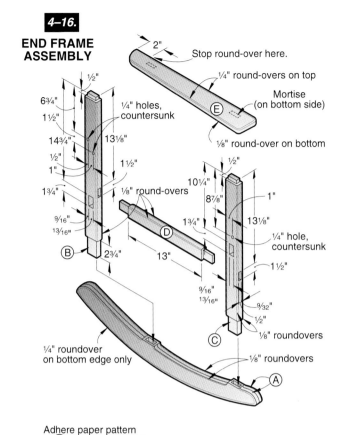

2"
Stop round-over here.
¼" round-overs on top
Mortise (on bottom side)
⅛" round-over on bottom
½"
6¾"
1½"
¼" holes, countersunk
14¾" 13⅛"
½"
1"
1¾"
⅛" round-overs
1½"
10¼"
8⅞"
1"
1¾"
13⅛"
¼" hole, countersunk
1½"
9/16"
13/16"
(B) 2¾" 13" (D) (E) (C)
9/16"
13/16"
9/32"
½"
⅛" roundovers
⅛" roundovers
¼" roundover on bottom edge only
(A)

Adhere paper pattern to (A) with spray adhesive.

4–17.
ROCKER LAMINATION

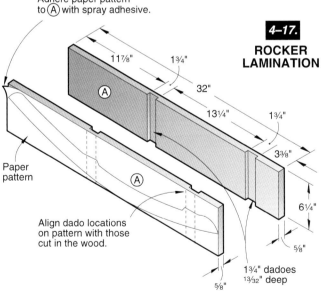

11⅞" 1¾"
32"
13¼" 1¾"
3⅜"
6¼"
Paper pattern
(A) (A)
Align dado locations on pattern with those cut in the wood.
1¾" dadoes 13/32" deep
⅝" ⅝"

shop TIP

● Another way to transfer a pattern is to photocopy it, lay the copy face down on the workpiece, and transfer the pattern with a clothes iron. Set the iron to its low setting (no steam), and run the iron over the pattern. Then, slowly peel up sections of the copy to make sure all the lines are transferred. If not, just iron over them again.

4 For securing the seat assembly to the end frames later, drill and countersink a pair of ¼" holes in each back leg (B) and one in each front leg (C).

5 Cut two armrest blanks (E) to $3\frac{1}{4} \times 21\frac{1}{4}$" from ¾"-thick white oak. Using **4–23** on *page 78* for reference, transfer the pattern to one of the pieces. Next, using the method described earlier, tape the armrests together, cut to shape, sand the edges smooth, separate the armrests, and remove the tape.

6 Mark the locations for the 9/16"-deep mortises on each armrest bottom.

7 Rout ⅛ " and ¼" roundovers along the edges of parts A, B, C, D, and E where shown on **4–15** and **4–16**.

8 Glue and clamp the two end-frame assemblies. Check each for square.

Add the Stretchers and Join the End Assemblies

1 Cut the stretchers (F) to size. Cut 1 1/16"-long tenons on the ends of each stretcher.

2 Glue the pair of stretchers between the end frames as shown in **4–21** *(page 78)*. (To ensure that the assembly stays square, clamp square corner braces in place until the glue dries.)

3 Position an armrest on the top of each end assembly, and verify that the marked mortises match the tenon locations on the top of the legs. Re-mark if necessary.

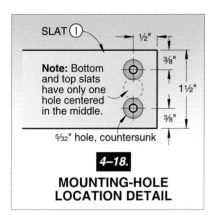

SLAT (I)

Note: Bottom and top slats have only one hole centered in the middle.

$\frac{1}{2}$"

$\frac{3}{8}$"

$1\frac{1}{2}$"

$\frac{3}{8}$"

$\frac{5}{32}$" hole, countersunk

4–18.

MOUNTING-HOLE LOCATION DETAIL

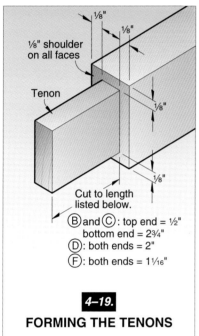

$\frac{1}{8}$"

$\frac{1}{8}$"

$\frac{1}{8}$" shoulder on all faces

Tenon

$\frac{1}{8}$"

$\frac{1}{8}$"

Cut to length listed below.

(B) and (C): top end = $\frac{1}{2}$"
bottom end = $2\frac{3}{4}$"
(D): both ends = 2"
(F): both ends = $1\frac{1}{16}$"

4–19.

FORMING THE TENONS

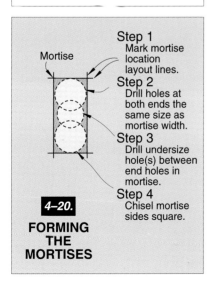

Mortise

Step 1 Mark mortise location layout lines.

Step 2 Drill holes at both ends the same size as mortise width.

Step 3 Drill undersize hole(s) between end holes in mortise.

Step 4 Chisel mortise sides square.

4–20.

FORMING THE MORTISES

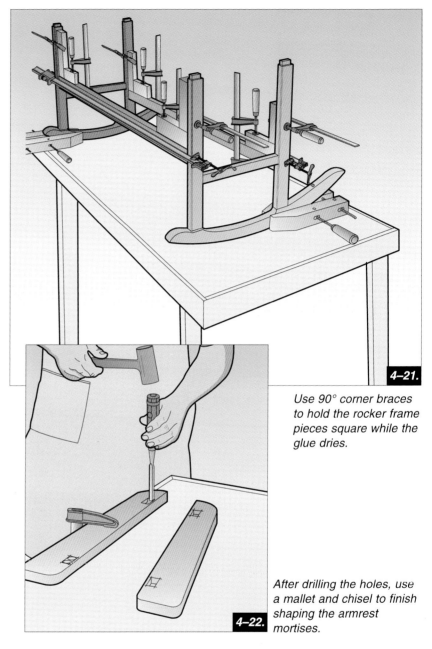

4–21.

Use 90° corner braces to hold the rocker frame pieces square while the glue dries.

After drilling the holes, use a mallet and chisel to finish shaping the armrest mortises.

4–22.

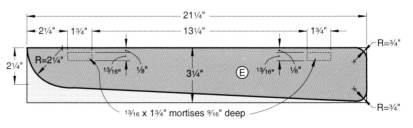

$21\frac{1}{4}$"

$2\frac{1}{4}$" $1\frac{3}{4}$" $13\frac{1}{4}$" $1\frac{3}{4}$"

R=$\frac{3}{4}$"

$2\frac{1}{4}$" R=$2\frac{1}{4}$" $\frac{13}{16}$" $\frac{1}{8}$" $3\frac{1}{4}$" (E) $\frac{13}{16}$" $\frac{1}{8}$"

R=$\frac{3}{4}$"

$\frac{13}{16}$ x $1\frac{3}{4}$" mortises $\frac{9}{16}$" deep

4–23.

ARMREST

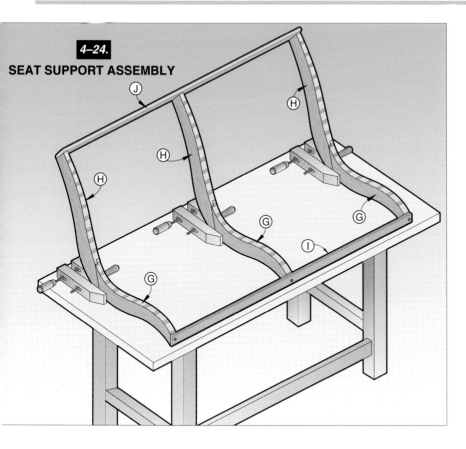

4–24.
SEAT SUPPORT ASSEMBLY

5 Enlarge the gridded Porch Rocker and Chair Seat Support pattern in **4–28** onto a 12 x 33" piece of paper. Tape the assembled supports together, and adhere the pattern outline to them, using spray adhesive. Cut out the supports, and sand the edges. Transfer the slat locations to each slat support assembly (G/H). Pry the pieces apart, remove the double-faced tape, and finish-sand the supports, being careful not to sand away the slat location lines.

6 Rout $\frac{1}{8}$" roundovers along the bottom and back edges of each slat support, where shown in **4–15,** on *page 76.*

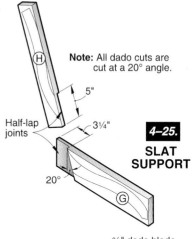

Note: All dado cuts are cut at a 20° angle.

Half-lap joints

5"

3¼"

20°

4–25.
SLAT SUPPORT

4 Drill overlapping holes $\frac{9}{16}$" deep where marked. Then, as shown in **4–22,** chisel the mortise sides square, and finish forming the mortise.

5 Glue an armrest to the top of each end-frame assembly. Sand the rocker assembly smooth.

Build the Slat-Support Assemblies

1 Rip and crosscut three pieces of 1$\frac{1}{16}$" mahogany stock to 4$\frac{3}{4}$ x 21" for the bottom-slat supports (G). Cut three pieces of the same stock to 3 x 23" for back-slat supports (H).

2 Using **4–25** for reference, mark the location of the half-

lap joint on one end of each of the slat supports (G, H).

3 Mount a $\frac{3}{4}$"-wide dado blade in your tablesaw. Elevate the blade to cut exactly half the thickness of your stock. (It is suggested that you use scrap the same thickness as the supports, and make test cuts to verify blade height.) Angle the miter gauge 20° from center. Cut a half lap on one end of each of the six slat supports, where shown on "Cutting the Half Laps" in **4–26**.

4 Dry-clamp the three supports (one G and one H per support) to check the fit. Then glue and clamp each of the three supports.

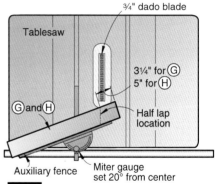

¾" dado blade

Tablesaw

3¼" for G
5" for H

Half lap location

G and H

Auxiliary fence   Miter gauge set 20° from center

4–26. **CUTTING THE HALF LAPS**

4–27. PORCH ROCKER GRIDDED PATTERN

4–28. PORCH ROCKER AND CHAIR SEAT SUPPORT GRIDDED PATTERN

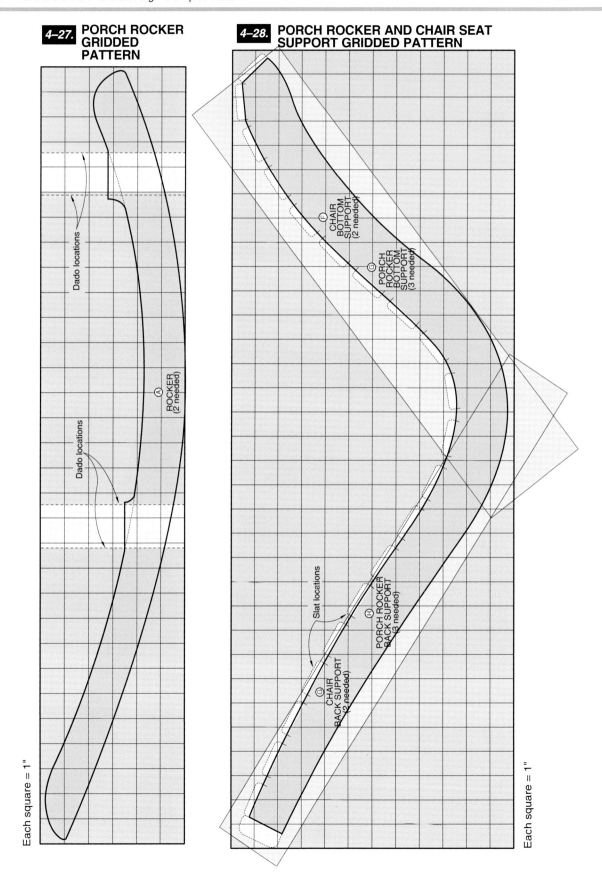

Dado locations

Dado locations

ⓐ ROCKER (2 needed)

Each square = 1"

Ⓕ CHAIR BOTTOM SUPPORT (2 needed)

Ⓖ PORCH ROCKER BOTTOM SUPPORT (3 needed)

Slat locations

Ⓗ PORCH ROCKER BACK SUPPORT (3 needed)

Ⓖ CHAIR BACK SUPPORT (2 needed)

Each square = 1"

Fasten the Slats to the Slat Supports

1 From $5/16$"-thick oak (plane thicker stock to size), cut 20 seat slats (I) to $1\frac{1}{2}$ x 48". From $3/4$" stock, cut the top slat (J) to size.

2 Rout a $1/8$ " roundover along the top edges and ends of each $5/16$" slat (I) and a $1/2$" roundover along the top edges and ends of the top slat (J). Next, rout a $1/8$" roundover along the bottom front edge of the top slat.

3 Drill the countersunk screw holes in each slat, where dimensioned in **4–15**, on *page 76*. (Clamp a fence and a stop block to your drill-press table to consistently position the holes from slat to slat.)

4 As shown in **4–24** (on *page 79*), place the three slat supports on your benchtop. Attach a large handscrew clamp to each to hold the pieces upright.

5 Screw the top slat (J) to the three slat supports. Then, fasten one of the $5/16$" slats (I) to the opposite end of the assembly, where shown in the Screw-Hole Detail drawing in **4–15**.

6 Following the layout marks on the slat supports, fasten the remaining seat slats (I).

Complete the Porch Rocker

1 With a helper, position the seat assembly on the rocker assembly where dimensioned in

Porch rocker table and chair

the yellow tinted boxes in **4–15**. Once the seat assembly is correctly positioned, clamp the seat in place.

2 Using the previously drilled $1/4$" holes in the front and rear legs as guides, drill $1/4$" holes through the slat supports. Using $1/4$" machine screws, fasten the two assemblies together.

3 Working from the back inside, drill a $7/32$" shank hole through the back seat support (H) and a $9/64$" pilot hole 1" deep into the inner edge of the armrests. Drive a #12 x 2" flathead brass wood screw through the support, into the armrest.

4 Remove the screws, and separate the seat assembly from the rocker assembly. Finish-sand both assemblies and apply the finish. (Three coats of spar varnish were applied to the rocker shown on *page 75*.) Later, fasten the two assemblies back together.

TABLE AND CHAIR FOR PORCH ROCKER

These companions to the porch rocker just presented are a practical twosome that feature the same easy-to-assemble slatted construction and stubborn resistance to whatever nature decides to dish out. Why not build several for your deck, porch, or patio?

CHAIR

Make the Legs, Rails, and Armrests

1 Cut the legs (A, B) to size, adding 1" to the finished length shown in the Materials List. (Honduras mahogany was used for the table and chair shown above.)

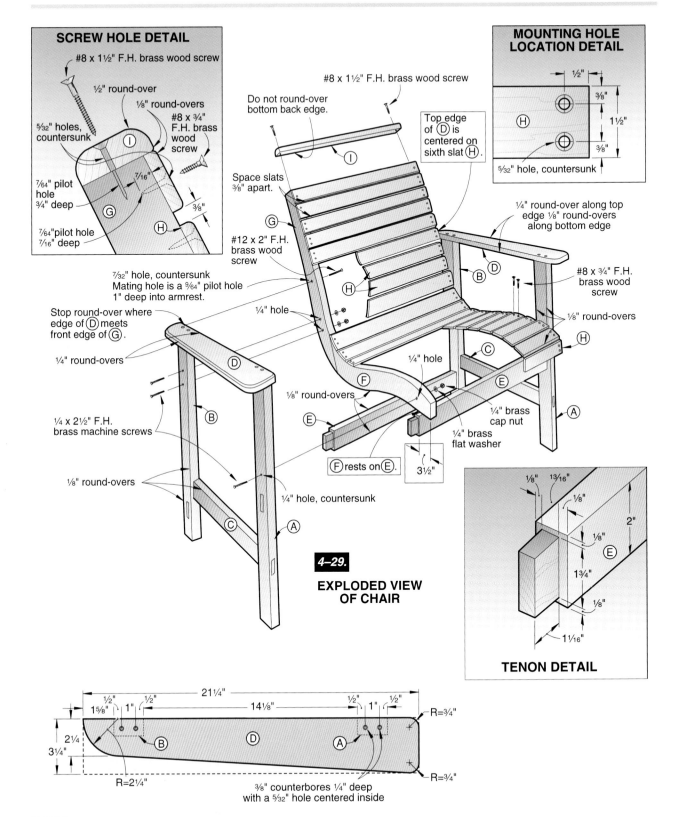

SCREW HOLE DETAIL

#8 x 1½" F.H. brass wood screw

½" round-over

⅛" round-overs

#8 x ¾" F.H. brass wood screw

5/32" holes, countersunk

7/64" pilot hole ¾" deep

7/64" pilot hole 7/16" deep

7/16"

3/8"

MOUNTING HOLE LOCATION DETAIL

½"

3/8"

1½"

3/8"

5/32" hole, countersunk

#8 x 1½" F.H. brass wood screw

Do not round-over bottom back edge.

Top edge of (D) is centered on sixth slat (H).

Space slats 3/8" apart.

#12 x 2" F.H. brass wood screw

¼" round-over along top edge ⅛" round-overs along bottom edge

#8 x ¾" F.H. brass wood screw

⅛" round-overs

7/32" hole, countersunk Mating hole is a 9/64" pilot hole 1" deep into armrest.

Stop round-over where edge of (D) meets front edge of (G).

¼" round-overs

¼" hole

¼ x 2½" F.H. brass machine screws

⅛" round-overs

¼" hole, countersunk

⅛" round-overs

¼" hole

¼" brass cap nut

¼" brass flat washer

(F) rests on (E).

3½"

4–29.

EXPLODED VIEW OF CHAIR

⅛" 13/16"

⅛"

2"

⅛"

1¾"

⅛"

1 1/16"

TENON DETAIL

21¼"

½" ½"

1 5/8" 1"

14⅛"

½" 1" ½"

R=¾"

2¼"

3¼"

R=2¼"

R=¾"

3/8" counterbores ¼" deep with a 5/32" hole centered inside

4–30.

ARMREST

CHAIR CUTTING DIAGRAM

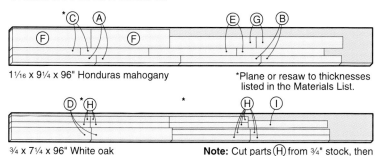

$1\frac{1}{16}$ x $9\frac{1}{4}$ x 96" Honduras mahogany

*Plane or resaw to thicknesses listed in the Materials List.

$\frac{3}{4}$ x $7\frac{1}{4}$ x 96" White oak

Note: Cut parts (H) from $\frac{3}{4}$" stock, then resaw in half to form $\frac{5}{16}$" slats.

Materials List for Chair

PART	FINISHED SIZE			MATL.	QTY.
	T	W	L		
A* front legs	$1\frac{1}{16}$"	2"	$21\frac{1}{2}$"	HM	2
B* back legs	$1\frac{1}{16}$"	2"	$20\frac{1}{4}$"	HM	2
C rails	$\frac{3}{4}$"	2"	$18\frac{1}{8}$"	HM	2
D armrests	$\frac{3}{4}$"	$3\frac{1}{4}$"	$21\frac{1}{4}$"	WO	2
E stretchers	$1\frac{1}{16}$"	2"	$23\frac{1}{8}$"	HM	2
F* seat slat supports	$1\frac{1}{16}$"	$4\frac{3}{4}$"	21"	HM	2
G* back slat supports	$1\frac{1}{16}$"	3"	23"	HM	2
H slats	$\frac{5}{16}$"	$1\frac{1}{2}$"	21"	WO	20
I top slat	$\frac{3}{4}$"	2"	21"	WO	1

*Initial dimensions shown.
Materials Key: HM = Honduras mahogany; WO = White oak.
Supplies: $\frac{1}{4}$ x $2\frac{1}{2}$" flathead brass machine screws with brass flat washers and cap nuts; #8 x $\frac{3}{4}$" and $1\frac{1}{2}$" flathead brass wood screws; #12 x 2" flathead brass wood screws; 2" galvanized deck screws; clear exterior finish.

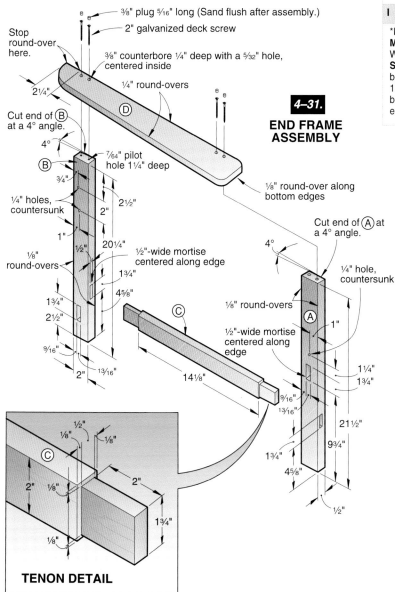

4–31.

END FRAME ASSEMBLY

TENON DETAIL

Miter-cut the top end of each leg at 4° to give the legs the finished length stated in the Materials List.

2 Cut the rails (C) to size from $\frac{3}{4}$" Honduras mahogany.

3 Using the dimensions in **4–31**, carefully mark the mortise and $\frac{1}{4}$" hole centerpoints on each leg (A, B). Following the four-step procedure in **4–32**, drill and chisel the mortises through the legs.

4 Next, drill and countersink a $\frac{1}{4}$" hole in each front leg (A) and two in each back leg (B).

5 Mark the tenon locations on the ends of each rail (C). (See the Tenon Detail drawing in **4–31**. Then, cut tenons on both ends of each rail.

Step 1 Mark mortise location layout lines.
Step 2 Drill holes at both ends the same size as mortise width.
Step 3 Drill undersize hole(s) between end holes in mortise.
Step 4 Chisel mortise sides and corners square.

4–32.
FORMING THE MORTISES

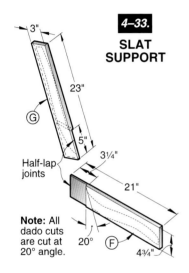

4–33.
SLAT SUPPORT

3"
23"
G
5"
Half-lap joints
3¼"
21"
Note: All dado cuts are cut at 20° angle.
20°
F
4¾"

6 Cut two armrest blanks (D) to 3¼ x 21¼" from ¾"-thick white oak. Using **4–29** for reference, transfer the outline to one of the blanks. Tape the armrest blanks together (using double-faced tape), with the edges and ends flush. Band-saw the armrests to shape, sand the edges smooth, and separate the armrests. Proceed to remove the tape.

7 Mark (but don't drill) the centerpoints for two pairs of screw mounting holes on the top of each armrest.

Construct the End-Frame Assemblies

➤*Note: Construct your chair using water-resistant glue, slow-set epoxy, or resorcinol glue so it can stand up to the elements.*

1 Rout ⅛ " and ¼" roundovers along the edges of parts A, B, C, and D where shown in **4–29** and **4–31** (*pages 82 and 83*).

2 Glue and clamp a rail (C) between a front and back leg. Using a framing square, check that the legs are square to the rail.

3 Clamp an armrest on the top of each end-frame assembly (A/B/C). Verify that the marked mounting holes are located on the top of the legs. Re-mark the holes if necessary.

4 Drill the mounting holes through the armrests and into the top ends of the legs. Screw the armrests to the leg tops, plug the holes, and sand the plugs flush.

Add the Stretchers and Join the End Assemblies

1 Cut the stretchers (E) to size. Cut 1¹⁄₁₆"-long tenons on the ends of each stretcher.

2 Rout ⅛" roundovers along the edges of each stretcher.

3 Glue the pair of stretchers between the end frames. (To ensure that the end assemblies

will stay square to the stretchers, clamp square corner braces in place and leave them there until the glue dries.) Sand the chair frame.

Make the Slat-Support Assemblies

1 Cut two pieces of 1¹⁄₁₆" mahogany to 4¾ x 21" for the bottom-slat seat supports (F) and two pieces to 3 x 23" for the back-slat supports (G).

2 Using **4–32** for reference, mark the location of a half-lap joint on one end of each slat support (F, G).

3 Mount a ¾"-wide dado blade to your tablesaw and an auxiliary wooden fence to your miter gauge. Elevate the blade to cut exactly half the thickness of your stock. (Using scrap the same thickness as the supports, make test cuts to verify blade height.) Angle the miter gauge 20° from center, and clamp a stop to your auxiliary miter-gauge fence. Cut a half lap on one end of each of the four slat supports, where dimensioned in **4–32**.

4 Dry-clamp the two supports (one F and one G per support) to check the fit. Then glue and clamp each of the two slat supports.

5 Enlarge the Porch Rocker and Chair Seat Support pattern in **4–28** (*page 80*). Tape the assembled slat supports (F, G) together,

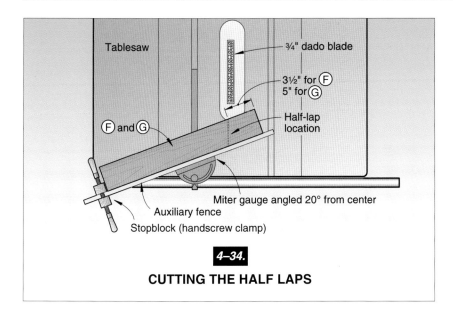

Tablesaw

¾" dado blade

3½" for Ⓕ
5" for Ⓖ

Ⓕ and Ⓖ

Half-lap location

Miter gauge angled 20° from center
Auxiliary fence
Stopblock (handscrew clamp)

4–34.

CUTTING THE HALF LAPS

Attach the Seat Assembly to the Chair Frame

1 With a helper, position the seat assembly on the chair frame, where dimensioned in the yellow tinted boxes in **4–29**. Once it is positioned, clamp the seat to the frame.

2 Using the previously drilled ¼" holes in the front and rear legs as guides, drill ¼" holes through the supports. Then connect the two assemblies together with ¼" brass machine screws, flat washers, and cap nuts.

3 Working from the back of the chair, drill a $7/32$" countersunk shank hole through the back seat supports (G) and a $9/64$" pilot hole 1" deep into the inside edge of the armrests. Drive a #12 x 2" flathead brass wood screw through each support and into the armrests.

4 Remove the wood screws and machine screws to separate the seat assembly from the chair frame. Finish-sand both assemblies, and apply a quality exterior finish. (Three coats of spar varnish were used on the chair shown on *page 81*.) Allow the finish to dry thoroughly; then fasten the two assemblies back together.

transfer the pattern outline to them, cut the supports to shape, and sand the edges. Using a try square, transfer the slat locations to the top edge of each slat support. Separate the pieces and finish-sand them, being careful not to sand away the slat location lines.

6 Rout ⅛" roundovers along the bottom and back edges of each slat support, where shown in **4–29**.

Fasten the Slats to the Slat Supports

1 From $5/16$"-thick white oak (plane thicker stock to size), cut 20 seat slats (H) to 1½ x 21". From ¾" stock, cut the top slat (I) to size.

2 Rout a ⅛" roundover along the top edges and ends of each $5/16$" slat (H) and a ½" roundover along the top edges and ends of the top slat (I).

(Refer to **4–28**.) Next, rout a ⅛" roundover along the bottom front edge of the top slat.

3 Drill countersunk screw holes in each slat where dimensioned in **4–29**. Note that the bottom and top two slats have only one hole per end. (Clamp a fence and a stop block to your drill-press table to consistently position the holes from slat to slat.)

4 Place the two slat supports on your benchtop. Clamp a large handscrew clamp to each to hold them upright.

5 Screw the top slat (I) to the slat supports. Fasten one of the $5/16$" slats (H) to the opposite bottom end of the assembly. Following the layout marks on the slat supports, fasten the remaining seat slats (H). Check that the slats are square to the supports.

Porch rocker table

TABLE

Build a Matching Table

To build the matching table, follow the same construction procedure used to build the chair, and refer to **4–35** and the Materials List for the table.

Using your router and a slot-cutting bit, rout $\frac{1}{4}$" spline slots $2\frac{1}{4}$" long in the mitered ends of the tabletop banding pieces (D, E). (See **4–38** for reference.) Next, turn the banding pieces on edge, and cut a $\frac{1}{8}$" groove along the inside edge of each to accommo-date the slats (F) on your tablesaw.

Materials List for Table

	PART	FINISHED SIZE			MATL.	QTY.
		T	W	L		
A	legs	$1\frac{1}{16}$"	2"	20"	HM	4
B	stretchers	$\frac{3}{4}$"	2"	$12\frac{1}{2}$"	HM	2
C	rails	$1\frac{1}{16}$"	2"	$9\frac{5}{8}$"	HM	2
D	bandings	$\frac{3}{4}$"	3"	$18\frac{1}{2}$"	HM	2
E	bandings	$\frac{3}{4}$"	3"	$13\frac{1}{2}$"	HM	2
F*	slats	$\frac{5}{16}$"	$1\frac{1}{2}$"	8"	WO	7

Materials Key: HM = Honduras mahogany; WO = White oak.
Supplies: 2" galvanized deck screws; clear exterior finish.

TABLE CUTTING DIAGRAM

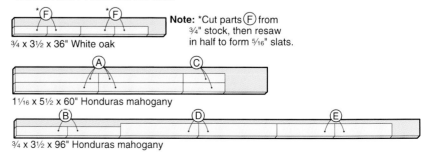

*F *F   Note: *Cut parts F from
$\frac{3}{4}$" stock, then resaw
in half to form $\frac{5}{16}$" slats.
$\frac{3}{4}$ x $3\frac{1}{2}$ x 36" White oak

A   C
$1\frac{1}{16}$ x $5\frac{1}{2}$ x 60" Honduras mahogany

B   D   E
$\frac{3}{4}$ x $3\frac{1}{2}$ x 96" Honduras mahogany

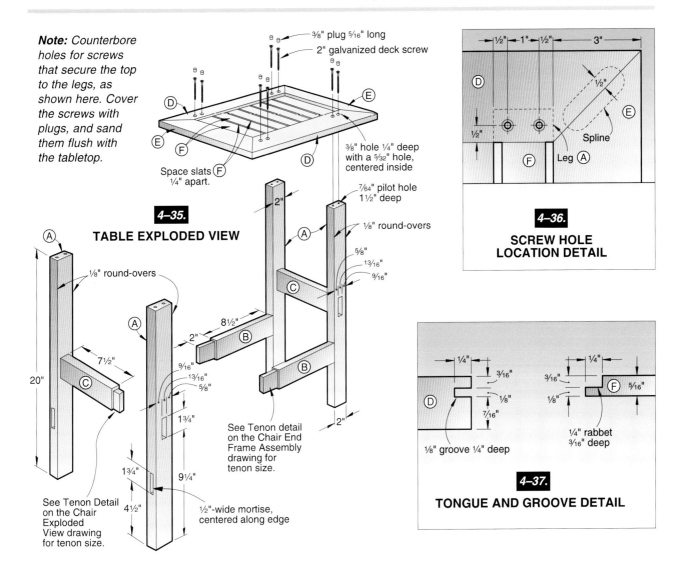

Note: *Counterbore holes for screws that secure the top to the legs, as shown here. Cover the screws with plugs, and sand them flush with the tabletop.*

$\frac{3}{8}$" plug $\frac{5}{16}$" long
2" galvanized deck screw

Space slats (F) $\frac{1}{4}$" apart.

$\frac{3}{8}$" hole $\frac{1}{4}$" deep with a $\frac{5}{32}$" hole, centered inside

4–35.
TABLE EXPLODED VIEW

$\frac{1}{8}$" round-overs

$\frac{7}{64}$" pilot hole $1\frac{1}{2}$" deep

$\frac{1}{8}$" round-overs

2"

$\frac{5}{8}$"
$\frac{13}{16}$"
$\frac{9}{16}$"

8½"

2"

$\frac{9}{16}$"
$\frac{13}{16}$"
$\frac{5}{8}$"

7½"

20"

$1\frac{3}{4}$"

$1\frac{3}{4}$"

9¼"

4½"

2"

See Tenon detail on the Chair End Frame Assembly drawing for tenon size.

See Tenon Detail on the Chair Exploded View drawing for tenon size.

½"-wide mortise, centered along edge

4–36.
SCREW HOLE LOCATION DETAIL

½" — 1" — ½" — 3"

½"

½"

Spline

Leg (A)

4–37.
TONGUE AND GROOVE DETAIL

¼"
$\frac{3}{16}$"
$\frac{1}{8}$"
$\frac{7}{16}$"

$\frac{1}{8}$" groove ¼" deep

$\frac{3}{16}$"
¼"
$\frac{1}{8}$"
$\frac{5}{16}$"

¼" rabbet $\frac{3}{16}$" deep

Use your tablesaw fitted with a dado blade and a miter-gauge fence to cut ¼" rabbets across the ends of the slats (F). Check the fit of the slat ends into the grooves cut in the banding pieces.

Assemble the table base, then the tabletop. Screw the two assemblies together, and complete the project by applying a clear exterior finish.

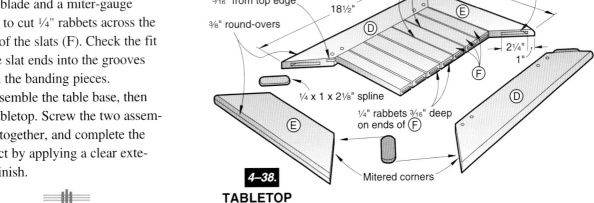

Space slats (F) ¼" apart.

$\frac{1}{8}$" groove ¼" deep $\frac{3}{16}$" from top edge

$\frac{3}{8}$" round-overs

18½"

$13\frac{1}{2}$"

¼" spline slot $2\frac{1}{4}$" long
Note: Spline slot starts 1" in from outside end.

$2\frac{1}{4}$"
1"

¼ x 1 x $2\frac{1}{8}$" spline

¼" rabbets $\frac{3}{16}$" deep on ends of (F)

Mitered corners

4–38.
TABLETOP

NOSTALGIC PORCH SWING

Made of white oak and hung from chains, this old-time favorite provides swinging seating for adults or kids.

Make the Seat and Back Support Pieces

1 Rip and crosscut three pieces of $1\frac{1}{16}$" oak stock to $4\frac{1}{4} \times 22$" for the seat supports (A). (See the Cutting Diagram.) For the back supports (B), rip and crosscut three $3\frac{1}{4} \times 24$" pieces.

2 Mount a $\frac{3}{4}$"-wide dado on your tablesaw. Elevate the dado (about $\frac{17}{32}$") to cut half laps on the ends of the support pieces. (Using scraps of the same thickness as the supports, make test cuts to adjust the blade height.) Place the miter gauge in the table's slot, and angle it 65° to the right. Cut a half lap on one end of each of the three seat support pieces to the dimensions shown in **4–41**. Now, angle the miter gauge to 65° to the left, and cut the half laps on the back support ends.

3 Dry-assemble the three supports (one A and one B per set). Using two-part resorcinol glue, assemble and clamp the half laps until the glue cures. Remove the clamps.

Porch swing

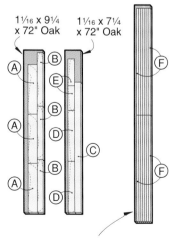

Materials List for Nostalgia Porch Swing

PART	FINISHED SIZE			MATL.	QTY.
	T	W	L		
A* seat supports	$1\frac{1}{16}$"	$4\frac{1}{4}$"	$21\frac{1}{4}$"	WO	3
B* back supports	$1\frac{1}{16}$"	$3\frac{1}{4}$"	$23\frac{1}{2}$"	WO	3
C cross-support	$1\frac{1}{16}$"	3"	$58\frac{1}{2}$"	WO	1
D* arms	$1\frac{1}{16}$"	3"	$24\frac{1}{2}$"	WO	2
E* arm supports	$1\frac{1}{16}$"	3"	$12\frac{3}{4}$"	WO	2
F seat slats	$1\frac{1}{16}$"	$\frac{3}{4}$"	$47\frac{1}{2}$"	WO	28

*Initially cut parts oversized, and trim to finished size according to instructions.
Material Key: WO = White oak.
Supplies: two $\frac{5}{16} \times 5$" eyebolts; two $5\frac{5}{16} \times 4$" eyebolts; six $\frac{5}{16}$" nuts; eight $\frac{5}{16}$" flat washers; $1\frac{1}{2}$" and $2\frac{1}{2}$" galvanized deck screws; $\frac{1}{2}$" oak dowel rod; 2/0 passing-link zinc-plated chain; four quick links for chain.

PORCH SWING CUTTING DIAGRAM

$1\frac{1}{16} \times 9\frac{1}{4}$ x 72" Oak $1\frac{1}{16} \times 7\frac{1}{4}$ x 72" Oak

$1\frac{1}{16} \times 7\frac{1}{4}$ x 96" Oak (2 needed)

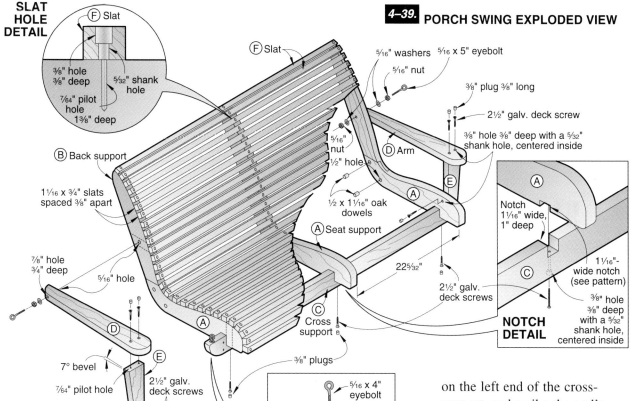

SLAT HOLE DETAIL

(F) Slat

$3/8"$ hole $3/8"$ deep
$5/32"$ shank hole
$7/64"$ pilot hole $1\,3/8"$ deep

4–39. **PORCH SWING EXPLODED VIEW**

(F) Slat

$5/16"$ washers
$5/16"$ nut
$5/16$ x 5" eyebolt

$3/8"$ plug $3/8"$ long
$2\,1/2"$ galv. deck screw
$3/8"$ hole $3/8"$ deep with a $5/32"$ shank hole, centered inside

(B) Back support

$1\,1/16$ x $3/4"$ slats spaced $3/8"$ apart

$5/16"$ nut
$1/2"$ hole
(D) Arm
(E)
(A)

$7/8"$ hole $3/4"$ deep
$5/16"$ hole

$1/2$ x $1\,1/16"$ oak dowels
(A) Seat support

$22\,5/32"$

(A)
Notch $1\,1/16"$ wide, 1" deep
(C)
$1\,1/16"$-wide notch (see pattern)
$3/8"$ hole $3/8"$ deep with a $5/32"$ shank hole, centered inside

NOTCH DETAIL

$2\,1/2"$ galv. deck screws

(C)
Cross support

$3/8"$ plugs

(D)
(A)
(E)
$7°$ bevel
$7/64"$ pilot hole
$2\,1/2"$ galv. deck screws
$3/8"$ plugs $3/8"$ long

$5/16$ x 4" eyebolt
$5/16"$ hole
$7/8"$ wide $3/4"$ deep
1"
(C)

BOLT DETAIL

4 Enlarge the gridded porch swing seat/back patterns in **4–44** *(page 92)*. Tape the patterns together so the dowel center-points register, then position the pattern on one of the support assemblies. Trace the outline on the assembly and, as shown in **4–40**, on, mark the centerpoints for the dowel and screw holes and the notch. Trace the pattern onto the other supports.

5 Drill the two $1/2"$-diameter holes for the dowels in each support. Cut six $1\,1/8"$ lengths of $1/2"$ dowel. Glue a dowel in each of the holes. Drill the $1/8"$-diameter screw holes located near the front edge on the inside of the two outside seat supports.

6 Using a bandsaw or jigsaw, cut the support assemblies to shape. (Cut outside the line, then sand to it.) Finish-sand.

7 For the cross-support (C), rip and crosscut a piece of $1\,1/16"$ oak to 3 x $58\,1/2"$. With your drill press, drill the bolt hole at each end of the cross-support, using the dimensions in the Bolt Detail drawing in **4–39**. Now, finish-sand the piece.

8 Make an enlarged copy of the Cross-Support End pattern in **4–44** *(page 92)*. Place the pattern

on the left end of the cross-support, and scribe the end's shape and the notch on the piece. Flip over the pattern, and mark the opposite end of the cross-support the same way. Locate the center notch where shown in **4–39**. Now, saw the cross-support ends to shape.

9 Cut the three $1\,1/16"$-wide and 1"-deep notches in the cross support. (Notch the piece on your tablesaw using a miter gauge and dado head, and finish the notches with a wood chisel.) Next, angle the dado head $7°$ from perpendicular; set the blade height ($1\,1/16"$ maximum as indicated in **4–44**); and, using the miter gauge, saw the $1\,1/16"$ notches in the bottom edge of all the seat supports at the same time, as shown in **4–42**. Finish cleaning out the notches with a chisel.

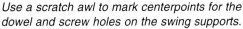

4–40.

Use a scratch awl to mark centerpoints for the dowel and screw holes on the swing supports.

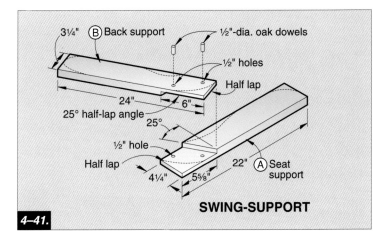

4–41.

SWING-SUPPORT

Make the Arms, Arm Supports, and Seat Slats

1 Enlarge the gridded patterns for the arms (D) and arm supports (E) from **4–44** on *page 92*. Cut the patterns to shape with a scissors.

2 From $1\frac{1}{16}$"-thick oak, rip and crosscut two pieces to $3\frac{1}{4}$ x 25" for the arms (D), and two pieces to $3\frac{1}{4}$ x 13" for the arm supports (E). Set the arm-support pieces aside temporarily. Trace the Arm Pattern outline onto the arm pieces (label them top left and top right), and mark the centerpoints for the screw holes and the centerline for the $\frac{5}{16}$" horizontal bolt hole. Band-saw the arms to shape, and sand the edges. (Tape the identical pieces together, top face to top face, using double-faced tape, and then sand them with your disc sander.)

3 With a try square, extend the bolt's centerline down the edge of each arm piece, find the centers on each edge, and mark them. Separate the pieces and remove the tape. Turn one of the arms on edge, and, with a spade bit or Forstner bit, bore a $\frac{7}{8}$"-diameter hole $\frac{3}{4}$" deep. (Hold the arm in a handscrew clamp, and clamp that assembly to the drill-press table for drilling.) Bore the other arm. Switch to a $\frac{5}{16}$" bit, center it in the $\frac{7}{8}$" hole, and drill through the arm. (When drilling, place scrap under the arm to avoid chip-out.) Drill the second arm the same way.

4 Rout a $\frac{1}{4}$" roundover along the top edge of both arms, starting at the point indicated on the pattern.

5 Tape the two arm-support pieces together using double-faced tape. Trace the Arm-Support pattern onto the top of one piece. Band-saw the pieces to shape, and sand the edges. Now, separate the pieces, and finish-sand the surfaces of the arm and arm-support pieces.

6 Lay out one left and one right arm support, and position the screw hole centerpoints accordingly. Drill and counter-bore the $\frac{3}{8}$" screw holes $\frac{3}{8}$" deep in the arm and arm-support parts. Next, using your tablesaw, cut a $7°$ bevel on the flat or top end of each arm support (see **4–39**). To correctly orient the supports, place the straight sides up against the seat supports, and angle the bevels toward the back of the swing.

7 From $1\frac{1}{16}$" oak, cut 28 seat slats (F) to $\frac{3}{4}$ x $47\frac{1}{2}$". Sand a slight roundover along the top edges and ends of each slat.

shop TIP

● **Dowels reinforce the swing supports' half-lap joints. Moisture in the air can swell dowel pins so they don't fit. Forcing them runs the risk of splitting the bored pieces. To shrink dowels down to size, place them on a paper towel inside a microwave oven set on high for 30 seconds. Remove the dowels and check them for fit. Microwave them for an additional 15 to 30 seconds if necessary.**

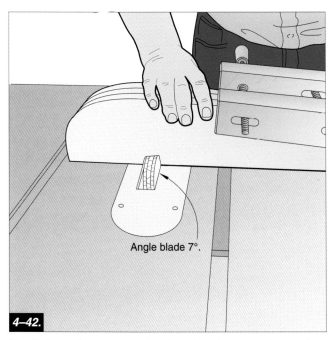

Angle blade 7°.

4–42.

Notch the swing supports by clamping them together and running all three through your tablesaw in a single pass.

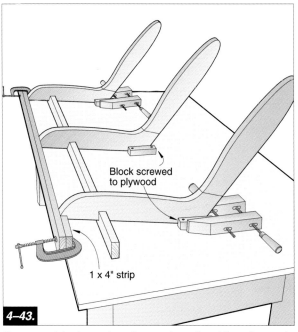

Block screwed to plywood

1 x 4" strip

4–43.

To assemble the swing, first make a jig with a sheet of plywood, a 1 x 4, handscrew clamps, and stop blocks, as shown here.

8 Drill three counterbored screw holes in each slat where dimensioned in the Slat Hole Detail drawing in **4–38**. (Set up a fence and a stop block to consistently position the slats when drilling.)

Assemble the Swing

1 Place the assembled seat supports upside down over the edge of a bench or table so the backs point toward the floor. Place the cross-support over the seat supports and engage the mating notches. Once in place, drill the $\frac{3}{8}$" counterbore and $\frac{7}{64}$" pilot holes through the cross-supports and into the seat supports. (For this job, a portable electric drill can be used.) Apply resorcinol glue to the mating areas, and then drive a $2\frac{1}{2}$" galva-

nized deck screw into each hole. (See the Notch Detail in **4–39** on *page 89*.)

2 Place a 4 x 8' sheet of $\frac{3}{4}$" plywood on your bench or table. Rip and crosscut a 54"-long piece of 1 x 4 (nominal) pine or fir, and screw it to the front edge of the plywood. Next, lay one of the seat slats against the 1 x 4 and clamp stop blocks at both ends. Remove the slat and place the assembly from the previous step on top of the plywood. Align the tips of the seat supports so they center between the stop blocks and against the 1 x 4 as shown in **4–43**. Square the seat supports to the cross-support.

3 Position three scrap blocks against the seat supports at

the back, and screw them to the plywood. Clamp the seat supports to these blocks.

4 Place the first seat slat on the top edge of the 1 x 4, align it with the end supports, and then glue and screw it to the supports. (Drill $\frac{7}{64}$" pilot holes into the supports before driving the $1\frac{1}{2}$" galvanized deck screws.) Place the second slat in position, allowing a $\frac{3}{8}$" gap on the front edge, and attach it the same way. Maintaining a $\frac{3}{8}$" spacing, glue and screw on the remaining seat slats, working back across the swing and the back. (To keep all slats square with the front, always measure off the first slat.)

5 Glue and screw on the arm supports to the cross-support. (Apply the glue, place the straight side of the supports against the seat supports with the bevel pointing down toward the back of the swing, align the parts at the bottom, and then clamp them in place. Next, drill $7/64$" pilot holes into the cross-support, and then drive in your deck screws.) Drive a $2\frac{1}{2}$" galvanized deck screw through each of the outside seat supports into the arm supports where shown in **4–44**.

6 Position the right arm on the arm support, center the screw holes, and then temporarily clamp the back end of the arm to the back support so the arm sits squarely on the arm support's beveled edge. Drill $7/64$" pilot holes (through the arm holes) into the arm supports. Drive in one screw to temporarily hold the arm. Switch to a $5/16$" bit, place it in the hole in the end of the arm, and drill a hole through the back support. Unclamp and remove the arm.

7 Assemble the eyebolt as shown in **4–39**, and insert it through the arm. Apply glue to the mating parts on the arm, arm support, and back supports. Insert the eyebolt through the back support, add a washer, and then the second nut. Drive the two screws

through the arm and into the arm support. Tighten the nut on the eyebolt. Attach the other arm the same way.

8 Attach the eyebolts in the ends of the cross-support as shown in the Bolt Detail drawing in **4–39** (*page 89*).

9 Using a $3/8$" plug cutter, make 97 plugs from scrap $3/4$" oak. Glue the plugs in the countersunk screw holes. Now, sand the plugs so they're flush with the surrounding surface.

10 Apply the finish of your choice. (Two wipe-on coats of an oil-based wood preservative

were applied to the swing shown on *page 88*, which is being used outdoors. This kind of product applies easily and can be reapplied as needed without much surface preparation.

11 Attach the chain to the eyebolts (use either S-hooks, lap links, or quick links—available where you buy the chain), and hang the swing. Adjust its height to a comfortable level for you. Cut the links with a hacksaw to remove unneeded chain. Now sit back, swing and sway, and enjoy the fruits of your labor.

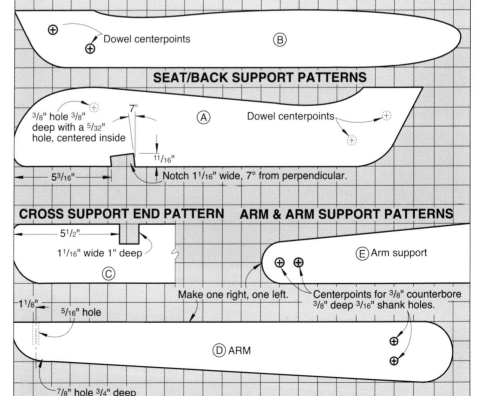

4–44. **SCALED PATTERNS** 1 square = 1"

Sitting-pretty settee

SITTING-PRETTY SETTEE

Combining the beauty and weather resistance of Honduran mahogany with the durability of mortise-and-tenon joinery makes this project go anywhere. For exterior use, you might want to paint it as shown; indoors, it will look equally exquisite in a natural finish.

Make the Legs

➤ *Note: You'll need 2½ x 2½" mahogany stock to make the settee's front and rear legs. You can either laminate thinner stock, or purchase 3 x 3" turning squares and saw or plane them to 2½" square. Also, if you intend to use the settee outdoors, be sure to use water-resistant glue, resorcinol, or slow-set epoxy for the adhesive.*

1 Rip and crosscut two rear legs (A) and two front legs (B) to the sizes listed in the Materials List. Chamfer both ends of the rear legs and the bottom end of the front legs. (You can chamfer with the tablesaw blade at 45°.)

2 To form the curved section (C) at the top of each front leg, refer to **4–45**, then start by crosscutting a 12¾" length of 2½" square mahogany for the curved sections. Rip the piece to 1" thickness. Then, enlarge the Front Leg pattern (**4–52**, *page 98*), and lay out the two curved leg sections (including the tenons) on the stock.

Materials List for Sitting-Pretty Settee

PART	FINISHED SIZE			MATL.	QTY.
	T	W	L		
A rear legs	2½"	2½"	32¼"	HM	2
B* front legs	2½"	2½"	23¼"	HM	2
C* curves	1 9/16"	2½"	6⅛"	HM	2
D* side rails	¾"	3"	17¼"	HM	2
E center rail	¾"	3"	17"	HM	1
F lower rails	¾"	1½"	17¼"	HM	2
G* stretcher	¾"	1½"	46½"	HM	1
H seat rail	¾"	3"	46"	HM	1
I seat rail	¾"	1¾"	46"	HM	1
J armrests	¾"	3¼"	18¾"	HM	2
K backrest top	¾"	3"	46"	HM	1
L backrest bottom	¾"	1¼"	46"	HM	1
M splats	¼"	1 1/64"	13"	HM	22
N* spacers	¼"	½"	15/16"	HM	46
O seat slats	¾"	2¼"	44"	HM	2
P seat slats	¾"	2¼"	48½"	HM	6

*Initially cut the parts oversized, and trim them to finished size according to the instructions.
Material Key: HM = Honduras mahogany.
Supplies: #8 x 1¼" flathead wood screws; water-resistant glue, resorcinol, or slow-set epoxy; finish.

CUTTING DIAGRAM

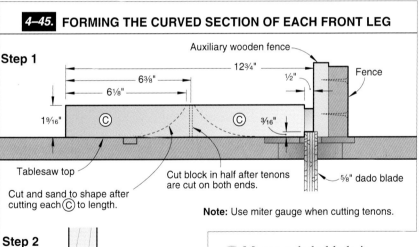

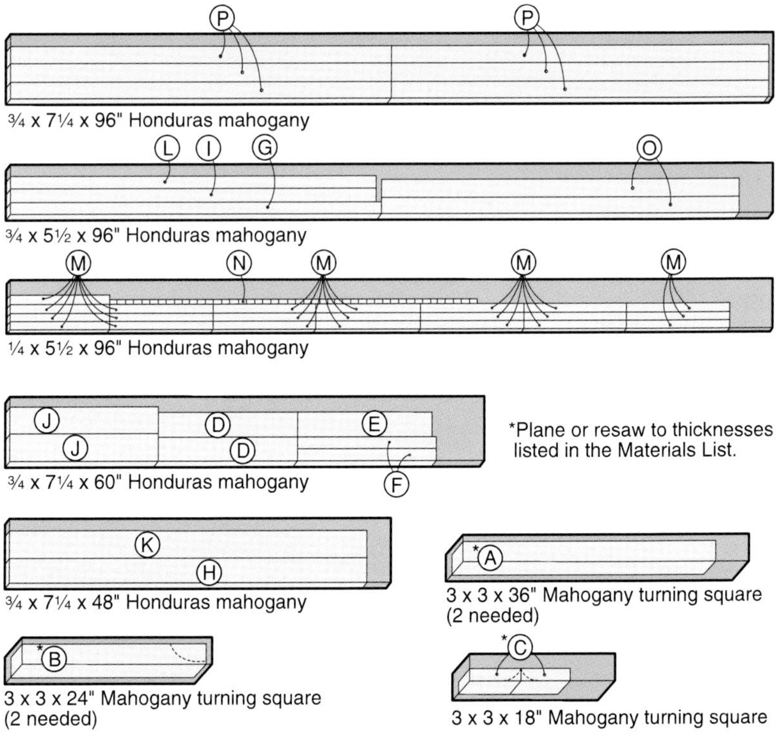

¾ x 7¼ x 96" Honduras mahogany

¾ x 5½ x 96" Honduras mahogany

¼ x 5½ x 96" Honduras mahogany

¾ x 7¼ x 60" Honduras mahogany

*Plane or resaw to thicknesses listed in the Materials List.

¾ x 7¼ x 48" Honduras mahogany

3 x 3 x 36" Mahogany turning square (2 needed)

3 x 3 x 24" Mahogany turning square (2 needed)

3 x 3 x 18" Mahogany turning square

4–45. FORMING THE CURVED SECTION OF EACH FRONT LEG

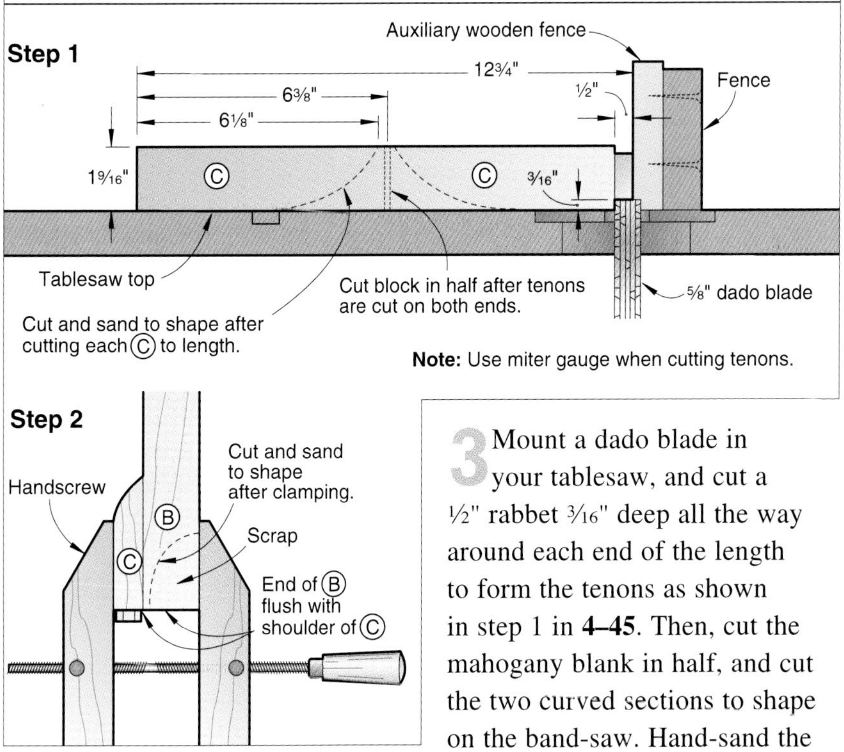

Step 1

Auxiliary wooden fence

12¾"

6⅜"

6⅛"

½"

Fence

1 9/16"

3/16"

Tablesaw top

Cut and sand to shape after cutting each (C) to length.

Cut block in half after tenons are cut on both ends.

⅝" dado blade

Note: Use miter gauge when cutting tenons.

Step 2

Handscrew

Cut and sand to shape after clamping.

Scrap

End of (B) flush with shoulder of (C)

3 Mount a dado blade in your tablesaw, and cut a ½" rabbet 3/16" deep all the way around each end of the length to form the tenons as shown in step 1 in **4–45**. Then, cut the mahogany blank in half, and cut the two curved sections to shape on the band-saw. Hand-sand the curved edge of each curved section smooth.

4 As shown in Step 2 of **4–45**, clamp parts B and C together, with the shoulder of the tenon of each curved section (C) flush with the top end of each front leg member (B). Later, remove the clamps, and lay out the curved shape on the front top edge of each front leg member (B), using the front leg pattern as a guide. Cut the legs to shape and sand them smooth.

Form the Leg Mortises

1 Mark the mortise center points on the two rear legs (A) and the two front legs (B)

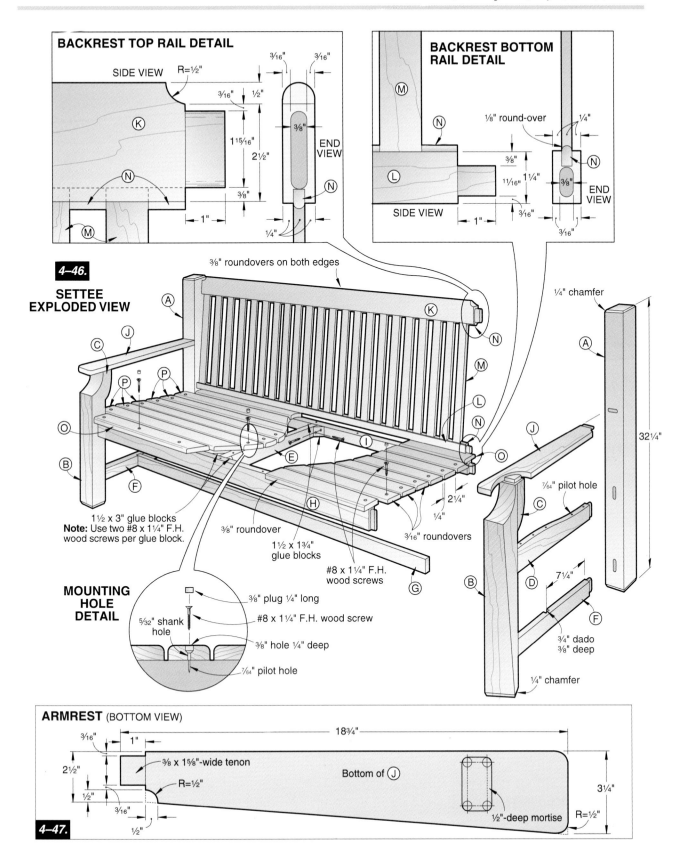

BACKREST TOP RAIL DETAIL

SIDE VIEW   R=$\frac{1}{2}$"

K

N

M

$\frac{3}{16}$" $\frac{1}{2}$"

$1\frac{15}{16}$"

$2\frac{1}{2}$"

$\frac{3}{8}$"

1"

$\frac{3}{16}$" $\frac{3}{16}$"

$\frac{3}{8}$"

END VIEW

N

$\frac{1}{4}$"

BACKREST BOTTOM RAIL DETAIL

M

N

L

SIDE VIEW

$\frac{1}{8}$" round-over

$\frac{3}{8}$"

$\frac{11}{16}$" $1\frac{1}{4}$"

$\frac{3}{16}$"

1"

$\frac{1}{4}$"

N

$\frac{3}{8}$"

END VIEW

$\frac{3}{16}$"

4–46.

SETTEE EXPLODED VIEW

$\frac{3}{8}$" roundovers on both edges

$\frac{1}{4}$" chamfer

A   K   N

C   J

P   P

O

B   F

$1\frac{1}{2}$ x 3" glue blocks
Note: Use two #8 x $1\frac{1}{4}$" F.H. wood screws per glue block.

E   I   H

$\frac{3}{8}$" roundover

$1\frac{1}{2}$ x $1\frac{3}{4}$" glue blocks

#8 x $1\frac{1}{4}$" F.H. wood screws

G

$\frac{3}{16}$" roundovers

$2\frac{1}{4}$"

$\frac{1}{4}$"

M   L   N   O

A

$32\frac{1}{4}$"

J

$\frac{7}{64}$" pilot hole

C

B   D

$7\frac{1}{4}$"

F

$\frac{3}{4}$" dado $\frac{3}{8}$" deep

$\frac{1}{4}$" chamfer

MOUNTING HOLE DETAIL

$\frac{5}{32}$" shank hole

$\frac{3}{8}$" plug $\frac{1}{4}$" long

#8 x $1\frac{1}{4}$" F.H. wood screw

$\frac{3}{8}$" hole $\frac{1}{4}$" deep

$\frac{7}{64}$" pilot hole

ARMREST (BOTTOM VIEW)

$\frac{3}{16}$"   1"

$18\frac{3}{4}$"

$2\frac{1}{2}$"

$\frac{1}{2}$"

$\frac{3}{16}$"

$\frac{1}{2}$"

$\frac{3}{8}$ x $1\frac{5}{8}$"-wide tenon

R=$\frac{1}{2}$"

Bottom of J

$\frac{1}{2}$"-deep mortise

$3\frac{1}{4}$"

R=$\frac{1}{2}$"

4–47.

where shown in **4–48**. (Remember that you are working in pairs of As and Bs, and that the mortises in one A must be a mirror image of those in the other.) Mark all the mortise center points on each pair before drilling to ensure that you mortise the correct edges of each leg.

2 Form the mortises, following the multistep sequence outlined in the Rear Leg drawing in **4–48**.

Cut and Tenon the Other Frame Members

1 Cut the side rails (D), center rail (E), and the lower rails (F) to the sizes listed in the Mate-rials List. Cut the stretcher (G) to size plus 1" in length. Cut the seat rails (H, I), armrests (J), backrest top (K), and backrest bottom (L) to size. (Do not make the contour cuts on D, E, and J yet; you'll cut them to shape after tenoning.)

2 Cut tenons on both ends of the side rails (D), lower rails (F), seat rails (H, I), the back end of the armrests (J), and both ends of the backrest top and bottom (K, L). Refer to the gridded Side and Center Rail pattern in **4–53** for the tenon sizes on the side rails (D). See the Armrest drawing in **4–47** for the tenon size on the armrest, and refer to the details on the Exploded View drawing in **4–46** for tenon sizes

on the backrest top and bottom (K, L). Cut the tenons on the remaining pieces (F, H, I) using the shoulder dimensions in **4–49**.

3 Cut a ¾" dado ⅜" deep in each lower rail (F) where shown on the Exploded View in **4–46**.

4 Cut the side rails (D) and center rail (E) to shape, using an enlarged copy of the Gridded Side and Center Rail patterns in **4–53** as a guide.

5 Cut the armrests to final shape using the Armrest drawing in **4–47** as a guide.

Assemble the End Sections

1 Dry-clamp the legs (A, B) and rails (D, F) together. Square each assembly, and slide the tenon on the armrest into its mating mortise in the rear leg. Hold the armrest firmly against the tenoned top of the front leg, and mark the location of the mortise needed on the bottom side of each armrest. Remove the armrest.

2 To form the mortise on the bottom side of each armrest, use a flat-bottomed bit, and drill a ½"-deep hole at each corner of your layout lines. Next, drill overlapping holes to remove stock, and finally chisel the mortise clean.

3 Check the fit of the end sections again with the

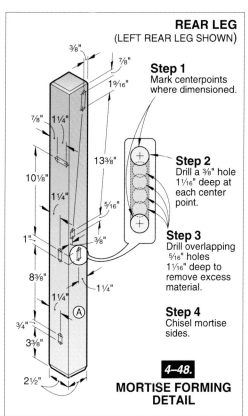

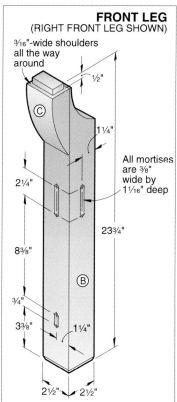

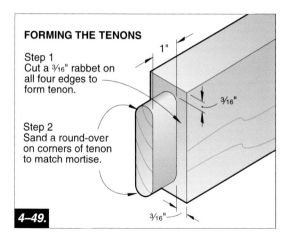

FORMING THE TENONS

Step 1
Cut a $\frac{3}{16}$" rabbet on
all four edges to
form tenon.

1"

$\frac{3}{16}$"

Step 2
Sand a round-over
on corners of tenon
to match mortise.

$\frac{3}{16}$"

4–49.

armrests in position. Now, glue and clamp the end sections together, checking both for square. Position the armrests, but do not glue them to their mating parts at this point. You'll do this later, after the seat slats have been attached.

Complete the Frame and Build the Backrest

1 Dry-clamp the seat rails (H, I) and backrest top and bottom (K, L) between the end assemblies and check them for square. Measure the distance between the dadoes in the lower rails (F), and cut the stretcher (G) to fit. Remove the clamps and disassemble.

2 Using the Backrest Top Rail Detail in **4–46** *(page 95)* as a guide, cut or rout a $\frac{1}{4}$" groove $\frac{3}{8}$" deep, centered along the bottom edge of the backrest top rail (K) and along the top edge of the bottom rail (L). (You can cut the grooves on the tablesaw fitted with a $\frac{1}{4}$" dado blade. If doing so, use a featherboard to keep the pieces pressed firmly against the fence when dadoing.)

3 Rip 11 strips $1\frac{1}{64}$" wide x 13" long from $\frac{3}{4}$" mahogany stock. Now, resaw each strip to obtain two $\frac{1}{4}$ x 1 $\frac{1}{64}$"-wide strips for the splats (M). (Insert the backrest top and bottom rails into their mating mortises, and measure the length needed for the splats.) To form the spacers (N), start by cutting two strips $\frac{1}{4}$ x $\frac{1}{2}$ x 30" long. Rout or sand a $\frac{1}{8}$" roundover along one edge of each long strip. Now, set a stop and cut the spacers (plus a few extra) to length ($\frac{15}{16}$").

4 Measure and mark the lengthwise-center of the backrest top rail (K) and the center of one spacer (N). As shown in **4–50**, position the marked spacer in the groove, and align its center mark with the center-line on the backrest top rail. Working from the center out, glue and clamp the splats and spacers in position, checking each splat for square. If the spacers on

Check each splat for square before gluing and clamping them onto the backrest's top rail. Glue spacers between the splats.

Before you glue on the bottom rail, align the splats by clamping on a pair of scrap strips of 1 x 2, as shown.

4–50.

4–51.

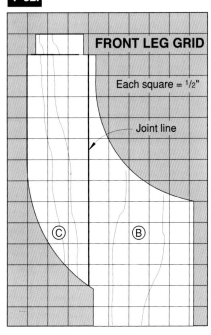

4–52.

FRONT LEG GRID

Each square = $1/2$"

Joint line

© B

4–53.

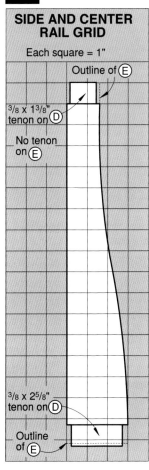

SIDE AND CENTER RAIL GRID

Each square = 1"

Outline of Ⓔ

$3/8 \times 1^3/8$" tenon on Ⓓ

No tenon on Ⓔ

$3/8 \times 2^5/8$" tenon on Ⓓ

Outline of Ⓔ

Build the Seat

1 Glue and clamp the seat rails (H, I) and the backrest assembly between the end sections, checking for square.

2 Clamp the center rail (E) between the seat rails, centered from end to end. Cut four triangular-shaped glue blocks to the size stated on the Exploded View drawing (**4–46**, on *page 95*). One at a time, hold a glue block in position against the center rail, and drill $7/64$" pilot holes and $5/32$" shank holes. Finally, glue and screw the glue blocks to the framework to hold the center rail in position.

3 Cut the seat slats (O, P) to size. Rout a $3/16$" roundover along the top edge of each part. Cut several strips of scrap wood $1/4$" wide for use as spacers. Clamp the front slat (O) to the bench, placing it flush with the front edge of the front legs (B). Now, work toward the back, spacing the slats $1/4$" apart with the scrap-wood spacers.

4 Once you have clamped all the slats in position, drill the plug, shank, and pilot holes to the sizes indicated in the Mounting Hole Detail drawing in **4–46**.

5 Now, screw the slats in place, starting with the front slat. For each slat, remove the clamps, then glue and screw the slat to the bench framework. Proceed toward the back of the seat, installing one slat at a time.

each end extend past the groove, trim them to the length required.

5 Once you have glued all the spacers and splats in position in the backrest top rail, clamp a scrap strip on each side of the splats to align them as shown in **4–51**, on *page 97*. Now, run a bead of glue down the groove in the backrest bottom rail, and tap this part onto the ends of the splats as shown in **4–51**. As soon as all the splats are positioned in the groove in the bottom rail, flip over the assembly to keep the glue in the groove from running down the splats. Wipe off excess glue with a wet rag immediately.

6 Again, starting at the center, glue the spacers in position, trimming the end spacers if they protrude. Check the fit of the backrest assembly (K, L, M, N) into the mortises in the rear legs. Separate the backrest assembly from the rear legs.

7 Rout a $3/8$" roundover along the top edges of the backrest top rail (K). Then, mark and cut a $1/2$" radius on each top corner of the backrest top rail. Sand each sawn radius smooth with a $1/2$" drum sander.

shopTIP

● Too often, you don't see spots of glue film on your project until after you've started to apply the stain or finish. A good way to expose glue smears is to wipe all joints and adjacent areas with mineral spirits or lacquer thinner. The glue smears will remain light-colored, but the surrounding wood will become dark. Be careful not to soak the wood with the solvent.

6 Plane or resaw a piece of mahogany to $5/16$" thickness and cut 32 plugs $3/8$" in diameter from it. (You can use a plug cutter chucked in a drill press.) Plug the screw holes in the seat slats with these plugs, and sand them flush.

7 Glue and clamp the armrests (J) in position.

Finish the Settee

1 Sand the settee smooth, starting with 100-grit sand paper and working through progressively finer grits to 180.

2 Stain and finish the settee as desired. For indoor use, you can leave the mahogany unstained, and finish the settee with clear polyurethane. For outdoor use, as shown on *page 93*, you can apply two coats of white urethane exterior enamel. For a natural-finish outdoor settee, you also could apply a clear exterior penetrating finish.

SIX-SERVER PICNIC SUITE

This rustic redwood (you could use cedar, too) table has six sides and six matching benches that tuck away underneath. Redwood was used to withstand the sun and rain and for its beautiful wood tones (which were preserved with a clear wood finish). Don't let the angle-cutting scare you off; you can cut all the top and bench pieces using just a few settings on your saw.

Six-server picnic suite

Build the Table

Note: Rip $1/4$" from each edge of all 2 x 6 stock for a 5" finished width. This removes the factory-rounded edges for tighter fitting, better looking joints.

1 Cut table leg parts A and B to length. Cut the 45° chamfer on one end of each A as shown in **4–58** *(page 102)*.

2 To cut the half-lap joints in leg parts B, start by fitting your saw with a dado blade. Now raise the blade to half the thickness of the redwood stock you are

CUTTING DIAGRAM FOR PICNIC SUITE

$1\frac{1}{2}$ x $3\frac{1}{2}$ x 96" Redwood (2 x 4)(14 needed)

$1\frac{1}{2}$ x $5\frac{1}{2}$ x 96" Redwood (2 x 6)(13 needed)

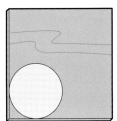

$\frac{3}{4}$ x 24 x 24" Exterior plywood

using. Test the depth of cut on a scrap of the same thickness as B. Set a stop on the fence $2\frac{1}{2}$" from the blade, and cut the half-lap joints on each end of B.

3 Lay out and mark the stopped half-lap joints on A, 5" in from the squared end as shown in **4–57**. Mark the joints in pairs (one top part A and one base part A) for ease and uniformity in cutting the parts.

4 With your blade still set at the height used to cut the half-lap joints, set a stop on your saw so that a $2\frac{1}{2}$" notch is cut into one side of A. (As shown in **4–54**, clamp a stop to the carriage of your radial arm saw to cut the stopped half-lap joints. You also could use a router and jig to cut the dado.) Now set a stop on the fence and cut the stopped half-lap joint into six As; then move the stop on the fence to the other side of the blade, and cut the remaining six As.

5 Using a router fitted with a straight bit and an edge guide, clean out the stopped half-lap joints. (Set the edge guide so the straight bit does not cut more than $2\frac{1}{2}$" in from the edge. While the guide prevents you from cutting too far in, you will need to clamp on stops for the side cuts—or just eyeball the guide. If you don't want to use the radial arm saw, you can use this same routing process to cut the entire stopped half lap.) Clean out the two rounded corners of each recess with a mallet and chisel. Check the fit of the half-lap joint of each B into the stopped half-lap joint of each A.

Materials List for Picnic Suite

PART		FINISHED SIZE			MATL.	QTY.
		T	W	L		
A	feet	$1\frac{1}{2}$"	5"	$30\frac{1}{8}$"	R	12
B	legs	$1\frac{1}{2}$"	5"	25"	R	6
C*	core blocks	$2\frac{5}{8}$"	$3\frac{1}{4}$"	5"	R	2
D*	top stretchers	$1\frac{1}{2}$"	$3\frac{1}{2}$"	$30\frac{1}{8}$"	R	6
E*	base stretchers	$1\frac{1}{2}$"	$4\frac{5}{8}$"	$10\frac{1}{8}$"	R	6
F*	top 1	$1\frac{1}{2}$"	$3\frac{1}{2}$"	$25\frac{7}{8}$"	R	6
G*	top 2	$1\frac{1}{2}$"	$3\frac{1}{2}$"	$21\frac{1}{2}$"	R	6
H*	top 3	$1\frac{1}{2}$"	$3\frac{1}{2}$"	$17\frac{1}{8}$"	R	6
I*	top 4	$1\frac{1}{2}$"	$3\frac{1}{2}$"	$12\frac{7}{8}$"	R	6
J*	top 5	$1\frac{1}{2}$"	$3\frac{1}{2}$"	$8\frac{1}{2}$"	R	6
K*	top 6	$1\frac{1}{2}$"	$3\frac{1}{2}$"	$4\frac{1}{8}$"	R	6
L	stabilizer	$\frac{3}{4}$"	$12\frac{1}{2}$" diameter		P	1
M	bench feet	$1\frac{1}{2}$"	5"	$12\frac{7}{8}$"	R	24
N	bench legs	$1\frac{1}{2}$"	5"	16"	R	12
O*	stretchers	$1\frac{1}{2}$"	$3\frac{1}{2}$"	$17\frac{3}{8}$"	R	6
P*	seat 1	$1\frac{1}{2}$"	$3\frac{1}{2}$"	$16\frac{5}{8}$"	R	6
Q*	seat 2	$1\frac{1}{2}$"	$3\frac{1}{2}$"	21"	R	6
R*	seat 3	$1\frac{1}{2}$"	$3\frac{1}{2}$"	$25\frac{3}{8}$"	R	6

*Initially cut oversized. Then, trim each to finished size according to the instructions.
Materials Key: R = Redwood; P = Exterior plywood.
Supplies: epoxy; #12 x $1\frac{1}{4}$" flathead wood screws; #10 x $1\frac{1}{4}$" panhead sheet-metal screws; #8 x $2\frac{1}{2}$" flathead wood screws; #10 x 2" flathead wood screws; #10 x 3" flathead wood screws; 1 x 1 x $\frac{1}{8}$" aluminum angle; clear exterior finish.

shop TIP

● **To determine which teeth of a dado blade cut farthest to the right and left, set the blade at its widest setting and align a try square against one side of the blade. Move the square away from the blade until just one tip touches the square. Mark the back side of that tip with paint or a permanent marker. Do the same for the other side of the blade, but mark it with a different color. Presto—you can quickly spot the two outside teeth that determine the width of the cut.**

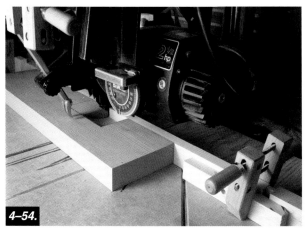

4–54.

Clamping a stop block to a radial arm saw's carriage ensures accurate joints.

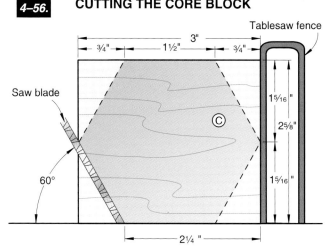

4–56. **CUTTING THE CORE BLOCK**

6 Mix epoxy and brush it onto the mating surfaces of two As and one B. (When brushing epoxy onto the end grain, apply a first coat, and then apply the second coat just before clamping and screwing to ensure adequate adhesion.) Clamp two As to each B and check them for square. Countersink and install two #12 x 1¼" wood screws into each half-lap joint. The head of the screw should rest just below the surface of the redwood to avoid hitting it when sanding later. Set the assembly aside to dry. Make the other five table legs in the same manner.

7 Sand each assembly smooth with 80-grit paper, and use a ¼" roundover bit to rout all the edges except the top edge of the top A.

8 With a hacksaw, cut 12 pieces of 1 x 1 x ⅛" aluminum angle to 29". On six pieces, cut one end at 30°. Then cut the ends of the other six at 30° in the opposite direction, as shown in **4–55**. The pieces join at a 60° angle when later mounted to the bottom side of the tabletop. Chamfer the outer ends of the other leg at 45° to match the angle on the outside ends of part A.

9 Clamp the aluminum pieces together, and lay out the screw holes as dimensioned in **4–55**. Drill two $\frac{7}{32}$" holes through the angle for each 2 x 4. Now drill six $\frac{7}{32}$" holes in each 2 x 4 to mount the angle to part A of the A/B assembly. File or sand all sharp edges and burrs from the angle pieces.

10 Using #10 x 1¼" panhead sheet-metal screws, fasten the aluminum supports to both sides of all As. (Use a 2 x 4 scrap to position the aluminum the thickness of D below the top edge.)

11 Construct each core block (C) by cutting and laminating with epoxy two 12" pieces of 2 x 4. After the epoxy dries, cut the block to 2¾ x 3¼", as dimensioned in **4–56**. Now, tilt the blade at 60° and set the fence 2$\frac{7}{16}$" away from the base of the blade as illustrated in **4–56**. Crosscut the two 5" part C blocks from the 12" lamination.

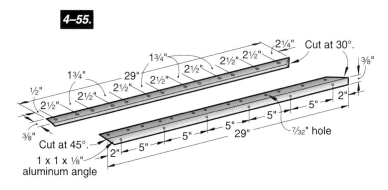

4–55.

ANGLE FOR TABLE

Assemble the Base

1 Working on a large, flat surface, set all six leg assemblies upside down to form a rough hexagon. Set one core block in the center of the legs. Use a band clamp to position and align the legs around the block. Repeat this with the other block.

2 Set your saw to cut a 60° angle; cut one linear piece of scrap into six equal lengths and form a hexagon with the pieces to verify the angle. Miter all six Ds at 60° to finished length and position them as shown in **4–60**. Slide the pieces under the aluminum and check that they true up the hexagon snugly; trim the angles if necessary. Using #10 x 1¼" panhead screws, fasten each D to the aluminum angle on the A/B assembly.

3 Miter parts E to finished length. Then clamp hand screws to B to hold each flush with the top of A, drill pilot holes, and "toe-screw"

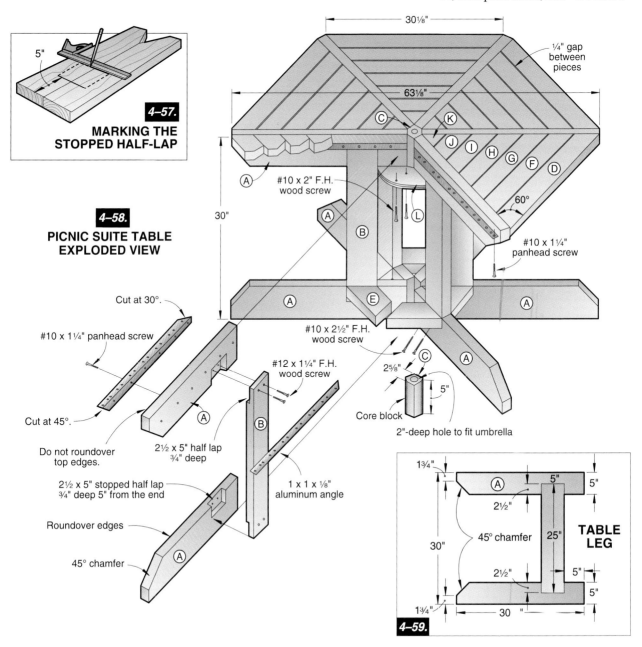

4–57.
MARKING THE STOPPED HALF-LAP

4–58.
PICNIC SUITE TABLE EXPLODED VIEW

4–59.

TABLE LEG

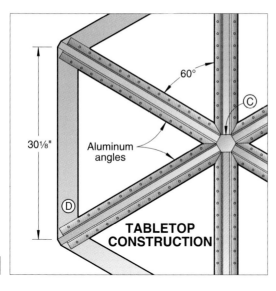

60°

30⅛"   Aluminum angles

Ⓒ

Ⓓ

TABLETOP CONSTRUCTION

4–60.

each E to the A/B assembly, as shown in **4–63,** on *page 104*.

4 Toe-screw the base core block (C) in place. (Drive the screws at an angle from the bottom edge of A into the core block.)

5 With a helper, turn the table right side up, and miter-cut one each of F, G, H, I, J, and K to finished length. Set the pieces into position on the aluminum angle, and check for a good fit at the ends and for the ¼" gap between pieces. (Rip scrap stock to ¼", then crosscut it to 2" to form the spacers. Next, position the tabletop pieces in one of the hexagonal sections with the spacers in place for consistent spacing.) Then miter-cut the rest of the tabletop pieces to the same finished lengths.

6 Fasten the tabletop pieces (F, G, H, I, J, K) to the aluminum angle, starting with F and working in. Be careful to keep a consistent ¼" gap between the pieces by using scrap spacers or by measuring.

7 Cut a 12½"-diameter disc (L) from ¾" exterior plywood to fit between the legs for additional stability in the base. Waterproof L with a coat of epoxy, and position it while the epoxy is still wet. (Brushing on a coat of epoxy is a quick and simple method of sealing the plywood.) Fasten L to the bottom of the tabletop center with #10 x 2" wood screws. Now epoxy the upper hexagonal block C in place at the top's center.

8 Sand the entire table assembly smooth with 100-grit paper. Remember that people will come in contact with the table and bench surfaces, so be extra careful to sand off any sharp edges remaining on these pieces. (The picnic suite shown on *page 99* had a few gouges that were filled with a mixture of wood patch

and cherry stain to match the redwood. Any rough spots were belt-sanded with 80-grit sandpaper, then finish-sanded with a pad sander and 100-grit paper.)

Build the Benches

➤*Note: Many of the construction techniques used in building the table are repeated in this section.*

1 Lay out and cut the half-lap joints in M and N. Chamfer the outside end of the M pieces to match those of the table legs.

2 Epoxy and screw the bench supports together, positioning the screws so they are not in the path of the dado to be cut in step 6. After the epoxy dries, sand the assembly smooth with 80-grit paper. Then, with a router and a ¼" roundover bit, roundover all edges of the assembly except the top inside edge of each.

3 Rip and crosscut stock for the rails (O) to length, plus 2".

4 Cut 12 pieces of aluminum angle to 12". Lay out the hole

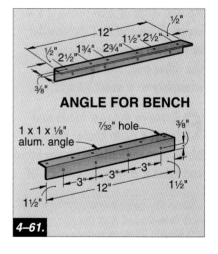

½"
12"
1½" 2½"
½" 2½" 1¾" 2¾"
⅜"

ANGLE FOR BENCH

1 x 1 x ⅛"
alum. angle

⁷⁄₃₂" hole   ⅜"

3" 3" 3"
12"

1½"

1½"

4–61.

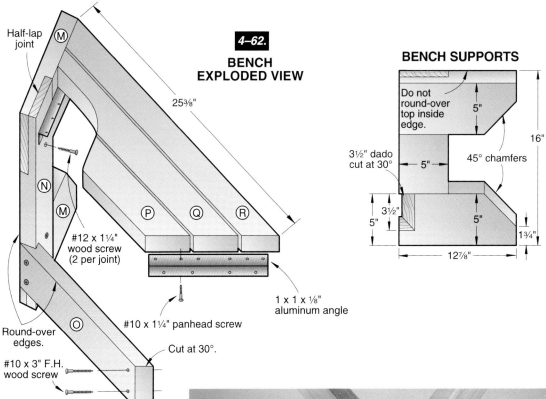

Half-lap joint

M

25⅜"

4-62.
BENCH
EXPLODED VIEW

N

M

P   Q   R

#12 x 1¼" wood screw (2 per joint)

Round-over edges.

O

#10 x 1¼" panhead screw

#10 x 3" F.H. wood screw

Cut at 30°.

1 x 1 x ⅛" aluminum angle

BENCH SUPPORTS

Do not round-over top inside edge.

5"

16"

3½" dado cut at 30°

5"

45° chamfers

3½"

5"

5"

1¾"

12⅞"

sequence on the angle and drill the holes as dimensioned in **4–61**.

5 Cut dadoes in each leg. To do this, you'll need to make an auxiliary fence: First tilt the tablesaw blade to 30°, then bevel-rip one edge of a 24"-long 2 x 4 scrap. Glue and nail the smaller of the two resulting pieces onto the other one, and fasten the assembly to a miter gauge.

6 Remove the saw blade and insert a dado blade. Set the blade perpendicular with the table and raise it above the surface of

Clamp the base assembly together, and "toe-screw" it to the top's radial members, as shown here.

4-63.

4–64.

To cut dadoes in the bench legs, make an auxiliary fence and fasten it to the miter gauge. Clamp legs to the fence.

the table the thickness of O. Mark the location of the dadoes in the M/N assemblies. Position one assembly against the auxiliary miter-gauge fence with the inside of the assembly facing out. Nail stops to each end of the miter gauge fence to make a finished dado 3½" wide; then cut six of

the dadoes to size as shown in **4–64**, making sure the screws are not in the path of the cut. Now remove the fence from the miter gauge and move it to the slot on the other side of the blade. To cut the other six dadoes, reposition and reattach the fence.

7 Attach the aluminum angle to the M/N assemblies.

8 Miter-cut bench parts P, Q, and R to size. Fasten them to the top faces of the aluminum angles with screws driven in from the bottom.

9 Epoxy and screw O into the dado using two #10 x 3" wood screws at each joint. After the epoxy dries, use a handsaw to trim the ends of O flush with the outside edge of the leg assembly.

10 File or sand all sharp edges and burrs from the aluminum, then sand the completed benches smooth.

Finish the Redwood Table and Benches

1 Apply redwood exterior finish to the table and benches. (Several applications of a penetrating-oil exterior wood finish were applied to the bench and tables on *page 99*.) Renew the finish periodically.

5

Structures With Style

Nothing defines outdoor spaces with more visual interest than a structural element such as an arbor or pergola. Arbors (like the one shown on the opposite page) can usher you into a backyard sanctuary, mark the entrance to a flower garden, or lead visitors down the path to your door. On *page 116*, you'll find a less elegant, but no less pleasing, arbor that, combined with a comfy bench, invites you to rest a while. For a contrast in style, look to *page 123* for an architectural structure you'll be proud to situate in a place of honor. And despite its impressive grandeur, it is easy to build.

Compared with an arbor, a pergola is more like a pavilion. But the pergola design on *page 126* can be easily sized to fit any space. Build it to enhance a deck, shelter a patio, or define

a quiet space on the lawn or lakeside. Step-by-step instructions are provided for the entire project, from planning to completion, so you'll have it built in no time at all.

TRELLISED ARBOR

The rewarding project shown on the facing page is destined to draw you into your workshop for a few evenings or weekends. It combines two straightforward joinery methods: biscuits and interlocking notches. Better still, you don't need a workshop full of tools to build it—just a tablesaw or portable circular saw, a bandsaw or jigsaw, and a biscuit joiner.

Make the Arches

➤ *Note: Use medium-density overlay (MDO) plywood for the arches (A), arch trim (B), and rings (G). This plywood, found at specialty lumberyards and building supply centers, provides excellent weather resistance and smooth surfaces for painting. For maximum durability, use the type*

Trellised arbor

Mark the 18" radius on the blank. Rotate the blank 180°, and mark the radius again. Band-saw or jigsaw the blank to form two trim pieces. Sand their edges smooth. Using one piece as a template, mark two trim pieces on each of the remaining blanks. Now, cut the arches and remaining trim pieces to shape, and sand them smooth.

4 Referring to the Arch Assembly drawing in **5–1** (on *page 109*), glue and nail two trim pieces (B) to one face of each arch, aligning them with the marked outlines. Repeat on the opposite side of each arch.

5 Cut the top keys (C) to the size listed. On one key, lay out its tapered sides, where dimensioned in the Top Key drawing in **5–1**. Cut the sides, and sand them smooth. Using this key as a template, mark the remaining pieces. Cut and sand them to shape. Center the keys on opposite sides of the arches with their top edges flush, and glue and nail them in place.

6 Cut the brackets (D) and corbel caps (E) to size. Drill countersunk shank holes through the back face of the brackets and bottom face of the corbel caps, where shown in the Arch Assembly drawing in **5–1**. Center and clamp the brackets to the arches with their top edges flush, and drive the screws. Center the corbel caps on the bottom of the arches flush against the brackets, and drive the screws.

that has an amber or green face on both sides. Also, you'll find it easiest to finish the arbor's parts as you complete them. See "How to Finish Cedar Outdoor Projects" on page 116 for details.

1 From ¾" plywood, cut two pieces for the arches (A) to the overall dimensions listed in the Materials List, shown on *page 108*. Then, cut four 6¾ x 7¼" blanks for the trim (B). You'll cut two trim pieces from each blank as described in *Step 3*.

2 Using a trammel, mark the 16" radius for the arch and the 18" radii for the trim locations on the arches, where dimensioned on the Arch Assembly drawing (**5–1**). (Refer to the Shop Tip "How to Use a Trammel" on *page 110*.) Then, draw the 90° lines to locate the trim (B) where dimensioned.

3 Adhere a trim blank to one of the trim-location outlines on an arch blank using double-faced tape. Position the blank with a 7¼"-long edge at the top, and align the blank with the outline's 90° sides.

CUTTING DIAGRAM

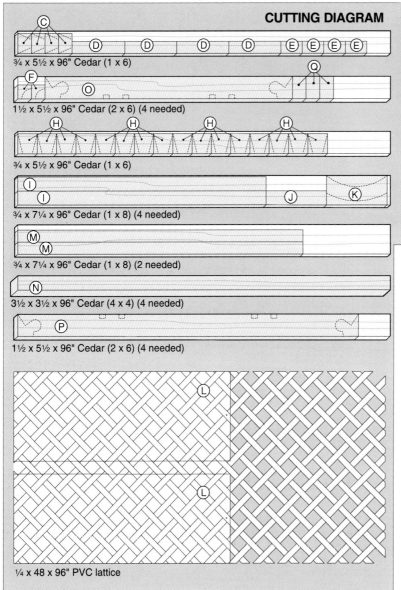

¾ x 5½ x 96" Cedar (1 x 6)

1½ x 5½ x 96" Cedar (2 x 6) (4 needed)

¾ x 5½ x 96" Cedar (1 x 6)

¾ x 7¼ x 96" Cedar (1 x 8) (4 needed)

¾ x 7¼ x 96" Cedar (1 x 8) (2 needed)

3½ x 3½ x 96" Cedar (4 x 4) (4 needed)

1½ x 5½ x 96" Cedar (2 x 6) (4 needed)

¼ x 48 x 96" PVC lattice

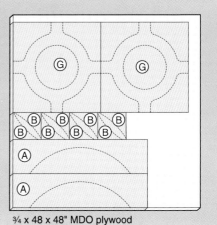

¾ x 48 x 48" MDO plywood

Materials List for Trellised Arbor

PART		FINISHED SIZE			MATL.	QTY.
		T	W	L		
ARCH ASSEMBLIES						
A	arches	¾"	8½"	34½"	P	2
B*	trim	¾"	6½"	7"	P	8
C	top keys	¾"	5"	3½"	C	4
D	brackets	¾"	3"	13½"	C	4
E	corbel caps	¾"	3"	5½"	C	4
F	corbels	1½"	3½"	3½"	C	8
RING ASSEMBLIES						
G	rings	¾"	22½"	22½"	P	2
H	ring keys	¾"	5"	5"	C	16
LATTICE FRAMES						
I	stiles	¾"	3½"	64¼"	C	8
J	bottom rails	¾"	3½"	15½"	C	4
K*	top rails	¾"	6¼"	15½"	C	4
L	lattice	¼"	22¼"	56"	L	2
M	supports	¾"	3"	73¾"	C	4
POSTS AND JOISTS						
N	posts	3½"	3½"	96"	C	4
O	main joists	1½"	5½"	64"	C	4
P	cross-joists	1½"	5½"	88"	C	4
Q	joist blocks	1½"	5½"	3½"	C	12

*Parts initially cut oversized. See the instructions.
Materials Key: P= Medium-density overlay (MDO) plywood; C = Cedar; L = Diagonal-pattern PVC lattice.
Supplies: #20 biscuits (16); 4d galvanized finish nails; 10d galvanized box nails; construction adhesive; 1¼", 1½", 2", and 2½" deck screws; #8 x 1" flathead wood screws (2); ¼ x 27½ x 39½" plywood; 8"-diameter tube forms (4); concrete (one 50-pound bag per 1' length of tube form);½ x 3" concrete hex-sleeve anchors (4) with mating washers and nuts; bolt-down standoffs (4); acrylic caulk.
Blades and Bits:½" masonry bit.

7 Cut the corbels (F) to the size listed. Referring to the Corbel drawing in **5–1**, mark the radius on one of the corbels. Cut and sand the radius to shape. Using this piece as a template, mark the remaining corbels, and cut and sand them to shape. Center four corbels on the brackets (D), flush against the corbel caps (E). Drill countersunk shank holes in the corbels, where shown in the Arch Assembly drawing (**5–1**), and drive the screws. Set aside the arch assemblies and the remaining corbels.

Ring Assemblies

1 From ¾" plywood, cut two 22½"-square pieces to form the rings (G). Mark centerlines across the width and length of each piece on both faces. Referring to the Ring drawing in **5–2** (*page 110*) lay out the ring shape on one face of each piece. On both faces of the pieces, draw lines 1¼" from their edges for aligning the wide end of the ring keys (H), where shown in **5–2**.

2 Jigsaw the rings (G) to shape, as shown in **5–3**, cutting close to the lines. Finish-sand to the lines using a 1"-diameter drum sander.

3 Cut the ring keys (H) to the size listed. As you did for the top keys (C), taper the ring keys' sides, where dimensioned in the Ring Key drawing in **5–2**.

4 Mark a centerline across the edge of the keys at the wide end, where shown in **5–4**, for aligning them with the rings' centerlines. Now, align four keys with the marks on one side of a ring, and glue and nail them in place. Repeat for the other side and for both sides of the other ring. Set the ring assemblies aside.

Make the Lattice Frames

1 Cut the stiles (I) and bottom rails (J) to the sizes listed. Also, cut four ¾ x 7¼ x 15½" blanks to form the top rails (K). Referring to **5–5** (*page 112*), dry-assemble a lattice frame on a flat surface, locating the top-rail blank below the top of the stiles, where dimensioned. Clamp the frame together.

2 Mark the two radii on the frame's top, where dimensioned. Then, mark the locations for the frame-joining #20 biscuits on the stiles and rails, where shown. Separate the parts.

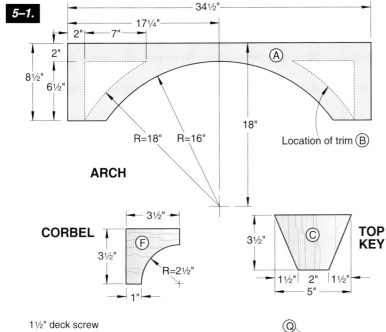

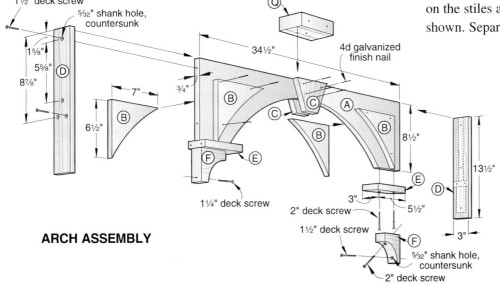

ARCH ASSEMBLY

shop TIP

How to Use a Trammel

Sometimes a large radius places a trammel's centerpoint off the stock, as with this arbor's arch and trim. To keep the trammel level, locate the centerpoint on a piece of scrap the same thickness as the stock being marked. Also, to keep the trammel beam level, adjust the projection of the centerpoint pin and pencil from the trammel heads as necessary.

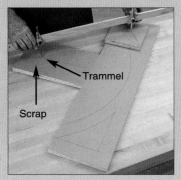

Trammel

Scrap

3 Cut and sand the top rail and stiles to shape. Cut the biscuit slots in the stiles and rails. Glue and clamp the frame together with the biscuits, and check for square. Repeat the process to assemble the other three frames.

4 Using your tablesaw or a jigsaw, cut the PVC lattice (L) to size. The lattice flexes easily, so use a support stand or a helper to keep it flat while you cut it.

5 Place a frame on your workbench, and position a lattice panel on it, aligning the panel and frame's bottom edges and centering the panel side-to-side. Referring to the Side Assembly View in **5–7** *(page 112)*, drill a countersunk shank hole at the top center of the lattice, where

shown, and screw it to the frame's top rail (K). (Use only one screw, to allow for expansion and contraction of the lattice.) Position another frame on top of the lattice, aligning it with the bottom frame. Place a ring assembly (G/H) in approximate position at the top of the frame.

6 Cut the supports (M) to size. Draw lines across the width of the supports $1\frac{1}{4}$" from each end for aligning the lattice frame and ring assemblies, where shown on the Side Assembly (**5–7**) and Support Details (front-face) drawings (**5–8**).

7 From scrap, cut four $\frac{5}{8}$ x 1 x 6" spacers and two $\frac{3}{8}$ x 1 x 6" spacers. Place the $\frac{5}{8}$" spacers under the frame assembly (one

under each end of the stiles) and the $\frac{3}{8}$" spacers under the ring assembly, where shown in **5–7**. (This centers the assemblies on the supports.)

8 Position a support against each side of the frame and ring assemblies, align the assemblies with the supports' marks, and clamp the parts together. Drill countersunk shank holes on the back face of the supports, where shown on the Side Assembly View (**5–7**) and Support Detail (back-face) drawings (**5–8**), and screw the supports to the frame and ring as shown in **5–6**. Repeat this process to assemble the remaining lattice frames, ring assembly, and supports. Set the assemblies aside.

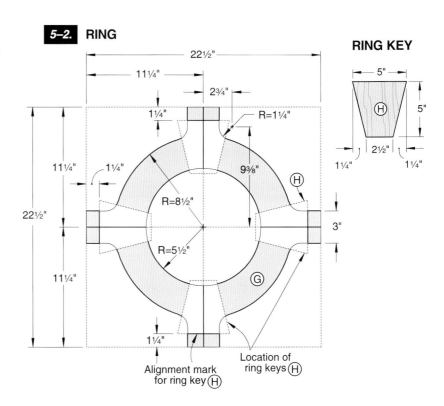

5–2. **RING**

RING KEY

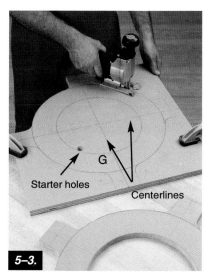

5–3.

Jigsaw the outside of the ring first. Then drill a ¾" starter hole in the ring's center, and cut out the center.

Starter holes

Centerlines

G

Make the Posts and Joists

1 Select the four straightest 8'-long 4 × 4 posts (3½ × 3½" actual size) you can find for N. Avoid twisted or warped posts, which will make it difficult to assemble the arbor. Check that each post measures the same length, as some could be slightly longer than 8'. Trim the posts as necessary and set them aside.

➤ *Note: The arbor shown on* page 107 *was installed on concrete footings; the cedar posts were anchored to the footings with bolt-down standoffs. If you plan to embed the posts in concrete, use pressure-treated posts, and allow for the extra buried length.*

2 Cut the main joists (O), cross-joists (P), and joist blocks (Q) to size. Lay out the 1½" notches 1" deep in the joists where

dimensioned in **5–9**. Mount a dado blade set in your tablesaw, and cut the notches. Or, use a portable circular saw to cut a series of kerfs to define the notches, and then clean out the openings with a mallet and chisel.

➤ *Note: Because the actual size of lumber can vary, measure the thickness of the posts and joists, and adjust the notch layouts as necessary to compensate for thickness differences.*

3 Lay out the decorative ends on the joists where dimensioned in **5–9**. Miter-cut the joists' 35° ends, and jigsaw the cutouts. Drill countersunk shank holes through the joists' outside faces, where shown. Then, attach the joist blocks (Q) to the inside faces of the two main joists (O) and two cross-joists (P), as shown in **5–9** and **5–10**. Use a scrap the width of your posts as a spacer to position the outer joist blocks on the cross-joists, as shown. Set the cross-joists aside.

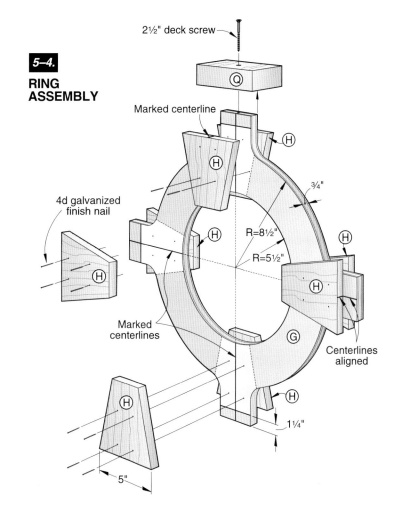

5–4.

RING ASSEMBLY

2½" deck screw

Q

Marked centerline

H

¾"

4d galvanized finish nail

H

H

R=8½"

R=5½"

H

Marked centerlines

G

Centerlines aligned

H

1¼"

H

5"

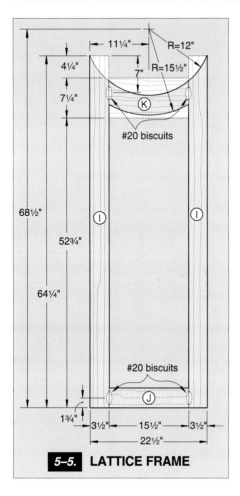

5–5. **LATTICE FRAME**

(labels on lattice frame drawing: 11¼", R=12", 4¼", 7", R=15½", 7¼", K, #20 biscuits, 68½", I, I, 52¾", 64¼", #20 biscuits, J, 1¾", 3½", 15½", 3½", 22½")

Below: *With the lattice frame and ring assemblies centered on the supports with spacers and aligned with the supports' marks, screw the supports to the assemblies.*

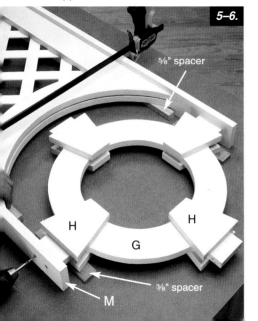

5–6.

(labels: ⅝" spacer, H, H, G, ⅜" spacer, M)

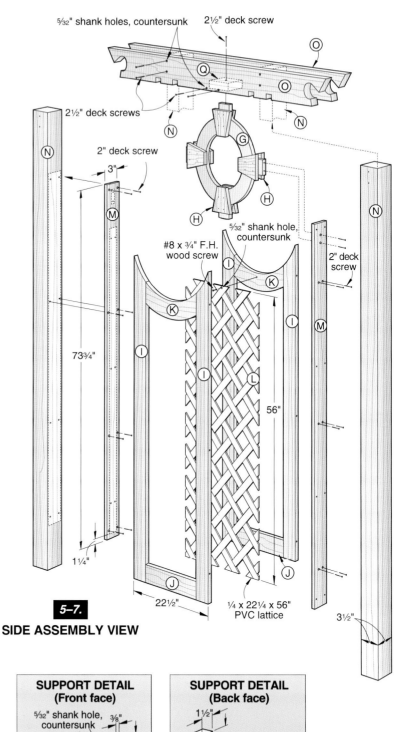

5–7.

SIDE ASSEMBLY VIEW

(labels on side assembly view: 5/32" shank holes, countersunk; 2½" deck screw; O; Q; O; N; 2½" deck screws; N; G; 2" deck screw; 3"; M; H; H; H; 5/32" shank hole, countersunk; N; 2" deck screw; #8 x ¾" F.H. wood screw; I; K; 73¾"; I; K; I; I; M; L; 56"; J; J; 22½"; ¼ x 22¼ x 56" PVC lattice; 1¼"; J; 3½")

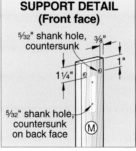

SUPPORT DETAIL (Front face)

(labels: 5/32" shank hole, countersunk; ⅜"; 1"; 1¼"; 5/32" shank hole, countersunk on back face; M)

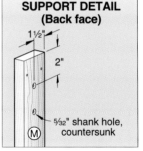

SUPPORT DETAIL (Back face)

(labels: 1½"; 2"; 5/32" shank hole, countersunk; M)

5–8. **SUPPORT DETAILS**

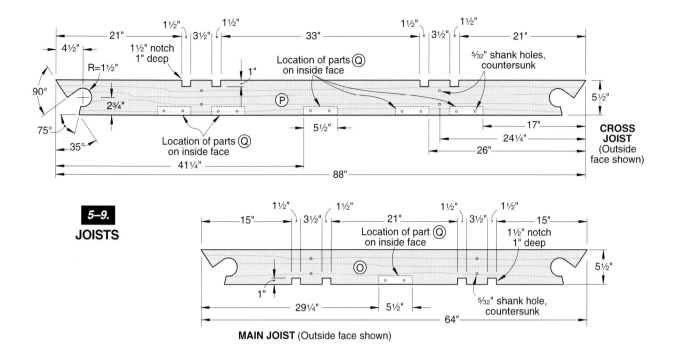

5–9.
JOISTS

MAIN JOIST (Outside face shown)

Assemble the Arbor Sides

1 After painting the parts, lay a lattice frame/ring assembly on your workbench. From scrap $\frac{1}{4}$" hardboard, cut four 1 × 6" spacers. Place the spacers under the assembly's supports (M), one at each end.

2 As shown in **5–11**, place a post (N) alongside each support, and position a main joist/block assembly (O/Q) across the posts with their top edges aligned and the posts centered between the pairs of joist notches. Slide up the lattice frame/ring assembly so the ring contacts the joist block (Q). Clamp the assembly together.

3 Drill countersunk shank holes in the supports (M) and the joist block (Q), where shown in the Side Assembly (**5–7**), and drive the screws into the posts and ring. (You'll need to angle your drill slightly when drilling the holes in the supports.) Also, screw the joist to the posts. With the aid of a helper, turn the assembly over. Place the opposing main joist (the one without a block) in position, and clamp. As before, drill the holes in the supports, and screw the supports and joist to the posts. Repeat this process to assemble the arbor's other side.

Put in the Footings and Install the Arbor

➤ *Note: You'll find the concrete tube forms, anchors, and bolt-down standoffs needed for the footings at home centers. Also, before you dig the footing holes, call the One Call phone number for your state or province, and ask to have the buried pipes and wires on your property located and marked. If you can't find the number, call the North American One Call Referral System at 888/258-0808.*

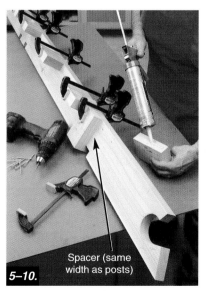

Spacer (same width as posts)

5–10.

Apply a bead of construction adhesive to the joist blocks, clamp them to the joists, and secure them with 2½" deck screws.

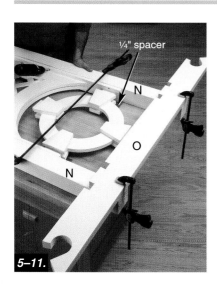

¼" spacer

N

O

N

5–11.

With the lattice frame/ring assembly supported on spacers, and the posts and joist clamped in position, drive the screws to secure the assembly.

1 Cut a piece of ¼" plywood to 27½ x 39½" for a marking template. Place the plywood on the ground where you plan to install the arbor, and mark the ground at each corner for the concrete footings.

2 Referring to **5–12**, dig 8"-diameter holes centered on the markings to the necessary depth using an auger or a posthole digger. For a neater job and added protection against heaving, place an 8"-diameter tube form in each hole, as shown. Fill the tubes with concrete, and level them. Check for level between adjacent and diagonally opposite footings.

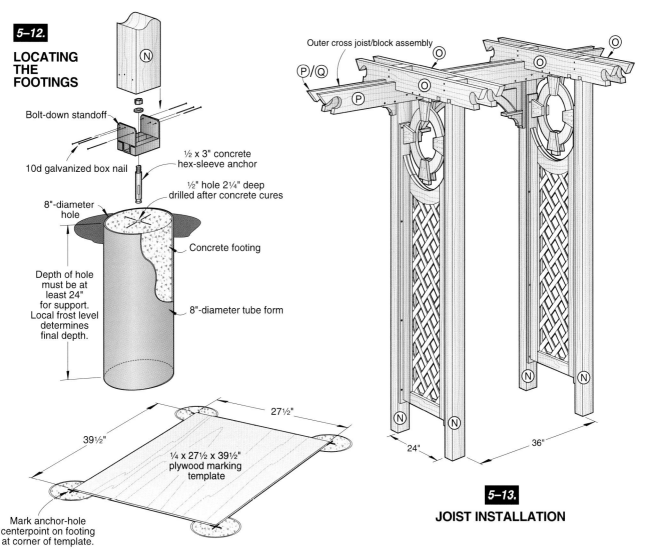

5–12.

LOCATING THE FOOTINGS

N

Bolt-down standoff

10d galvanized box nail

½ x 3" concrete hex-sleeve anchor

½" hole 2¼" deep drilled after concrete cures

8"-diameter hole

Concrete footing

Depth of hole must be at least 24" for support. Local frost level determines final depth.

8"-diameter tube form

27½"

39½"

¼ x 27½ x 39½" plywood marking template

Mark anchor-hole centerpoint on footing at corner of template.

Outer cross joist/block assembly

O

O

O

P/Q

P

O

N

N

N

N

N

24"

36"

5–13.

JOIST INSTALLATION

5–14.

With the posts captured between the cross-joist's outer blocks (Q), raise the joist assembly and slip its notches into those in the main joists (O).

5–15.

Clamp the arch assembly to the cross-joist blocks (Q). Then screw the blocks to the arch and the brackets to the posts.

3 When the concrete has cured, center the plywood template on the footings, as shown in **5–12**, and make a mark at the corners on the footings. Using a ½" masonry bit, drill a 2¼"-deep hole in each footing to receive a ½ x 3" concrete hex-sleeve anchor. Drive an anchor into each hole. (Back off each anchor's nut just enough to protect the bolt's top threads while you drive the anchor.) Mount a bolt-down standoff on each anchor, leaving the anchor's nut loose. Adjust the standoffs' spacing to exactly 24 x 36" (the spacing between the arbor's posts), then tighten the anchor nuts.

4 Retrieve the cross joists that you set aside earlier. With the aid of two helpers, stand the arbor's two side assemblies

upright in the standoffs. While your helpers hold the assemblies vertical, lift an outer cross joist/block assembly (P/Q) into position, where shown in **5–13** and **5–14**. Clamp the cross-joist to the main joists. Do not drive the screws yet.

5 Lift an arch assembly into position with its top flush against the cross-joist blocks (Q) and its brackets (D) centered on the posts (N), where shown in **5–16**. Clamp and fasten the assembly, as shown in **5–15**.

5–16.
ARCH INSTALLATION

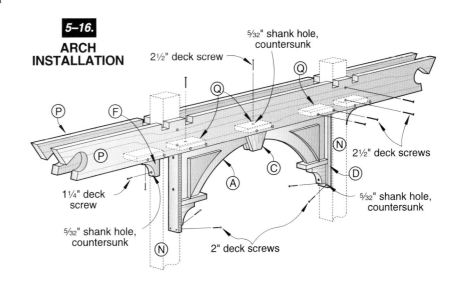

How to Finish Cedar Outdoor Projects

When you plan to paint cedar, be sure to properly prime it first. Otherwise, the colored extracts, resins, and oils that cedar contains may leach out and discolor the paint.

The U.S. Forest Products Laboratory has done extensive research on finishing cedar, and offers these tips:

5–17.

Priming the knots.

● *After sanding the parts, apply a quality, exterior latex, stain-blocking primer to "lock up" the troublesome substances and prevent them from seeping into the paint. Although an oil-based primer also does a good job as a stain blocker, USFPL tests have found that it can become brittle with age and flake, whereas a latex primer remains flexible.*

● *Prime the knots first, as shown in 5–17. When dry, prime the complete parts, giving extra attention to thirsty end-grain areas. Recoat any areas where you see significant residual discoloration. Let the primer cure for one week, and then cover it with a quality exterior latex paint.*

6 As you did before, lift and clamp the remaining cross-joist/block assembly (P/Q) in position on the arbor's opposite side, and mount the other arch assembly. Place the remaining cross-joists (P) in position, where shown in **5–15**, inserting them through the arbor side assemblies and clamping them to the main joists. Now, screw all of the cross-joists to the posts, and screw the inside cross-joists to the joist blocks (Q).

7 Finally, retrieve the four corbels (F) that you set aside earlier. Center the corbels on the posts and cross-joist outer blocks, where shown in **5–16**. Drill countersunk shank holes, where shown, and drive the screws. Drive 10d galvanized box nails through the standoffs into the posts. Touch up the screw and nail holes with acrylic caulk and paint. (If you use stainless-steel screws, you can omit this step.)

COMFORTABLE ARBOR BENCH

Adorn your backyard with a graceful accent and provide a restful place with this slatted bench and finger-jointed arbor combination.

Build a Pair of Arches

1 From $1\frac{1}{16}$" stock, cut the arch-top segments (A) and arch uprights (B) to the sizes listed in the Materials List plus 1" in length. (The pieces for the arbor bench on the following page were cut from $1\frac{1}{16}$"-thick cedar deck boards. If your stock is thicker, you'll need to plane it to $1\frac{1}{16}$" thickness to work with a finger-joint router bit. Redwood, mahogany, white oak, or teak would also work well for this project. Cut a couple of extra arch-top segments: They'll come in handy when testing the finger-joint bit setup in *Step 3*.)

2 Using **5–19** for reference, miter-cut the arch-top segments (A) to length. (Test-cut scrap stock first to verify an accurate 22.5° miter cut.)

3 Fit your table-mounted router with a finger-joint bit. (See the Shop Tip "Gluing Boards End to End" on *page 118*.) Then, rout finger joints across the miter-cut ends of the arch-top segments and across the top ends of the

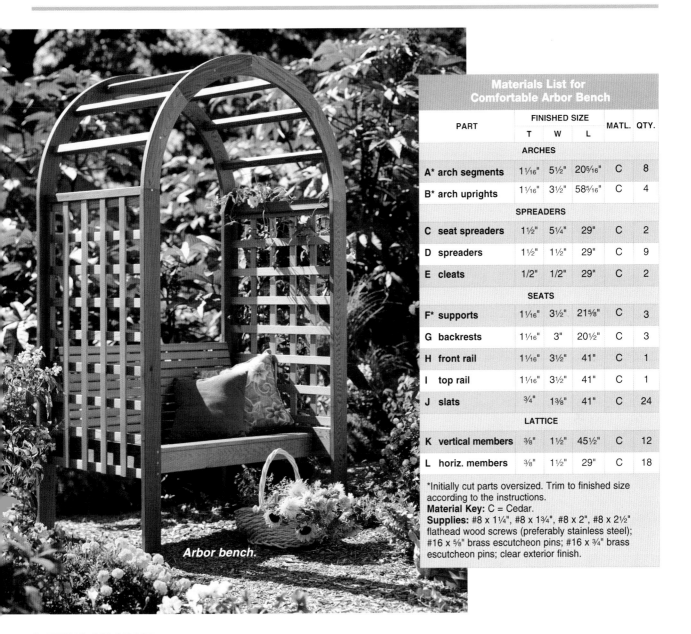

Arbor bench.

Materials List for Comfortable Arbor Bench

PART	FINISHED SIZE			MATL.	QTY.
	T	W	L		
ARCHES					
A* arch segments	$1\frac{1}{16}$"	$5\frac{1}{2}$"	$20\frac{5}{16}$"	C	8
B* arch uprights	$1\frac{1}{16}$"	$3\frac{1}{2}$"	$58\frac{5}{16}$"	C	4
SPREADERS					
C seat spreaders	$1\frac{1}{2}$"	$5\frac{1}{4}$"	29"	C	2
D spreaders	$1\frac{1}{2}$"	$1\frac{1}{2}$"	29"	C	9
E cleats	$1/2$"	$1/2$"	29"	C	2
SEATS					
F* supports	$1\frac{1}{16}$"	$3\frac{1}{2}$"	$21\frac{5}{8}$"	C	3
G backrests	$1\frac{1}{16}$"	3"	$20\frac{1}{2}$"	C	3
H front rail	$1\frac{1}{16}$"	$3\frac{1}{2}$"	41"	C	1
I top rail	$1\frac{1}{16}$"	$3\frac{1}{2}$"	41"	C	1
J slats	$3/4$"	$1\frac{3}{8}$"	41"	C	24
LATTICE					
K vertical members	$3/8$"	$1\frac{1}{2}$"	$45\frac{1}{2}$"	C	12
L horiz. members	$3/8$"	$1\frac{1}{2}$"	29"	C	18

*Initially cut parts oversized. Trim to finished size according to the instructions.
Material Key: C = Cedar.
Supplies: #8 x $1\frac{1}{4}$", #8 x $1\frac{3}{4}$", #8 x 2", #8 x $2\frac{1}{2}$" flathead wood screws (preferably stainless steel); #16 x $\frac{5}{8}$" brass escutcheon pins; #16 x $\frac{3}{4}$" brass escutcheon pins; clear exterior finish.

CUTTING DIAGRAM

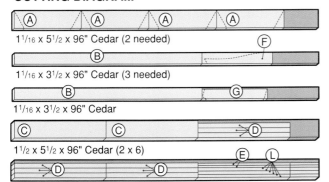

$1\frac{1}{16}$ x $5\frac{1}{2}$ x 96" Cedar (2 needed)

$1\frac{1}{16}$ x $3\frac{1}{2}$ x 96" Cedar (3 needed)

$1\frac{1}{16}$ x $3\frac{1}{2}$ x 96" Cedar

$1\frac{1}{2}$ x $5\frac{1}{2}$ x 96" Cedar (2 x 6)

$1\frac{1}{2}$ x $5\frac{1}{2}$ x 96" Cedar (2 x 6)

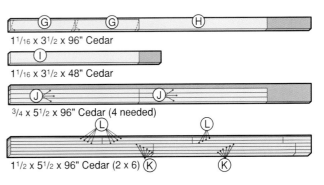

$1\frac{1}{16}$ x $3\frac{1}{2}$ x 96" Cedar

$1\frac{1}{16}$ x $3\frac{1}{2}$ x 48" Cedar

$3/4$ x $5\frac{1}{2}$ x 96" Cedar (4 needed)

$1\frac{1}{2}$ x $5\frac{1}{2}$ x 96" Cedar (2 x 6)

uprights (B). (Cut $1\frac{1}{16}$"-thick scrap stock first, to verify the settings.) Crosscut the uprights to their final length.

4 Clamp a board measuring approximately $\frac{3}{4} \times 4 \times 72$" to one edge of your workbench where shown in **5–20**. Now, dry-clamp four arch-top segments together in the configuration shown in **5–18**. (For photo clarity, the boards used to align the segments for clamping were stained.) Check the fit. Remember, if you trim these four segments, you'll need to do the same for the remaining four to keep both arch tops the same exact shape.

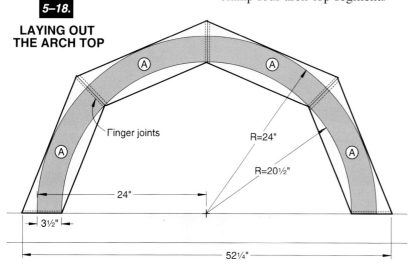

5–18.
LAYING OUT THE ARCH TOP

Finger joints
R=24"
R=20½"
24"
3½"
52¼"

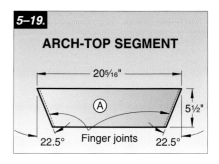

5–19.
ARCH-TOP SEGMENT

$20\frac{5}{16}$"
5½"
22.5° Finger joints 22.5°

shop TIP

5–20.

Gluing Boards End to End

Gluing boards end to end is not a simple matter because the hollow fibers of end grain act like straws and draw adhesive away from a joint. Also, the ends of these "straws" provide little surface area for the glue to adhere to. Fortunately, a finger joint, which you can cut with a router bit, solves both of these problems by exposing face grain and greatly increasing the surface area of the joint.

Left: Check the fit, then glue and clamp the arch-top segments together with long clamps and clamping boards.

5–21.

After sanding the finger joints smooth, use a trammel to mark a pair of arcs on one face of each arch.

5–22.

Sawhorses come in handy when gluing and clamping the uprights to the previously assembled arched top.

5 Glue and clamp the segments together as shown in **5–20**. Place waxed paper between your workbench and the segments at each glue joint to prevent the arch top from being glued to your workbench. Wipe off the excess glue with a damp cloth.

6 After the glue has dried (use water-resistant glue and leave the arch-top pieces clamped up overnight), sand the joints smooth. Use a trammel to mark two arcs on the clamped-together arch top, referring to **5–18** and **5–21**. Repeat the process to form and mark the second arch top.

7 Band-saw or jigsaw the arches' tops to shape, cutting just outside both marked arcs and then sanding to the line.

8 Using a pair of sawhorses with extra-long tops, glue and clamp the uprights to the arch tops as shown in **5–22**.

9 Sand the arches, and clamp them together surface-to-surface with the edges flush. Mark the hole centerpoints on the top arch where shown in **5–23**. Drill a $5/32$" shank hole through both arches at each mark. Use a drill press or drill guide to keep the holes perpendicular to the arch face. Separate the arches, and countersink the shank holes on *the front face of the front arch* and *the back face of the rear arch*.

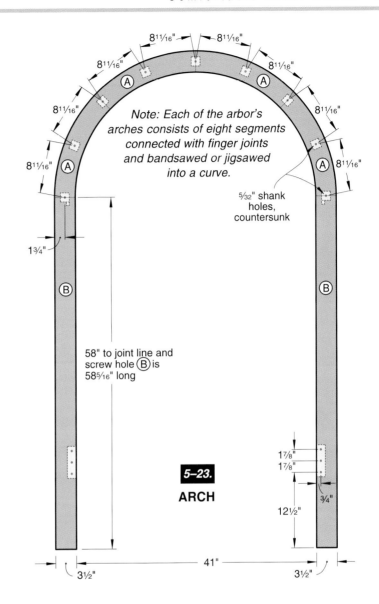

Note: Each of the arbor's arches consists of eight segments connected with finger joints and bandsawed or jigsawed into a curve.

$5/32$" shank holes, countersunk

58" to joint line and screw hole (B) is $58 5/16$" long

5–23.
ARCH

$8^{11}/16$" (×16)
$1^3/4$"
$1^7/8$"
$1^7/8$"
$3/4$"
$12^1/2$"
41"
$3^1/2$"
$3^1/2$"

10 Rout a $1/8$" roundover along both inside and outside edges of each arch.

Add the Spreaders

1 Cut the spreaders (C, D) and cleats (E) to size.

2 Glue and clamp the cleats (E) to the bottom side of two of the spreaders (D) where shown on the Spreader Detail drawing in **5–24**.

3 Rout $1/8$" roundovers along all edges of the spreaders and combination spreader/cleats.

4 Mark centerpoints on the ends of each spreader (D). Drill a $3/32$" pilot hole at each marked point. Using exterior screws (stainless steel is recommended), screw the spreaders (C, D) between the arches (A, B).

Make a Contoured Seat for Comfortable Sitting

1 To form the seat supports (F), cut three pieces of $1\frac{1}{16}$" stock to $3\frac{1}{2}$" wide by $22\frac{1}{8}$" long. Then, cut the backrests (G) to the size listed in the Materials List.

2 Using **5–28** *(page 122)*, machine the supports and backrests to fit in the configuration shown in **5–29**. See the machining drawings (**5–26** and

5–27). Enlarge the Seat Support pattern (**5–30**) to full size and transfer it to the seat supports (F). Cut them to shape.

3 Glue and clamp the three supports (F, G) together.

4 Cut the front rail (H) and top rail (I) to size. Bevel-rip the front edge of the top rail at 15°. Referring to **5–24** and **5–25**, rout $\frac{1}{8}$" roundovers, drill the mounting holes, and screw the rails to the seat supports (F/G) where shown.

5 Cut the seat slats (J) to size. Rout $\frac{1}{8}$" roundovers along the top edges of each. Then, rout a $\frac{1}{2}$" roundover on the slat you'll use across the front of the seat. Drill the mounting holes, and screw the slats to the seat framework (F-I), spacing them $\frac{1}{4}$" apart where shown **5–25**. (When adding the slats, start at the top of the backrest pieces and work down. On the seat, start at the front of the seat supports and work to the back.)

6 Screw the seat assembly in place between the arches.

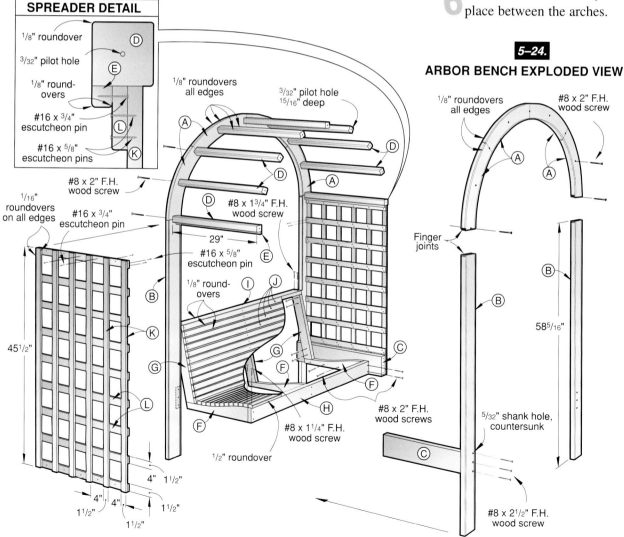

SPREADER DETAIL

5–24.
ARBOR BENCH EXPLODED VIEW

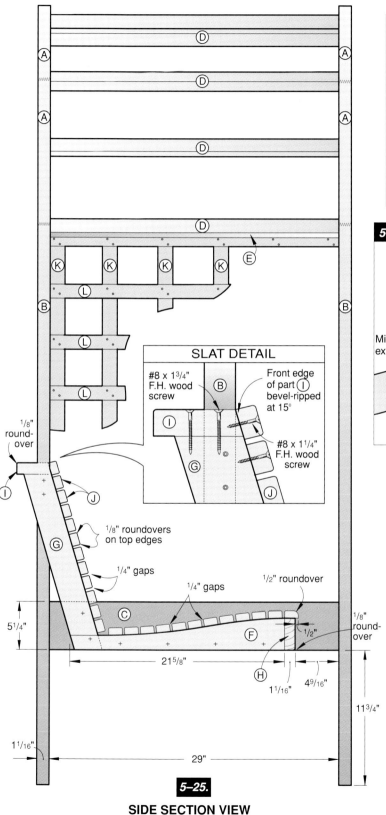

5–25.

SIDE SECTION VIEW

SLAT DETAIL

#8 x 1 3/4" F.H. wood screw

Front edge of part (I) bevel-ripped at 15°

#8 x 1 1/4" F.H. wood screw

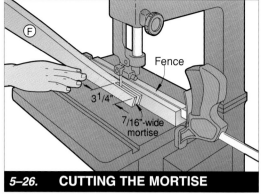

5–26. **CUTTING THE MORTISE**

Fence

3 1/4"

7/16"-wide mortise

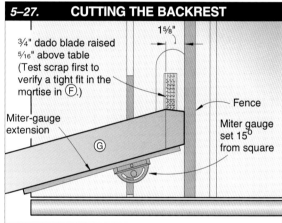

5–27. **CUTTING THE BACKREST**

1 5/8"

3/4" dado blade raised 5/16" above table (Test scrap first to verify a tight fit in the mortise in (F).)

Miter-gauge extension

Fence

Miter gauge set 15° from square

Add the Lattice Sides

1 Joint one edge of a 2 x 6, then rip $3/8$ x $1\frac{1}{2}$" strips from the stock for lattice pieces (K, L). Next, rout $1/16$" roundovers along all edges of each strip.

2 Use two Ks and two Ls to form the perimeter framework to fit between the uprights (B). Glue and nail these four pieces together. Repeat for the other side of the arbor.

3 Cut a scrap piece of stock 4" wide by about 45" long. Use this as a spacer to position the Ls on the framework when gluing and nailing them in place. Repeat with the Ks.

4 Glue and nail the lattice assemblies to the arbor.

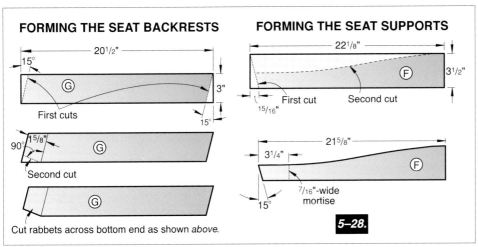

FORMING THE SEAT BACKRESTS

20½" · 15° · (G) · 3" · First cuts · 15°

1⅝" · 90° · (G) · Second cut

(G) · Cut rabbets across bottom end as shown *above*.

FORMING THE SEAT SUPPORTS

22⅛" · First cut · Second cut · (F) · 3½" · 15/16"

21⅝" · 3¼" · (F) · 15° · 7/16"-wide mortise

5–28.

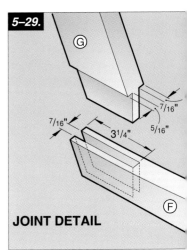

5–29.

(G) · 7/16" · 7/16" · 3¼" · 5/16" · (F)

JOINT DETAIL

Sand the Surfaces and Add the Finish

1 Check all surfaces, and sand where necessary.

2 Apply a quality exterior finish to the entire project. (You can brush it on, and also place a small amount of finish in pie tins, putting one under each upright.

This allows the finish to slowly wick into the end-grain upright ends to enhance the rot resistance of the wood.)

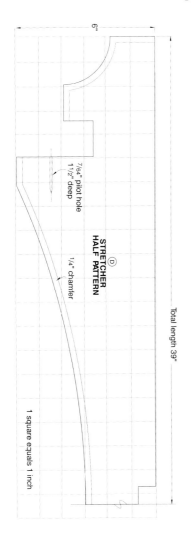

6" · 7/64" pilot hole 1½" deep · ¼" chamfer · **STRETCHER HALF PATTERN** · Total length 39" · 1 square equals 1 inch

3" · 1½" · 6¾" · (B) · 18" · Drill a ¾" counterbore 1⅜" deep before cutting curve · **PEDESTAL** · Drill a 7/32" pilot hole 2¾" deep into (C) · 3/8" shank hole · 3/8 x 4½" lag bolt · 1" nylon tack guides

11½" · 5/32" shank hole, countersunk on outside face · Blank is 11" wide x 11½" long · (C) · 2⅝" · 1½" · 11" · ¼" chamfer · R=6½" · 1 square equals 1 inch

For full-size pattern, enlarge 400%

5–30. **GRIDDED SEAT-SUPPORT PATTERN**

ARBOR/SWING COMBO

Arbor/swing combo

The construction method used for this project is very versatile. With a little imagination and planning, it can be adapted for a number of outdoor applications, including the pergola on *page 126*.

The porch swing from Chapter 4 (*page 88*) has been combined with a pergola-style arbor. The result is a great place to relax and watch your outdoor world go by. (The swing shown here was made out of cedar.)

Plant Four Posts on a Level Spot

1 Dig four 10"-diameter holes spaced where shown in **5–31** (*page 124*). To support the swing, the posts should extend at least 36" below grade. (Because of the frost line in the location for the

arbor/swing combo shown on this page, the posts extend 42" below grade; check your local requirements.) Dig holes deep enough to allow for a 6" layer of gravel at the bottom for drainage, as shown in **5–32**.

➤ *Note: The swing for the project shown on this page is 58½" wide. The pergola is sized to leave about 8" of clearance at each end between swing and posts. If you use a different swing, you may have to modify the pergola to maintain this clearance.*

Materials List for Arbor/Swing Combo

PART	FINISHED SIZE			MATL.	QTY.
	T	W	L		
A posts	5½"	5½"	†	PT	4
B post cap tops	1½"	5½"	5½"	C	4
C post cap bases	¾"	4½"	4½"	C	4
D main joists	1½"	5½"	106"	C	4
E cross-joists	1½"	5½"	50"	C	6

†Length varies depending on depth of frost line. See the instructions.
Materials Key: PT = Pressure-treated lumber; C = Cedar.
Supplies: ⅜" lag screws 4" long (16); ⅜" flat washers (20); 4" deck screws (32); 4d galvanized finish nails;⅜" eyebolts 8" long (2); ⅜" nuts (2); construction adhesive; primer; paint; gravel; concrete mix (approximately five cubic feet).

CUTTING DIAGRAM

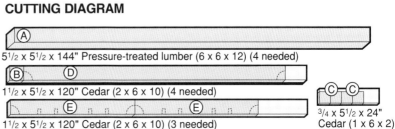

5½ x 5½ x 144" Pressure-treated lumber (6 x 6 x 12) (4 needed)

1½ x 5½ x 120" Cedar (2 x 6 x 10) (4 needed)

1½ x 5½ x 120" Cedar (2 x 6 x 10) (3 needed)

¾ x 5½ x 24" Cedar (1 x 6 x 2)

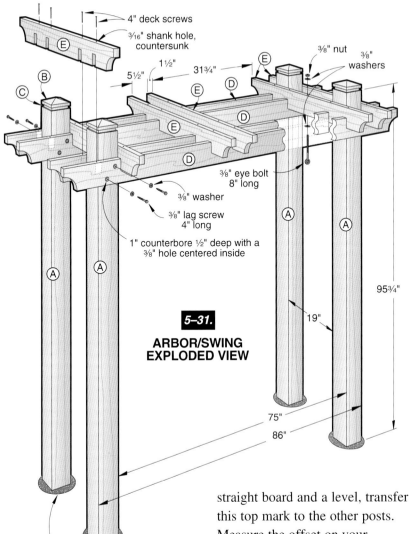

4" deck screws

3/16" shank hole, countersunk

3/8" nut

3/8" washers

1 1/2"

31 3/4"

5 1/2"

3/8" eye bolt 8" long

3/8" washer

3/8" lag screw 4" long

1" counterbore 1/2" deep with a 3/8" hole centered inside

95 3/4"

19"

5–31.

ARBOR/SWING EXPLODED VIEW

75"

86"

10"-diameter hole

this procedure on the other three posts, making them even in height.

4 Make four post caps (B/C), as explained in *Step 2* on *page 126*. Set them aside

Cut the Parts for the Overhead Grid

1 Cut the main joists (D) to the length in the Materials List. Form the end cutouts, shown in **5–33**, as explained in *Step 3* on *page 126*. Drill the counterbored 3/8" holes where shown.

2 Cut the cross joists (E) to the length in the Materials List. Form the end cutouts, shown in **5–34**, in the same manner as those in the main joists.

3 Turn the cross-joists upside down on a pair of sawhorses, and clamp them together with their ends and edges flush. Lay out the notch locations, where

2 Position four 6 x 6 x 12' (5 1/2 x 5 1/2" actual size) pressure-treated posts (A) in the holes, plumb them, and brace them in place. Make sure that the distance between the posts is the same at the top as at the grade. Set them in concrete, as shown in **5–32**.

3 When the concrete hardens, remove the bracing from the posts. Make a mark 95 3/4" up from grade on one post. Using a

straight board and a level, transfer this top mark to the other posts. Measure the offset on your portable circular saw between the edge of its base and the blade. Measure this offset distance down from the marked top line, and draw a level line around all four sides of each post. Temporarily nail a short board to one side of the first post with its top edge at this lower line. Setting your saw to its maximum depth, use the board to guide your saw as you make the cut. In this manner, work your way around the post's other three sides. Finish cutting through the post with a handsaw. Repeat

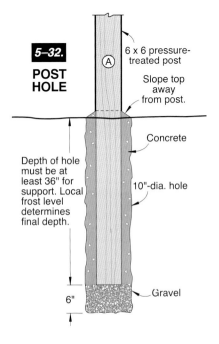

5–32.

POST HOLE

6 x 6 pressure-treated post

Slope top away from post.

Concrete

Depth of hole must be at least 36" for support. Local frost level determines final depth.

10"-dia. hole

6"

Gravel

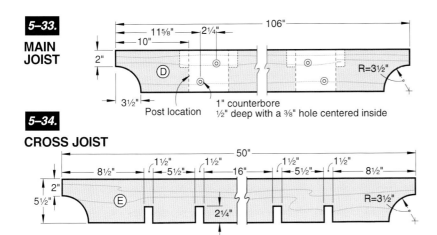

5–33.

MAIN JOIST

5–34.

CROSS JOIST

shown in **5–34**. Form the notches, as explained in *Step 4* on *page 127* of the Build-to-Suit Pergola.

➤ *Note: Check the actual dimension of your 6 x 6 posts. The spaces between the paired notches in the cross-joists (E) must match this dimension.*

4 Sand all your pergola parts with 120-grit sandpaper. Prime the parts, including the posts, with an exterior-grade latex primer. Take special care to coat the end grain and the notches.

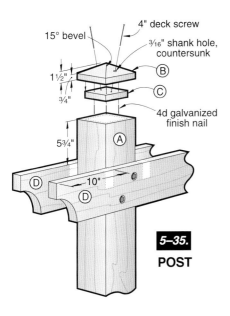

5–35.

POST

When the primer dries, lightly sand with 220-grit sandpaper. Finish the parts with two coats of exterior latex paint.

Assemble the Arbor/Swing Combo

1 Apply construction adhesive and glue, and screw the post caps (B/C) to the posts, as shown in **5–35**.

2 Clamp the main joists (D) to the posts, where shown in **5–31** and **5–35**. Make sure the joists are level from side to side and that the front pair of joists is level with the back pair. Using the counterbored holes in the joists as guides, drill pilot holes into the posts. Drive in the lag screws, as shown in **5–36**.

3 Place the cross-joists (E) where shown in **5–31**. The notches in the cross-joists fit over the main joists, as shown in **5–37**. Drill countersunk shank holes through the cross-joists at each notch. Drive 4" deck screws through the cross-joists into the main joists.

5–36.

Fasten the main joists to the posts with lag screws and flat washers.

5–37.

Drop the cross-joists in place over the main joists.

4 Drill ⅜" holes for the eyebolts, centered between the posts and in the thickness of the cross-joists, where shown on **5–31**. Touch up the paint where needed. With the paint dry, install the eyebolts, and hang the swing.

BUILD-TO-SUIT PERGOLA

With this airy pavilion, you can make your outdoor space special. It's easily sized to fit a deck (see the photo inset), patio, or yard.

This pergola has been designed to be infinitely adaptable. The one shown here occupies a 111 x 148" footprint, but you'll learn how to increase or decrease its dimensions as needed. You can build it as a freestanding structure on an existing deck or patio, or set its posts in the ground. Either way, you'll appreciate the simple way your pergola goes together like Lincoln Logs.

Cut the Parts for Your Pergola Kit

1 Cut four 6 x 6" (5½ x 5½" actual size) posts (A) to the length in the Materials List. To get a square cut, mark your cutting line on all four sides. Using a crosscut guide, cut all around the post to the full depth of your portable circular saw. Finish off the cut with a handsaw. Sand the posts to 120 grit, and set them aside.

2 For the post caps, start by cutting four 1½ x 5½ x 5½" cap tops (B) and four ¾ x 4½ x 4½" cap bases (C). Bevel the 1½"-thick cap tops, where shown in 5–38. (Use an auxiliary wooden fence on the tablesaw. To hold

Build-to-suit pergola

the blank, drive a wood screw through the back of the jig into the blank's center. Cut one face, rotate 90°, cut, and repeat until all four bevels are cut.) Glue and nail the cap bases, centered, to the cap tops, using an exterior glue and 4d galvanized nails. Sand the caps to 120 grit and set them aside. (Install the caps when the pergola is completely assembled.)

3 Cut the 2 x 6 main joists and side girders (D, E) to length. Make the marking/trimming template shown in 5–42, and use it to mark the 3½"-radius cutouts on the parts' ends, where shown in 5–41. Cut close to the lines, as shown in 5–39. Chuck a flush-trim bit in your handheld router. Clamping the template to each part to guide the bit, rout the final

profile. For smooth routing, rout from the cutout's "heel" to the part's end. Chuck a $\frac{1}{8}$" roundover bit in your router (to match the joists' factory edges), and rout the end profiles' edges.

Materials List for Build-to-Suit Pergola					
PART	**FINISHED SIZE**			**MATL.**	**QTY.**
	T	**W**	**L**		
A posts	5½"	5½"	107¾"	C	4
B post cap tops	1½"	5½"	5½"	C	4
C post cap bases	¾"	4½"	4½"	C	4
D main joists	1½"	5½"	168"	C	8
E side girders	1½"	5½"	168"	C	2
F blocking	1½"	5½"	22"	C	30
G upper bracket cleats	1½"	5½"	8⅜"	C	8
H end girders	1½"	5½"	131"	C	2
I stub joists	1½"	5½"	15½"	C	20
J* brackets	1½"	7¼"	40⅜"	C	8
K lower bracket cleats	¾"	3½"	10"	C	8
L* cove caps	¾"	¾"	7"	C	16
M* base trim	¾"	3¾"	7⅛"	C	16

*Parts initially cut oversized. See the instructions.
Material Key: C = Cedar.
Supplies: 1½" deck screws; 2" deck screws; 3" deck screws; 4" deck screws; ⅜ lag screws 3" long; ⅜" lag screws 4" long; ⅜" flat washers; 4d galvanized finish nails; steel post bases (4); construction adhesive; primer; paint.

Turn the joists and girders upside down on a pair of sawhorses, and clamp them together with their ends and edges flush. Using a square, draw lines across the parts' bottom edges (now facing up) for the 1½"-wide notches, where dimensioned in **5–41**. Using your portable circular saw, a straightedge, and a 1" chisel, form the notches, as shown in **5–43** and **5–44** (*page 129*). (These photos show cutting similar notches used for the arbor/swing combo on *page 123*.) Check the fit of your 1½" stock in the notch. For good appearance and easy assembly, you'll want a close but not tight fit.

Take two of the parts just notched, and clamp them together, with ends and edges flush. In the same manner as before, use a handsaw and chisel to deepen the notches to 2¾" (or half the actual width of your 2 x 6s). Mark these as the side girders (E) that, along with the end girders (H), form the pergola's outer frame. Sand the parts (D, E) to 120 grit, and set them aside.

Cut the blocking (F) and upper bracket cleats (G) to size. Sand them to 120 grit, and set them aside.

Cut the end girders (H) and the stub joists (I) to size. As with the main joists and side girders, use the template, jigsaw, and router to mark and form the end cutouts, where shown in **5–45**.

CUTTING DIAGRAM

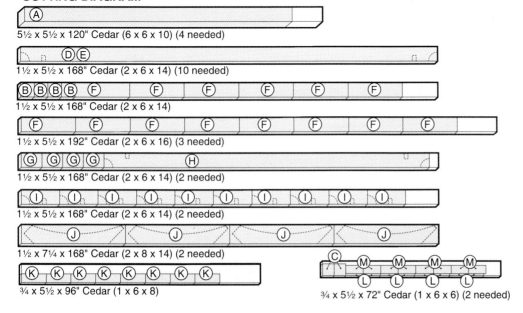

5½ x 5½ x 120" Cedar (6 x 6 x 10) (4 needed)

1½ x 5½ x 168" Cedar (2 x 6 x 14) (10 needed)

1½ x 5½ x 168" Cedar (2 x 6 x 14)

1½ x 5½ x 192" Cedar (2 x 6 x 16) (3 needed)

1½ x 5½ x 168" Cedar (2 x 6 x 14) (2 needed)

1½ x 5½ x 168" Cedar (2 x 6 x 14) (2 needed)

1½ x 7¼ x 168" Cedar (2 x 8 x 14) (2 needed)

¾ x 5½ x 96" Cedar (1 x 6 x 8)

¾ x 5½ x 72" Cedar (1 x 6 x 6) (2 needed)

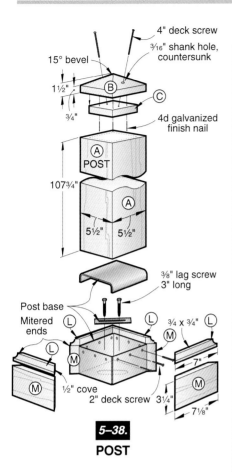

4" deck screw
15° bevel
$\frac{3}{16}$" shank hole, countersunk
$1\frac{1}{2}$"
B
C
$\frac{3}{4}$"
4d galvanized finish nail
A POST
$107\frac{3}{4}$"
A
$5\frac{1}{2}$" $5\frac{1}{2}$"
$\frac{3}{8}$" lag screw 3" long
Post base
Mitered ends
L L $\frac{3}{4} \times \frac{3}{4}$" L
M
L
M
M
$\frac{1}{2}$" cove
2" deck screw $3\frac{1}{4}$"
7"
M
$7\frac{1}{8}$"

5–38.
POST

5–39.

Use your jigsaw to cut the joist and girder ends to shape before smoothing the final profile with your router.

How to Plan Your Perfect Pergola

Using these instructions and *5–40* as a guide, you can easily customize a pergola to fit your needs. Here how.

Start with your pergola's footprint. This is simply the outside-of-post to outside-of-post length and width. Because 16' is the longest commonly available cedar 2 x 6, and the girders and joists extend beyond the footprint by 10" at each end, your footprint cannot exceed 172" x 172".

Although you can orient the main joists and side girders (D, E) in either direction, for planning purposes we'll refer to the outside-of-post to outside-of-post dimension parallel to these members as the footprint length. To find the length of the main joists and side girders (D, E), add 20" to the footprint's length. To find the length of the end girders (H), add 20" to the footprint's width.

Position the main joists (D) across the end girders (H), keeping the distance

$5\frac{1}{2}$"
24"±
$5\frac{1}{2}$"
24"±
$5\frac{1}{2}$"
Footprint length
24"±
$5\frac{1}{2}$"
10"
I
E F F
D
D
H
A B C
24"± $5\frac{1}{2}$"
24"± $5\frac{1}{2}$"
10"
Footprint width

5–40.

between the closed-spaced pairs at $5\frac{1}{2}$". Adjust the number of pairs and/or the length of the blocking (F) to evenly fill the distance between the posts. (We tried to keep the interval between the adjacent joist pairs in the neighborhood of 24".) The interval between the pairs is the length of the blocking (F).

Now, using the same spacing method (though not necessarily the same spacing), position the blocking and the stub joists (I) along the main joists.

8 Following the same procedure as with the main joists and side girders, form the notches in the end girders (H) and the stub joists (I), where shown in **5–45** (*page 130*). Note that the notches in the end girders are cut in their top edges to mate with the notches cut in the bottom edges of the side girders. As with the two side girders (E), extend the notches in the end girders to $2\frac{3}{4}$"

deep. Sand parts H and I to 120 grit, and set them aside.

9 Cut eight 2 x 8 blanks $41\frac{7}{8}$" long for the brackets (J). Using your circular saw or tablesaw and miter gauge, make the angled end cuts, where shown in **5–46** (*page 130*). Mark the centerpoint of the curve on one blank. Bend a narrow strip of hardboard to join the centerpoint and ends, and draw the curve.

5–41.

MAIN JOIST/BLOCKING ASSEMBLY.

168"

22"

5½"

1½"

1½"

23⅝"

5½"

1½"

5½"

1½"

15½"

3" deck screw

3" deck screw

8⅜"

1½"

R=3½"

8½"

1½"

2¼"

⁵⁄₃₂" shank hole, countersunk

3" deck screw

5–42.

¼" hardboard

6¼"

9¾"

R=3½"

¾ x ¾ x 9¾" stock

Rout ⅛" round-overs on these edges after the end profiles are shaped.

MARKING/ TRIMMING TEMPLATE.

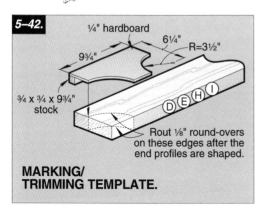

Jigsaw or band-saw the curved piece out, and then sand to the line. Use this completed bracket as a template to trace the curve on the other bracket blanks. Saw to the waste side of the lines. Then clamp the template bracket, in turn, to each of the sawn blanks, and use a flush-trim bit in your handheld router to smooth out the curves. Finish up by routing ⅛" roundovers where shown.

10 Cut the lower bracket cleats (K) to size. Rout the ¼" cove, and drill three shank holes countersunk from the back, and six shank holes countersunk from the front, in each piece, where shown in **5–47**. Sand the cleats to 120 grit.

➤ *Note: The 4/4 cedar that many lumberyards carry is about ⅞" thick and rough-sawn on one side. To get smooth faces and edges, plane a 1 x 6 x 8' board to ¾" thickness and rip and joint it to a 3½" width before cutting into 10" lengths.*

5–43.

Set your saw to cut 2¼" deep. Clamp a straightedge to the joists, and cut a series of kerfs to define the notches.

5–44.

Use a hammer and chisel to clean out the notches, smoothing their bottoms to a uniform depth.

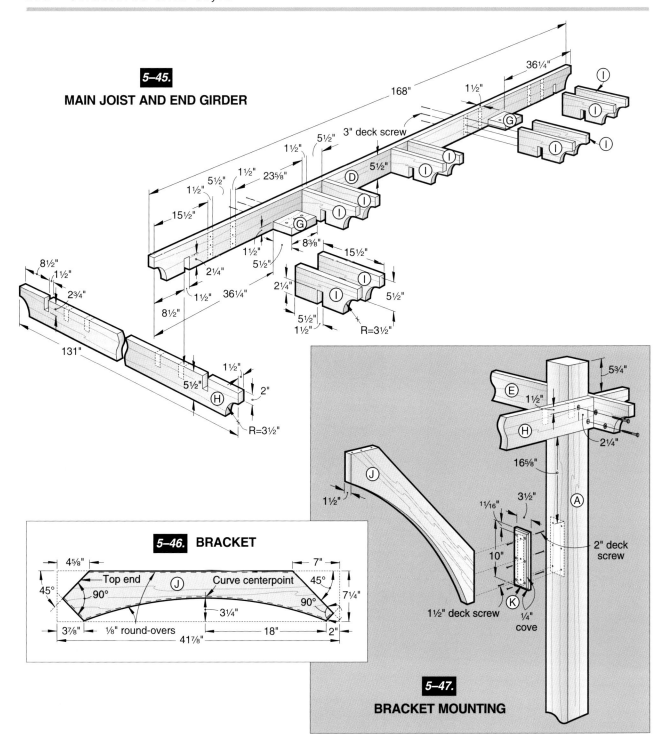

5-45.
MAIN JOIST AND END GIRDER

5-46. BRACKET

5-47.
BRACKET MOUNTING

For the cove caps (L) and base trim (M), plane two 1 x 6 x 6' cedar boards to ¾" thick. Joint one edge of each board. Rout a ½" cove in the jointed edges, and rip off a ¾"-wide strip for the cove caps (L). Joint the sawn edges of the remaining boards, and rip them to 3¼" width for the base trim (M). Sand the base and cap stock to 120 grit. You'll miter-cut the cove caps and base trim to fit around the posts after the pergola is in place.

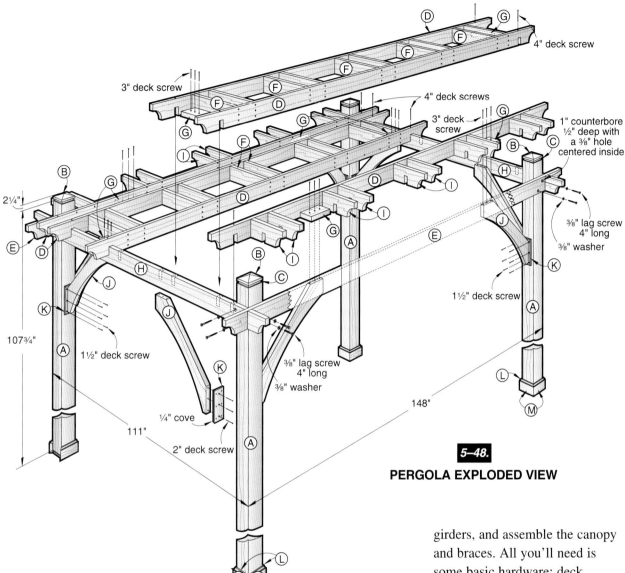

4" deck screw

3" deck screw

4" deck screws

3" deck screw

1" counterbore ½" deep with a ⅜" hole centered inside

2¼"

⅜" lag screw 4" long
⅜" washer

1½" deck screw

107¾"

1½" deck screw

⅜" lag screw 4" long
⅜" washer

148"

¼" cove

111"

2" deck screw

5–48.
PERGOLA EXPLODED VIEW

Prime all the pergola parts with an exterior-grade latex primer. Apply two coats to the end grain and the notches. When the primer dries, lightly sand the parts with 220-grit sandpaper. Finish the parts with two coats of exterior latex paint.

Assemble the Pergola

Now that you have made, primed, and painted all your pergola parts, you're just an afternoon away from transforming your yard's personality. Referring to **5–49** to **5–57**, create the subassemblies, erect the posts and

girders, and assemble the canopy and braces. All you'll need is some basic hardware: deck screws, lag screws, and steel post bases. To supply secure anchorage for the post bases, add blocking underneath the deck. When lag-screwing the girders to the posts, drill counterbored shank holes through the girders and ¼" pilot holes into the posts. When fastening parts with deck screws, drill only countersunk shank holes. The deck screws drive into the cedar without pilot holes.

2 Finish off your pergola by driving 3" deck screws through the side girders (E) and the end girders (H) into the upper bracket cleats (G). Remove the temporary braces from the posts. Drill countersunk shank holes through the post caps (B/C). Apply construction adhesive to the bottoms of the caps, and screw the caps to the tops of the posts. Touch up the paint where needed.

How to Assemble the Pergola

5–49.

Step 1. Screw together main joist/blocking (D/F) subassemblies, where dimensioned on **5–41**. Fasten the upper bracket cleats (G) to the subassemblies where shown on **5–41** and **5–48**.

5–50.

Step 2. Screw together the two main joist/stub joist (D/I) subassemblies, where dimensioned on **5–45**. Fasten the upper bracket cleats (G) to the main joists, where shown on the drawing.

5–51.

Step 3. Lay out your pergola's footprint, and lag-screw four post bases to the deck. Take diagonal measurements to check your layout for square. The post bases allow you to fine-tune their locations.

5–52.

Step 4. Lag-screw each end girder to two posts, where shown on **5–47**. Stand up these assemblies in the post bases, plumb them, and brace them in place. Screw the bases to the posts, as shown in **5–38**.

How to Assemble the Pergola (continued)

5–53.

5–54.

Step 5. *Slip the end notches of the side girders (E) into the notches of the end girders (H). The tops of both girders will be flush. Drill 1¼" pilot holes, and lag-screw the side girders to the posts.*

Step 6. *Hoist the main joist/stub joist assemblies (D/I) into place, slipping the stub joist and main joist notches over the side girders (E) and the end girders (H). Fasten with deck screws, as shown.*

5–55.

5–56.

5–57.

Step 7. *Position the main joist/ blocking assemblies (D/F), slipping the main joist notches over the end girders. Leave 5½" spaces between the main joists of adjacent assemblies. Fasten with screws.*

Step 8. *Screw the lower bracket cleats (K) to the brackets (J), where shown on 5–47. Screw the bracket assemblies to the posts and the upper bracket cleats (G), where shown on 5–47 and 5-48.*

Step 9. *Miter-cut the base trim (M) to fit around the post bases. Apply construction adhesive and band-clamp the pieces together, as shown. Miter-cut the cove cap (L) to fit around the post, and nail it in place.*

6

Gardener's Delights

Do you love to play in the dirt? If so, prepare yourself for the great gardening projects in this chapter. Whether flowers are your only passion or whether you also enjoy growing vegetables and herbs for the table, there are plenty of things to build in the following pages.

For starters, the planter shown on *page 135* is the ideal place to plant flowering annuals. But, it's also a great spot for container-sized vegetable plants, such as tomatoes. Combine it with the tuteur on *page 138*, and you'll have real pyramid power for growing climbing things. Or simply put the tower to use all by itself as a strong visual statement in your yard.

If you like to pot your plants, the potting bench on *page 142* will become the ideal place to get your hands dirty. If you don't like to get your knees as grimy

as your hands in the garden, look at the bench on *page 149*. It performs double duty, and is a breeze to build.

On *pages 152* and *158* you can treat yourself to a pair of trellises. One will accent a fence or a wall, and the other offers a place for plants to cling to and to climb wherever you place it. You'll probably want to make several. See *page 155* for a simply lovely window box that can house your colorful plantings from spring through fall.

PATIO-PERFECT PLANTER

Spruce up your outdoor spaces with this 19"-tall, cedar-trimmed planter. It accepts up to a 16" square or round pot for showing off pretty plantings.

Make the Box

1 Cut the sides (A) to the size listed in the Materials List. Glue and clamp the sides together, overlapping the ends as shown in **6–2** (*page 136*). Use an exterior-type adhesive, such as water-resistant glue or polyurethane glue. Check for square. Then drill countersunk shank holes where shown, and drive the screws.

2 Cut the support rails (B) to size. Using a dado blade, cut a 1½" notch 1¾" deep in the center of each rail. Glue and screw the rails together. Place the rails in the bottom of the box, and secure with screws, where shown.

Cedar-trimmed planter

Materials List for Patio-Perfect Planter

PART	FINISHED SIZE			MATL.	QTY.
	T	W	L		
A sides	¾"	16⅜"	17⅛"	MP	4
B support rails	1½"	3½"	16⅜"	C	2
C wide stiles	¾"	2¾"	17⅝"	C	4
D narrow stiles	¾"	2"	17⅝"	C	4
E* top and bottom rails	¾"	3"	13⅞"	C	8
F* center stiles	⅝"	4"	12⅜"	C	4
G top trim pieces	¾"	2⅝"	21⅜"	C	4
H* spline blanks	⅛"	2⅝"	5¼"	C	4

*Parts initially cut oversized. See the instructions.
Materials Key: MP = Medium-density overlay (MDO) plywood; C = Cedar.
Supplies: #8 x 1", #8 x 1¼", #8 x 1½", and #8 x 2½" stainless-steel flathead wood screws; 6d galvanized finish nails; spray adhesive; exterior-type adhesive.
Blades and bits: Dado-blade set; 45° chamfer router bit.

Add the Trim

1 Cut the wide stiles (C) and narrow stiles (D) to size. Mark a 1¼" radius at the bottom of a narrow stile (either corner is fine) where dimensioned in **6–4** *(page 136)*. Band-saw and sand the radius to shape. Using this stile as a template, mark the radius on a corner of each of the remaining narrow and wide stiles. Band-saw and sand these pieces.

2 Glue and clamp the narrow and wide stiles together, where shown in **6–2**. Note that the stile assemblies (C/D) at adjacent corners form mirror images. When the glue dries, screw the assemblies to the box, as shown in **6–1**, with their top edges flush.

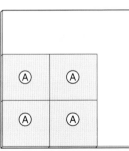

¾ x 48 x 48" MDO plywood

CUTTING DIAGRAM

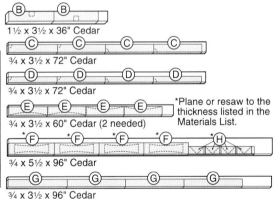

1½ x 3½ x 36" Cedar

¾ x 3½ x 72" Cedar

¾ x 3½ x 72" Cedar

¾ x 3½ x 60" Cedar (2 needed)

*Plane or resaw to the thickness listed in the Materials List.

¾ x 5½ x 96" Cedar

¾ x 3½ x 96" Cedar

3 From ¾"-thick cedar, cut eight 3 x 14" pieces for the top and bottom rails (E). Trim each rail's length to fit between the stile assemblies (C/D). Mark the rails and box so you can install the pieces in the same locations later.

With the stile assemblies clamped to the box (no glue), drill countersunk shank holes in the box, and drive the screws.

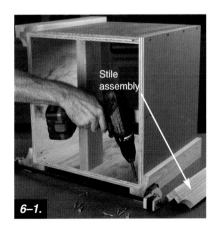

Stile assembly

6–1.

4 Using a flexible metal ruler or a thin strip of wood as a fairing strip, mark an arch on a rail (E), where dimensioned in **6–4**. Band-saw and sand the arch to shape. Using this rail as a template, mark the arch on the remaining rails; then cut and sand them.

5 From ¾"-thick cedar planed to ⅝"-thick, cut four 4 x 16⅜" pieces for the center stiles (F). Mark centerlines on the stiles and

rails (E), where shown in **6–3**. Position a top and bottom rail on a stile, and mark the rails' contours on the stile, as shown.

Align the rails' and stile's centerlines and their top and bottom edges. Scribe each rail's arch contour onto the stile.

6–2. PLANTER EXPLODED VIEW

6d galvanized finish nails

⅛" chamfer along top edges

⅛ x 2½" slot

#8 x 1¼" stainless-steel F.H. wood screw

5⁄32" shank hole, countersunk

#8 x 1" stainless-steel F.H. wood screws

5⁄32" shank hole, countersunk

#8 x 1½" stainless-steel F.H. wood screw

2½" stainless-steel F.H. wood screw

3⁄32" pilot hole ¾" deep

1½" notch 1¾" deep

#8 x 1½" stainless-steel F.H. wood screws

5⁄32" shank hole, countersunk

⅛" chamfer on bottom outside edge

SPLINE CUTTING DETAIL

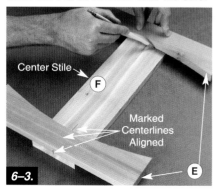

Center Stile

Marked Centerlines Aligned

6–3.

⅛" chamfer along all edges on outside face

No chamfer along this edge

⅛" chamfers

No chamfer along this edge

6–4.

SIDE VIEW OF THE PLANTER

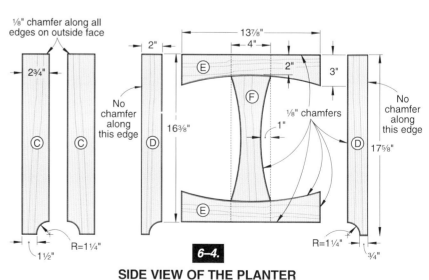

Identify the stile to match it to the rails, and keep the parts together. Repeat this process to mark the remaining stiles. Now, band-saw the stiles' ends to shape, and sand them to get a good fit between the rails.

6 Mark the arches on the sides of a center stile (F), where dimensioned on **6–4**. Band-saw and sand the arches to shape. Use this stile to mark the arches on the remaining pieces; then cut and sand them.

7 Remove the stile assemblies (C/D) from the box, and mark their locations. Sand all of the stiles and rails to 220 grit. Then chamfer the edges of the parts, where shown.

Make the Top

1 Cut the top trim pieces (G) to size. Miter-cut their ends, where shown in **6–2**. Glue the pieces together to form a frame, secure with a band clamp, and check for square.

2 Referring to Spanning Miters with Big Splines, cut a slot in each corner of the frame to receive the spline blanks (H), where shown in **6–2.**

3 Resaw a $\frac{1}{8}$"-thick strip from cedar for the spline blanks (H). Referring to the Spline-Cutting Detail in **6–2** and the Cutting Diagram, miter-cut four $2\frac{5}{8} \times 5\frac{1}{4}$" splines from the strip. Apply glue in the frame's slots, and

shop TIP

Spanning Miters with Big Splines

Mitered workpieces subjected to the rigors of Mother Nature will surely open up unless you have reinforced them in a substantial way. The best solution is to span the miters with hefty splines, like those for the planter's top trim (G), which offer plenty of face-grain gluing surface.

To safely support your workpiece while cutting the deep slots for the splines, build a V-block jig, as shown in 6–5. Raise your $\frac{1}{8}$"-thick tablesaw blade to the appropriate height for the required slot depth ($2\frac{1}{2}$" for the planter). Position your fence to center the blade on the width of the jig's $\frac{3}{4}$"-thick cleat. Clamp the frame in the jig, and cut out the slot, as shown in 6–6.

Right: Putting the V-block jig to use.

6–5. V-BLOCK JIG

6–6.

insert the splines. When the glue dries, flush-trim and sand the splines.

4 Chamfer the frame's top edges, where shown in **6–2**. Chisel the inside-corner edges to complete the chamfers. Now sand the frame.

Finish and Assemble the Planter

1 Remove the support rails (B) from the box. Brush two coats of paint or stain on the inside and outside surfaces of the box. (The planter shown on *page 135* was finished with a solid-color deck stain—acrylic latex.) Brush two coats of a water-repellent wood tone finish on all of the other parts.

2 Reattach the support rails (B) and stile assemblies (C/D) to the box. Fasten the top and bottom rails (E) by drilling countersunk shank holes on the inside of the box and driving in #8 × $1\frac{1}{4}$" screws. In the same way, fasten the center stiles (F) using #8 × 1" screws. Centering the assembled top trim (G) on the box, glue and nail it in place.

3 Finally, place a pot in the box, and plant flowers. The planter on *page 135* has a 16"-square, $13\frac{5}{8}$"-tall pot with a self-supporting rim that fits the box just right. For a pot less than $13\frac{5}{8}$" tall, elevate it by placing scrap cedar spacers on top of the support rails (B), as needed.

FLOWER-TOWER TUTEUR

Create a unique garden focal point and give climbing plants an upscale home with this geometric trellis structure. The roughly 50"-tall tuteur can be freestanding or mounted atop its companion planter, as described on *pages 134 to 137*. Need some ideas for plants? See Vine Ideas on *page 141*.

Make the Sides

1 From a $1\frac{1}{2} \times 5\frac{1}{2} \times 48$" cedar board (2 x 6) planed to 1" thick, cut the legs (A) to the size listed in the Materials List. Mark the locations for the rail blanks (B, C, D, E, F) on the legs, where dimensioned in the Side Assembly drawing (**6–8**).

2 Plane a $1\frac{1}{2} \times 5\frac{1}{2} \times 24$" cedar board to 1" thick. Rip sixteen $\frac{1}{4}$"-thick, 1"-wide strips from the edge of the board for the rail blanks (B through F), referring to the Cutting Diagram for layout. Crosscut the strips to the listed lengths.

3 From scrap $\frac{3}{4}$" plywood, make a $5 \times 19\frac{3}{8}$" spacer, and miter-cut its ends at $11\frac{1}{2}°$, where shown in the Side Assembly drawing (**6–8**).

4 Lay two legs (A) on your workbench with the markings visible, and position the spacer between them with the bottom edges flush. Clamp the legs to the spacer.

5 Glue and nail a rail blank (B) to the legs, where shown in the Side Assembly drawing (**6–8**), aligning it with the marks and roughly centering it end to end. Use an exterior-type adhesive, such as a water-repellent or

Tuteur

polyurethane glue. In the same way, attach a rail blank (C) to the legs with the top edges flush and the legs spaced 3" apart at the rail's bottom edge, where shown in the Top-Rail Detail drawing (**6–9**). Now, attach the other rail blanks (D, E, F) to the legs. When the glue dries, trim the rails' ends flush with the legs' outside edges, as shown in **6–7**.

PART	FINISHED SIZE			MATL.	QTY.
	T	W	L		
A legs	1"	1"	47"	C	4
B* rail blanks	$\frac{1}{4}$"	1"	22"	C	4
C* rail blanks	$\frac{1}{4}$"	1"	5"	C	4
D* rail blanks	$\frac{1}{4}$"	1"	18"	C	4
E* rail blanks	$\frac{1}{4}$"	1"	14"	C	4
F* rail blanks	$\frac{1}{4}$"	1"	10"	C	4
G* vertical trim strips	$\frac{1}{8}$"	$1\frac{1}{2}$"	32"	C	4
H base	$\frac{1}{2}$"	$3\frac{3}{4}$"	$3\frac{3}{4}$"	C	1
I cap	$\frac{1}{2}$"	$2\frac{1}{2}$"	$2\frac{1}{2}$"	C	1
J finial	$1\frac{1}{2}$"	$1\frac{1}{2}$"	6"	C	1
K mounting blocks	$\frac{3}{4}$"	$\frac{3}{4}$"	$3\frac{1}{2}$"	C	2

Materials List for Flower-Tower Tuteur

*Parts initially cut oversized. See the instructions.
Material Key: C = Cedar.
Supplies: #18 x $\frac{3}{4}$" galvanized nails; #8 x $1\frac{1}{2}$" stainless-steel flathead wood screws (3); spray adhesive; exterior-type adhesive.

CUTTING DIAGRAM

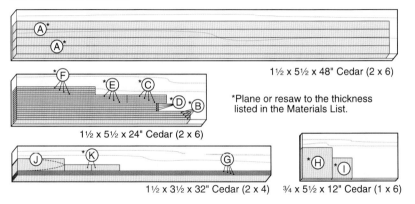

$1\frac{1}{2} \times 5\frac{1}{2} \times 48$" Cedar (2 x 6)

*Plane or resaw to the thickness listed in the Materials List.

$1\frac{1}{2} \times 5\frac{1}{2} \times 24$" Cedar (2 x 6)

$1\frac{1}{2} \times 3\frac{1}{2} \times 32$" Cedar (2 x 4)

$\frac{3}{4} \times 5\frac{1}{2} \times 12$" Cedar (1 x 6)

6–7.

Place the side assembly face down on scrap boards. Using a fine-tooth saw, trim the rails' ends even with the legs.

Adding a Tuteur to the Planter

For a winning combination, consider mounting the tuteur on the planter described on pages 134 to 137. This arrangement is shown in here. First, trim the tuteur's legs (A) flush with the bottom edge of the rails (B). Then, cut two mounting blocks (K) to the size listed in the Materials List. Glue the blocks to the inside face of two opposing rails B, where shown in 6–13. With the tuteur placed on the planter, drill a countersunk shank hole in each mounting block, and screw the blocks to the planter's top trim.

6–8.

SIDE ASSEMBLY

#18 x ¾" galvanized nail

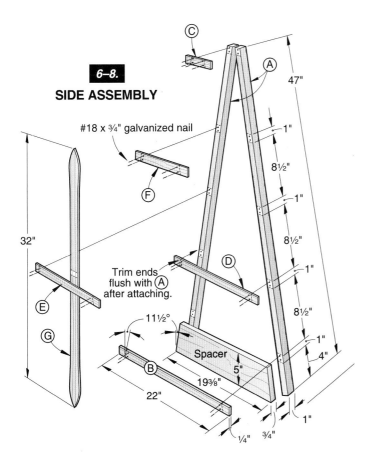

Trim ends flush with (A) after attaching.

Spacer

$11\frac{1}{2}°$

32"

47"

1"

$8\frac{1}{2}$"

1"

$8\frac{1}{2}$"

1"

$8\frac{1}{2}$"

1"

4"

5"

$19\frac{3}{8}$"

22"

1"

¼" ¾"

6–9.

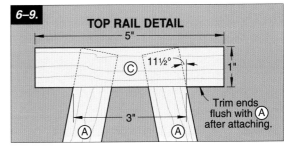

TOP RAIL DETAIL

5"

$11\frac{1}{2}°$

1"

3"

Trim ends flush with (A) after attaching.

From a $1\frac{1}{2}$ x $3\frac{1}{2}$ x 32" cedar board, rip four ⅛"-thick, $1\frac{1}{2}$"-wide strips for the vertical trim (G). Face-join the strips together using a few pieces of double-faced tape. Make two copies of the Vertical Trim pattern (**6–14**, on *page 141*). Adhere the patterns to the ends of a strip, and draw lines to connect them, where shown in the Vertical Trim drawing in **6–10** (*page 140*). Band-saw the strips to shape, and sand the curved edges smooth. Carefully separate the strips and remove the tape.

Glue a vertical trim strip (G) to the side assembly, where shown in the Side Assembly drawing (**6–8** , *page 139*) and the Exploded View drawing (**6–13**). Center it side-to-side in the assembly with an equal overhang above rail F and below rail D. Note that the trim fits behind rail E and in front of rails D and F.

8 Repeat the process to assemble the opposite side.

Assemble the Sides and Add a Top to the Tuteur

1 Position the two side assemblies upright and opposite each other. As shown in **6–11**, clamp the spacer between the assemblies, and attach the rail blanks (B through F) to the legs in the same order as before. (An

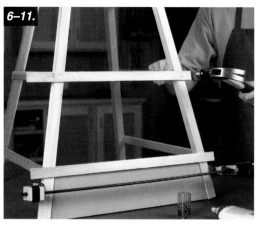

6–11.

Clamp the spacer between the assemblies' legs at one end. Attach the rail blanks, aligning them with the adjoining rails.

6–12.

Using a sanding block with 80-grit sandpaper, flatten the top edges of the rails (C) to receive the top assembly.

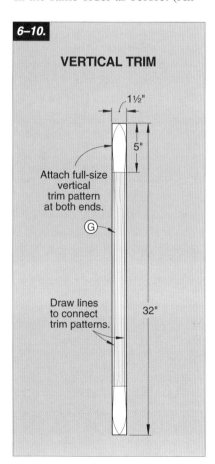

6–10.

VERTICAL TRIM

1½"

5"

Attach full-size vertical trim pattern at both ends.

(G)

Draw lines to connect trim patterns.

32"

6–13. TUTEUR EXPLODED VIEW

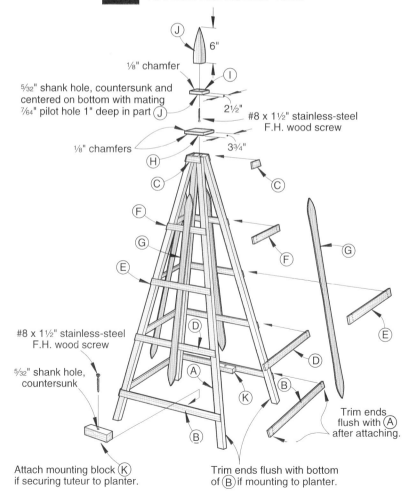

(J) 6"

⅛" chamfer

(I)

5/32" shank hole, countersunk and centered on bottom with mating 7/64" pilot hole 1" deep in part (J)

2½"

#8 x 1½" stainless-steel F.H. wood screw

⅛" chamfers

3¾"

(H)

(C)

(C)

(F)

(G)

(F)

(G)

(E)

(E)

(D)

#8 x 1½" stainless-steel F.H. wood screw

5/32" shank hole, countersunk

(D)

(A)

(B)

(K)

(B)

Trim ends flush with (A) after attaching.

Attach mounting block (K) if securing tuteur to planter.

Trim ends flush with bottom of (B) if mounting to planter.

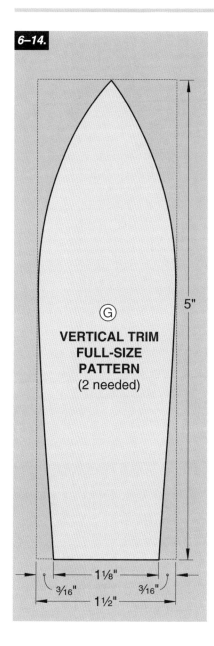

6–14.

VERTICAL TRIM
FULL-SIZE
PATTERN
(2 needed)

(G)

5"

1⅛"

³⁄₁₆" ³⁄₁₆"

1½"

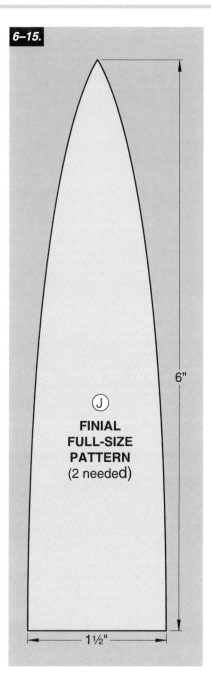

6–15.

FINIAL
FULL-SIZE
PATTERN
(2 needed)

(J)

6"

1½"

VINE IDEAS

Are you wondering what vines will work best with this tuteur? The selections below enjoy full sun and do well in most areas of North America. You'll want to tie miniature climbing roses and clematis to the tuteur for support, and help vines that have tiny rootlets, such as ivy, get a foothold by twining them around the structure. In areas with cold winters, bring tender vines indoors in fall before the first frost.

Annuals: *Sweet pea, hyacinth bean, climbing snapdragon, moonflower (specifically Ipomoea alba), morning glory, cardinal climber, Spanish flag, cypress vine, and nasturtium.*

Perennials: *Clematis, miniature climbing roses, and English ivy.*

Tender vines: *Mandevilla, passionflower, black-eyed Susan, and jasmine.*

air nailer is ideal for this.) Repeat the process on the opposite side. Trim the rails' ends, and install the remaining vertical trim (G).

From a ¾ x 5½ x 12" cedar board planed to ½" thickness, cut the base (H) and cap (I) to the sizes listed. Chamfer their edges, where shown in **6–13**.

Cut the finial (J) to the dimensions listed. Make two copies of the finial pattern in **6–15**. Adhere one pattern to the finial. Band-saw to the pattern lines. Adhere the other pattern to one of the curved sides, and band-saw again. Sand the finial smooth.

Center and glue the finial to the top of the cap (I). Drill a pilot and countersunk shank hole through the bottom of the cap, where shown, and drive in the screw. Center and glue this assembly to the base (H).

Sand flat the top of the tuteur, as shown in **6–12**. Then center, glue, and clamp the top assembly H/I/J to the rails (C).

Potting bench

Left: A look at the sturdy work surface and handy waste disposal opening.
Right: A look at the storage bins.

POTTING BENCH

This potting bench has gardener-friendly features: a galvanized-metal work surface with a handy waste disposal opening over a plastic garbage can; plastic storage bins concealed by doors; a tool rack and overhead shelf; plus wheels and a handle to make the whole setup mobile.

The bench shown above was built from rot-resistant cypress.

Random-width 4/4 and 8/4 boards were cut to the sizes listed. Cypress was used because clear, defect-free boards were available from the local lumber supplier for about the same price as western red cedar. However, to give you other options, the parts were sized so you can build the bench from cedar or pressure-treated lumber available in standard dimensional sizes (1x and 2x stock).

Build Two Frame Assemblies

Cut the four frame fronts/backs (A) and the eight frame cross members (B) to the lengths listed in the Materials List and shown in **6–16**.

➤*Note: If you use dimensional lumber, crosscut these pieces to length. Otherwise, you'll need to rip pieces to width, as well. To avoid splitting the lumber, drill holes for all screws.*

Materials List for Potting Bench

PART	FINISHED SIZE T	W	L	MATL.	QTY.
A frame fronts/backs	3/4"	3½"	42⅜"	C	4
B frame cross-members	3/4"	3½"	21¼"	C	8
C frame decking	3/4"	5½"	42⅜"	C	4
D supports	3/4"	3½"	10"	C	2
E back legs	1½"	3½"	57½"	C	2
F front legs	1½"	3½"	35"	C	2
G back	½"	42⅜"	30"	P	1
H end boards	3/4"	3½"	30"	C	10
I bottom skirt	3/4"	5½"	42⅜"	C	1
J corner blocks	3/4"	3/4"	5"	C	2
K divider panel	½"	21¼"	25¾"	P	1
L cleats	3/4"	3/4"	21¼"	C	4
M drawer guides	3/4"	2⅜"	21¼"	C	8
N top	½"	24"	45⅜"	P	1
O side skirts	3/4"	3½"	20¾"	C	2
P back skirt	3/4"	7¼"	42⅜"	C	1
Q shelf back	3/4"	7¼"	42⅜"	C	1
R shelf boards	3/4"	5½"	45⅜"	C	2
S shelf supports	3/4"	3½"	10¾"	C	3
T front filler	3/4"	3"	42⅜"	C	1
U end fillers	3/4"	3"	17¾"	C	2
V front/back trim	3/4"	3½"	56"	C	2
W end trim	3/4"	3½"	24¾"	C	2
X handle	1¼"	1¼"	25½"	F	1
Y door boards	3/4"	3½"	26¼"	C	12
Z door battens	3/4"	3½"	19½"	C	4
AA tool rack	3/4"	3½"	18"	C	1
BB mounting plate	3/4"	3½"	17"	C	1

Materials Key: C = Cypress; P = Plywood, C/D exterior grade; F = Fir closet pole.
Supplies: 1", 1¼", 1½", and 2" deck screws; tube of clear silicone caulk; 28-gauge galvanized steel 26 x 47⅜"; 20" plastic trash can; 7-gallon plastic bins (2) (Rubbermaid no. 2221); exterior glue; exterior finish.
Hardware: 6"-diameter wide metal-rimmed wheels with rubber tires, 1⅜" wide with ½" axle bore (2); 4" T-hinges (black) with screws (4); double roller catches (2); 6" black door pulls (2); ½" lag screws 4" long (4); ½" flat washers (4).

CUTTING DIAGRAM

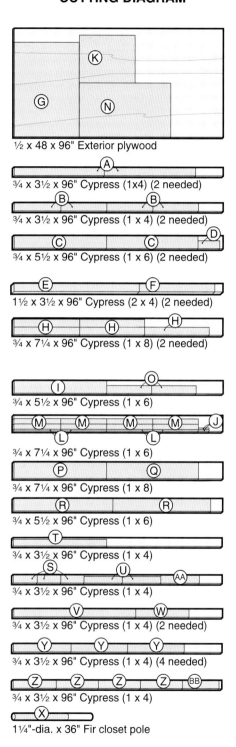

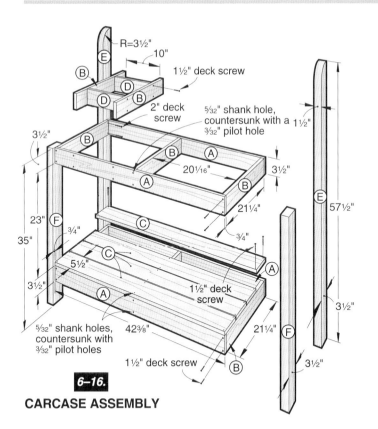

6–16.

CARCASE ASSEMBLY

6–17.

CARCASE DETAIL, TOP VIEW

2 Form two frame assemblies (A/B) by driving 1½" deck screws through the frame fronts/backs (A) into the cross members (B), where shown in **6–16**. For now, set aside one of the assemblies and the two extra frame cross members.

3 Cut four pieces of frame decking (C) to the size shown in the Materials List. Then align two pieces of the decking (C) with the front and back edges and the ends of one frame assembly (A/B), and screw the pieces in place. Add the remaining two pieces of frame decking with equal gaps between their edges. This assembly (A/B/C) will become the lower carcase frame.

4 The upper carcase frame will get additional bracing around the waste disposal opening. Cut two supports (D) to size. Screw the two remaining frame cross members (B) to the supports, where shown in **6–17**. Don't mount this assembly (B/D) to the upper frame (A/B) just yet.

Make Sturdy Legs

1 Mark the length of the back legs (E) and use a compass to lay out the 3½" radius at the upper end of each leg, where shown in **6–16**. Cut the radius on each leg using a jigsaw, then sand to the line. Then cut the front legs (F) to length.

2 Mark the vertical and horizontal location of the upper

and lower frame assemblies on the legs, where shown in **6–16**. As shown in **6–17** you'll see that the edge of the back legs extends 1¼" past the rear of the frames and that the front legs are ¾" forward of the frames.

3 To make assembly easier, cut two scrap-wood spacers to ¾ x 1¼ x 36". Lay the spacers on edge on the floor so they support the upper and lower frames (A/B). Align the frames with the marks on the legs, and clamp them into place. Attach the legs as shown in **6–18** to make the carcase assembly.

Add the Back, Ends, and Bottom Skirt

1 Cut to size the plywood back (G). Place the carcase assembly face down on the floor, and align the edge of the back (G) with the edge of the frame back (A) in the upper frame assembly.

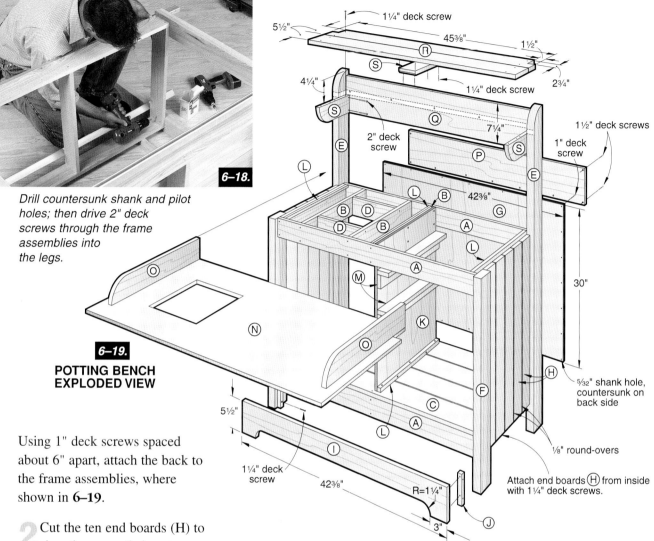

6–18.

Drill countersunk shank and pilot holes; then drive 2" deck screws through the frame assemblies into the legs.

6–19.

POTTING BENCH EXPLODED VIEW

1¼" deck screw

5½"

45⅜"

1½"

4¼"

1¼" deck screw

2¾"

2" deck screw

7¼"

1½" deck screws

1" deck screw

42⅜"

30"

⁵⁄₃₂" shank hole, countersunk on back side

⅛" round-overs

Attach end boards (H) from inside with 1¼" deck screws.

5½"

1¼" deck screw

42⅜"

R=1¼"

3"

Using 1" deck screws spaced about 6" apart, attach the back to the frame assemblies, where shown in **6–19**.

2 Cut the ten end boards (H) to size, then ease their outer edges with sandpaper or a ⅛" roundover bit. Align the end boards' upper ends with the top of the upper frame assembly (A/B), and leave equal spaces between them. Attach the end boards, as shown in **6–19** and **6–20**. Rest the carcase on its end to drive screws into the lower ends.

3 Attach the support assembly (B/D) you set aside earlier to the upper frame, where shown in **6–17**.

4 Cut the bottom skirt (I) to size, and mark the radius near each end, where shown in **6–19**. Connect the tops of the radii with a straight line. Cut out the opening, staying just to the waste side of the line, then sand it smooth.

5 Cut the two corner blocks (J) to size. Screw the corner blocks to the front legs (F) where shown. Next, screw the bottom skirt (I) to the corner blocks.

To give the bench a clean appearance, drive the 1¼" deck screws into the end boards from inside the carcase.

6–20.

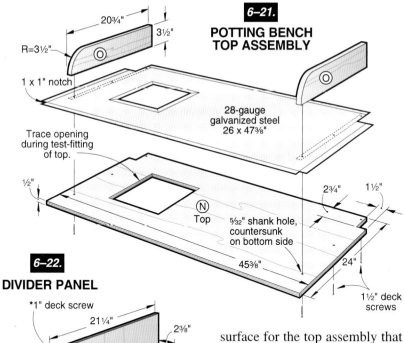

6–21.
POTTING BENCH TOP ASSEMBLY

20¾"
3½"
R=3½"
O
1 x 1" notch
28-gauge galvanized steel 26 x 47⅜"
Trace opening during test-fitting of top.
½"
N
Top
5/32" shank hole, countersunk on bottom side
2¾"
1½"
45⅜"
24"
1½" deck screws

6–23.

As you drill the holes at the corners of the rectangles, support the metal top on a sheet of scrap plywood.

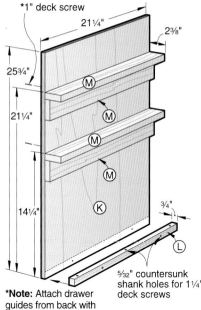

6–22.

DIVIDER PANEL

*1" deck screw
21¼"
2⅜"
25¾"
M
21¼"
M
M
M
14¼"
K
¾"
L
5/32" countersunk shank holes for 1¼" deck screws

*Note: Attach drawer guides from back with 1" deck screws.

6–24.

Align the plywood top with the sheet metal, and then place weights on the top. Let the silicone cure before bending the metal.

Make the Divider Panel and Drawer Guides

Cut the plywood divider panel (K) to size. Rip and crosscut the four cleats (L). Screw three of the cleats to the top frame assembly (A/B) where shown in **6–19**. (They provide a mounting surface for the top assembly that you'll add later.) Now drill countersunk holes for 1¼" deck screws through one of the cleats, and mount it flush with the edges and bottom end of the divider panel (K), where shown in **6–22**.

Cut the eight drawer guides (M). Glue pairs of the drawer guides together to make four L-shaped drawer guide assemblies, as shown in **6–22**. Screw two drawer guide assemblies to the divider panel (K).

Place the divider panel assembly (K/L/M) inside the carcase and screw it into the center frame cross member (B), where shown in **6–19**, on *page 145*. Use a framing square to position the divider on the frame decking (C), and drive screws through the cleat (L) into the decking. Now fasten the two remaining drawer guide assem-blies inside the carcase, aligning them with the drawer guide assemblies on the divider.

Cut a Metal-Clad Top

Cut the plywood top (N) to size, and notch the back corners, where shown in **6–21**. Test-fit the top onto the carcase assembly, and use a pencil to trace the perimeter of the supports (B/D) onto the underside of the top. Drill ½" holes near the corners of the layout, and cut the opening with a jigsaw.

2 Go to a local heating contractor or sheet-metal supplier, and purchase a sheet of 28-gauge galvanized steel cut to 26 x 47⅜". This size is 2" larger than the top (N) to allow 1" of metal to wrap around the edges and ends of the top.

3 Lay the sheet of steel face down on your workbench, and center the top (N) on it. Mark the notches for the back legs (E) and the perimeter of the waste opening using a permanent marker. Lift off the plywood top, and set it aside. Draw another rectangle on the steel whose sides are 1" inside the perimeter of the opening you just marked.

Now drill ½" holes within the inner rectangle, where shown in **6–23**, to serve as starting points

for your tin snips. Drill ⅛" holes in the corners of the outer rectangle. Wear heavy gloves as you cut the perimeter of the inner rectangle, and make diagonal cuts from each corner of the inner rectangle to the ⅛" hole. Also cut notches for the back legs, and small notches at the front corners that allow the metal to bend around the plywood.

4 Place the steel sheet face down on your workbench, and apply a bead of clear silicone caulk to the metal near the perimeter of the hole and the cutouts for the rear legs, and put small dots of silicone in a 6" grid pattern in the field of the metal.

(Don't use all of the caulk; you'll need some later.) Position the top (N) on the metal, as shown in **6–24**, and let the silicone cure.

5 Using a dead-blow mallet and wood scraps, wrap the metal around the edges of the waste opening and the perimeter of the top, as shown in **6–28**.

6 Cut the side skirts (O) to the length shown in **6–21**, then cut the radius at one end of each. Drive screws through the top (N) from underneath to attach the side skirts.

7 Wipe a thin layer of silicone onto the notches for the back

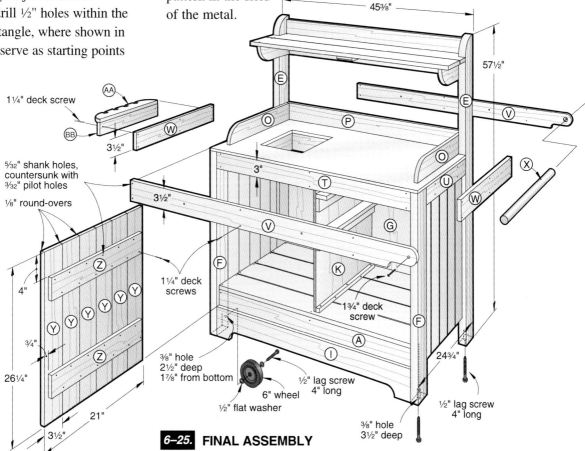

6–25. FINAL ASSEMBLY

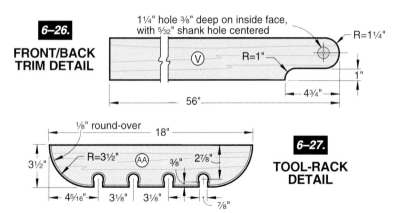

6–26.
FRONT/BACK TRIM DETAIL

1¼" hole ⅜" deep on inside face, with 5/32" shank hole centered

R=1¼"

(V) R=1"

1"

56"

4¾"

⅛" round-over 18"

3½"

R=3½" (AA) ⅜" 2⅞"

4 5/16" 3⅛" 3⅛" ⅞"

6–27.
TOOL-RACK DETAIL

6–28.

Wrap the metal around the perimeter, and then form the cut-out opening. The hardwood scrap keeps the metal from rising.

legs in the top (N) to seal the edges of the plywood. Then position the top on the carcase assembly, and drive 1¼" screws up through the cleats (L) and into the top.

8 Crosscut the back skirt (P) to size. Then align its top edge with the side skirts (O), where shown in **6–19** (on *page 145*), and screw the back skirt in place.

Add a Convenient Shelf

1 Cut the shelf back (Q) and the two shelf boards (R) to size. Notch both ends of one shelf board, where shown in **6–19**.

2 Cut the three shelf supports (S) to size. One support has square ends, and the other two have a radiused end that you cut with a jigsaw.

3 Screw the two radiused-end shelf supports (S) to the back legs (E), where shown on **6–19** (on *page 145*). Now attach the shelf boards (R) to the two outer shelf supports, then attach the

remaining shelf support to the shelf boards where shown.

4 Align the lower edge of the shelf back (Q) with the lower edges of the radiused shelf supports (S). Then screw the shelf back into the rear shelf board (R) and the radiused shelf supports (S).

Fasten the Fillers and Trim

1 Cut the front filler (T) and the end fillers (U) to size. Fasten these parts where shown in **6–25**, *page 147*.

2 Cut the front/back trim (V) to length. Then lay out and cut the shaped ends on both pieces, where shown in **6–26**, and bore the stopped holes that will receive the handle (X). Cut the end trim (W) to length. Now attach both pieces of end trim and the front trim.

3 Cut a length of 1¼"-diameter fir closet pole to length for the handle (X). Position the handle into the holes in the front/back trim (V), and screw the back trim into place with the

handle captured between the front and back trim.

Make and Attach the Doors

1 Crosscut twelve door boards (Y) and four door battens (Z) to size. Ease the edges on the door boards using your router and an ⅛" roundover bit. Butt six of the door boards edge to edge, face down on your workbench. Square up the boards, and attach the door battens (Z), where shown in **6–25**. Repeat for the other door.

2 Mount the hinges to the carcase, referring to the photo on *page 142* to see their locations. The rectangular plates of the T-hinges are spaced 2¼" from the bottom skirt (I) and front trim (V). Then attach the doors, leaving approximately an ⅛" gap between them. Mount each door pull centered on the width of the innermost door boards (Y) 2½" from the top of the door. To hold the doors closed, mount roller catches inside the doors and carcase.

Finishing Touches

1 Lay the potting bench on its back, and drill $\frac{3}{8}$" holes into the inner edges of the left-hand front leg (F) and back leg (E), where shown on **6–25**, on *page 147*. Place the washers and wheels onto the lag screws, and drive the screws into the legs, leaving enough clearance for the wheels to spin freely.

2 Drill holes into the ends of the other two legs, where shown in **6–25**. Drive lag bolts into these holes to act as leveling feet and to prevent moisture from wicking into the ends of the legs.

3 Cut the tool rack (AA) to size, then shape the radiused ends and the hole centerpoints, where dimensioned in the Tool-Rack Detail in **6–27**. Bore the holes using your drill press, and cut the opening from each hole to the edge. Sand the edges smooth, then rout a $\frac{1}{8}$" roundover on the edges of the tool rack.

4 Crosscut the mounting plate (BB), and glue and clamp it to the tool rack, forming the L-shaped assembly shown in **6–25** (on *page 147*). When the glue dries, screw the assembly to the end of the potting bench.

5 Before applying finish, use sandpaper to ease the remaining exposed edges on any bench parts you may come in contact with. Apply your choice of finish to the potting bench. The bench shown on *page 142* has

two coats of an exterior oil finish. To help prevent water from wicking under the metal top, run a bead of silicone around the seams where metal meets wood.

DOWN-TO-EARTH BENCH

Garden chores can bring you quite literally to your knees or, even worse, force you to crouch awkwardly in the bushes. This combination kneeling and sitting bench is a site for sore knees and aching back muscles.

Down-to-earth bench

Made of weather-resistant wood, it will keep you working comfortably throughout many growing seasons.

➤*Note: Truss-head cabinet screws were used to construct this bench. These specialty screws, often used for cabinet installation, are also suitable for outdoor use. They feature a large head for extra holding power. If you can't find them at a hardware store, substitute #10 x 2½" roundhead wood screws with washers.*

Make the Legs

1 Crosscut a 50" length from a 2 x 10. (Cedar was used for the bench shown above because of its light weight and rot resistance. Redwood would be another good choice.) Joint one edge of the stock, then rip the other edge to produce a board that is 8" wide.

2 Crosscut two 8"-long blanks for the legs (A), then crosscut the 8"-long seat (B). Set the seat

Materials List for Down-to-Earth Bench

PART	FINISHED SIZE			MATL.	QTY.
	T	W	L		
A legs	1½"	8"	15"	C	2
B seat	1½"	8"	18"	C	1
C* feet	1"	2½"	10½"	C	4

*Cut to size according to the instructions.
Material Key: C = Choice of redwood or cedar.
Supplies: #10 x 2½" truss-head cabinet screws or #10 x 2½" roundhead wood screws (14); #8 x ¾" roundhead wood screws (4); 1" O.D. x 1" I.D. fender washers (4); 1¼ x 8 x 6½" foam kneeling pads (2) (use 1¼ x 8 x 16½" foam kneeling pads, which are widely available at discount department stores and home centers); exterior finish.

aside for the moment. Mark a centerline the length of one leg blank.

Install a ¾" dado set in your tablesaw, and raise it ¾" above the table. Attach an extension to your miter gauge to reduce chip-out during the dadoing operation. Adjust your rip fence 1¼" from the inner edge of the dado set, and make the first dado cut in each leg. Move the rip fence away from the blade to produce a dado width that is the exact thickness of the seat (B).

Make an enlarged photocopy of the Leg gridded pattern in **6–34** on an 8 x 15" piece of paper, and adhere it to the outside surface of one of the legs. Center the centerline on the pattern with that on the leg blank. Attach the other leg blank face-to-face to the first, with the dadocs facing and the edges and ends flush.

CUTTING DIAGRAM

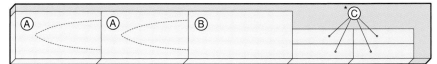

1½ x 9¼ x 72" Cedar (2 x 10)   *Plane or resaw to thickness listed in the Materials List.

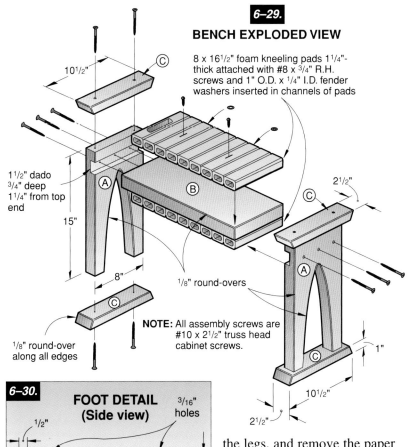

6–29.
BENCH EXPLODED VIEW

8 x 16½" foam kneeling pads 1¼"-thick attached with #8 x ¾" R.H. screws and 1" O.D. x ¼" I.D. fender washers inserted in channels of pads

10½"

1½" dado ¾" deep 1¼" from top end

15"

8"

⅛" round-over along all edges

⅛" round-overs

2½"

NOTE: All assembly screws are #10 x 2½" truss head cabinet screws.

10½"

2½"

1"

6–30.
FOOT DETAIL (Side view)   3/16" holes

1/2"
2"   10½"   2"   1"

Mark the centerpoints of the holes through the pattern and onto the wood with a scratch awl. Drill the holes.

Band-saw just to the waste side of the arched pattern lines on the leg blanks, then sand to the line. Sand the cutting line, using a sanding block. Separate

the legs, and remove the paper pattern from the wood.

Chuck a ⅛" roundover bit into your table-mounted router, and round over the arched pattern line on both sides of each leg.

Apply weatherproof glue to the dado, then glue and screw the legs to the seat.

➤ *Note: To maximize the holding power of the screws in the cedar, use a power screwdriver without drilling pilot holes into the seat.*

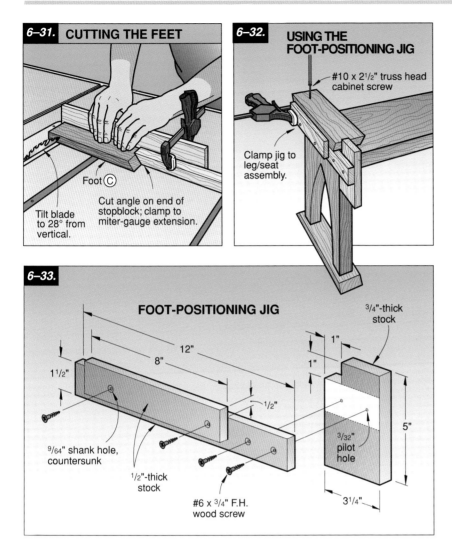

6–31. CUTTING THE FEET

Foot (C)

Tilt blade to 28° from vertical.

Cut angle on end of stopblock; clamp to miter-gauge extension.

6–32. USING THE FOOT-POSITIONING JIG

#10 x 2½" truss head cabinet screw

Clamp jig to leg/seat assembly.

6–33.

FOOT-POSITIONING JIG

¾"-thick stock

12"
8"
1½"
1"
1"
½"
5"
³⁄₃₂" pilot hole
3¼"

⁹⁄₆₄" shank hole, countersunk

½"-thick stock

#6 x ¾" F.H. wood screw

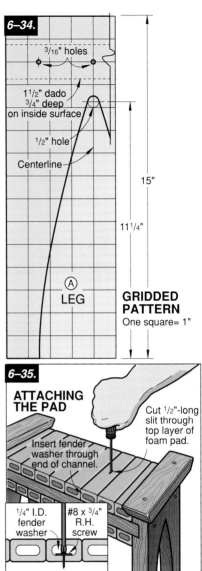

6–34.

³⁄₁₆" holes

1½" dado ¾" deep on inside surface

½" hole

Centerline

15"

11¼"

(A) LEG

GRIDDED PATTERN
One square= 1"

6–35.

ATTACHING THE PAD

Insert fender washer through end of channel.

Cut ½"-long slit through top layer of foam pad.

¼" I.D. fender washer

#8 x ¾" R.H. screw

If you use a denser wood or are driving the screws by hand, you may need to drill ⅛" pilot holes.

9 Rout ⅛" roundovers on the leg/seat assembly, where shown on the Exploded View in **6–29**. Do not round over the ends of the legs.

Make the Feet

1 Plane two 6 x 24" lengths of stock to 1" thickness. Rip to 2½" wide, then crosscut four blanks for the feet (C) to 11½" long.

2 Attach an extension to your tablesaw's miter gauge, as shown in the Cutting the Feet drawing (**6–31**). Tilt your blade to 28° from vertical, and miter-cut one end of each foot blank, as shown in the Foot Detail (**6–30**). Also miter-cut a piece of scrap wood to form a stop block. Then, clamp the stop block to the miter-gauge extension. Next, miter-cut the other end of each foot blank to a length of 10½".

3 Mark the centerpoints of the holes in the feet, where shown on the Foot Detail. Chuck a ³⁄₁₆" bit into your drill press, and drill the holes through the feet.

4 Clamp a fence flush with the bearing of the ⅛" roundover bit in your table-mounted router, and rout all edges and ends of the feet.

Use a Jig to Finish the Bench

1 Make a jig from scrap wood, as shown in the Foot-Positioning Jig drawing in **6–33**, *page 151*. Clamp the jig to the leg/seat assembly as shown in the Using the Foot-Positioning Jig (**6–32**). Position a foot, then drive the screws to secure it to the leg. Repeat for each foot.

2 Do any finish-sanding necessary, then apply your finish. The bench shown on *page 149* received two coats of a clear exterior penetrating-oil finish.

3 With a screwdriver, attach the pads to the stool, referring to Attaching the Pad (**6–35**).

WALL- OR FENCE-HUNG TRELLIS

This wall- or fence-hung trellis dresses up any outdoor area, and provides an attractive background for a climbing plant. But the real beauty lies in its simple construction method.

Lay Out and Shape the Uprights and Crossbars

➤ *Note: Begin your project at the lumberyard by selecting stock carefully. All the parts for the trellis frame come from two*

Wall- or fence-hung trellis

10'-long cedar 2 x 4s. Look for boards with straight grain; with no warp or twist; and with no knots or with small, tight knots that won't pop out. Also pick up a 4' cedar 1 x 4, and a 24 x 48" sheet of lattice. (Plastic lattice in a square 1½" pattern, available in home centers, was used for the trellis shown above.)

1 Rip two 10' 2 x 4s into 1½ x 1½"-wide strips. Then crosscut the strips to the lengths listed in the Materials List and **6–37** (*page 154*) to create the uprights (A, B) and crossbars (C, D).

2 Lay out and mark the locations of the dadoes in each piece, where dimensioned in **6–37**. Mark the area to be removed with an "X" to prevent confusion when you machine the dadoes.

6–36. WALL- OR FENCE-HUNG TRELLIS EXPLODED VIEW

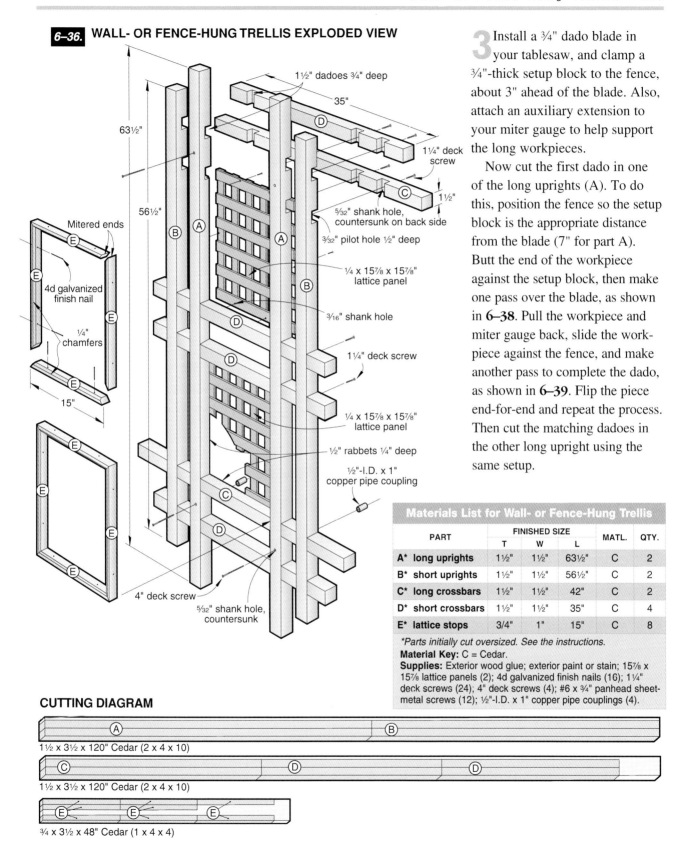

1½" dadoes ¾" deep

35"

63½"

56½"

1¼" deck screw

1½"

⁵⁄₃₂" shank hole, countersunk on back side

³⁄₃₂" pilot hole ½" deep

Mitered ends

4d galvanized finish nail

¼" chamfers

15"

¼ x 15⅞ x 15⅞" lattice panel

³⁄₁₆" shank hole

1¼" deck screw

¼ x 15⅞ x 15⅞" lattice panel

½" rabbets ¼" deep

½"-I.D. x 1" copper pipe coupling

4" deck screw

⁵⁄₃₂" shank hole, countersunk

3 Install a ¾" dado blade in your tablesaw, and clamp a ¾"-thick setup block to the fence, about 3" ahead of the blade. Also, attach an auxiliary extension to your miter gauge to help support the long workpieces.

Now cut the first dado in one of the long uprights (A). To do this, position the fence so the setup block is the appropriate distance from the blade (7" for part A). Butt the end of the workpiece against the setup block, then make one pass over the blade, as shown in **6–38**. Pull the workpiece and miter gauge back, slide the workpiece against the fence, and make another pass to complete the dado, as shown in **6–39**. Flip the piece end-for-end and repeat the process. Then cut the matching dadoes in the other long upright using the same setup.

Materials List for Wall- or Fence-Hung Trellis

PART	FINISHED SIZE			MATL.	QTY.
	T	W	L		
A* long uprights	1½"	1½"	63½"	C	2
B* short uprights	1½"	1½"	56½"	C	2
C* long crossbars	1½"	1½"	42"	C	2
D* short crossbars	1½"	1½"	35"	C	4
E* lattice stops	3/4"	1"	15"	C	8

*Parts initially cut oversized. See the instructions.
Material Key: C = Cedar.
Supplies: Exterior wood glue; exterior paint or stain; 15⅞ x 15⅞ lattice panels (2); 4d galvanized finish nails (16); 1¼" deck screws (24); 4" deck screws (4); #6 x ¾" panhead sheet-metal screws (12); ½"-I.D. x 1" copper pipe couplings (4).

CUTTING DIAGRAM

Ⓐ Ⓑ
1½ x 3½ x 120" Cedar (2 x 4 x 10)

Ⓒ Ⓓ Ⓓ
1½ x 3½ x 120" Cedar (2 x 4 x 10)

Ⓔ Ⓔ Ⓔ
¾ x 3½ x 48" Cedar (1 x 4 x 4)

4 Reposition the fence/setup block and cut the rest of the dadoes in the long uprights (A) using the same procedures. Then dado the short uprights (B), long crossbars (C), and short crossbars (D).

➤ *Note: The locations of the first two dadoes in the long uprights (A) match those in the long crossbars (C). Cut these pieces consecutively to eliminate extra fence setups. The dadoes in the short uprights (B) and the short crossbars (D) match one another as well.*

6–38.

Butt the workpiece against the setup block, holding it securely against the miter gauge. Then make the first cut.

6–39.

For the second pass, butt the workpiece against the fence. This doubles the dado width without changing the setup.

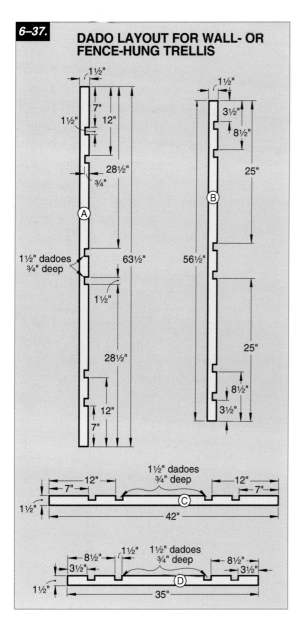

6–37.

DADO LAYOUT FOR WALL- OR FENCE-HUNG TRELLIS

Assemble, Finish, and Mount the Trellis

1 Predrill $5/32$" countersunk shank holes through the long crossbars (C) and short crossbars (D) before gluing them to the uprights. Center these holes in the dadoes, where shown in **6–36** (*page 153*).

2 Lay the long uprights (A) on a flat surface, about 16" apart and with the dadoes facing up. This will be the back side. Lay the short uprights (B) just outside the long uprights. Now spread an exterior-grade glue in the dadoes. Join the long and short crossbars to the uprights with the dadoes facing down to lock the pieces together. Using the shank holes in the crossbars as guides, drill $3/32$" pilot holes into the uprights. Then secure each joint with a $1\frac{1}{4}$" deck screw.

3 Chuck a $\frac{1}{2}$" rabbeting bit in your handheld router, and set it to make a $\frac{1}{4}$" deep cut. Rabbet the square areas of the trellis frame to receive the lattice panels, where shown in **6–36**. Square up the corners using a chisel. Cut lattice panels to fit the rabbeted openings, but don't install them yet.

4 Use your handheld router, equipped with a chamfering bit, to rout a $\frac{1}{4}$" chamfer along each edge of the 4'-long 1 x 4. Then rip a 1"-wide strip from each edge of the board. Chamfer and rip one edge of the remaining 1 x 4 again so you end up with three $3/4$ x 1 x 48" chamfered strips. Miter-cut the strips to

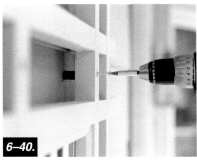

At first, attach all four mounting screws loosely. Then snug them down to hold the trellis firmly to the wall.

length to create the lattice stops (E). Attach the stops to the trellis frame using 4d galvanized finish nails, where shown in **6–41**.

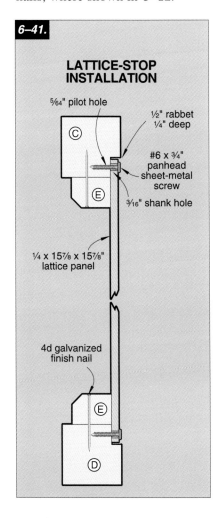

6–41.

**LATTICE-STOP
INSTALLATION**

$5/64$" pilot hole

$1/2$" rabbet
$1/4$" deep

C

#6 x $3/4$"
panhead
sheet-metal
screw

E

$3/16$" shank hole

$1/4$ x $157/8$ x $157/8$"
lattice panel

4d galvanized
finish nail

E

D

5 Stain or paint the trellis as you prefer. (The trellis shown on *page 152* was painted to match the exterior trim on the house where it was installed.) Then mount the lattice panels to the frame, where shown in **6–41**.

6 To mount the trellis to the wall, first drill $5/32$" counter-sunk shank holes through the long uprights for the mounting screws, where indicated in **6–36** (on *page 156*). Temporarily position the trellis, then push an awl or long nail through the pilot holes to mark the locations of pilot holes on the wall. To hold the trellis away from the wall, you can use spacers made from standard copper plumbing-pipe couplings ($1/2$" inside diameter x 1" long) purchased at the local hardware store. Hold the spacers between the trellis and wall, and secure the trellis with 4" deck screws, as shown in **6–40**.

**WINSOME
WINDOW BOX**

Give your favorite plants a place to hang out with the easy-to-build planter shown on the following page. Size it (or them) to the width of the windows at your house. The planter shown \was made with cedar, but you could substitute redwood or pres-sure-treated lumber if you like.

Build the Carcase

1 Cut the front (A), back (B), and sides (C) to the sizes in the Materials List on *page 156*. Cut $3/8$" dadoes in the ends of the front (A) and rear edges of the sides (C) as shown in **6–42**. Use the same dado setup to cut rabbets on the ends of the back (B) and front edges of the sides (C). Glue and clamp the front (A), back (B), and sides (C) with waterproof glue. Check for square.

2 Cut bottom supports (D) and (E) to size. Make sure these parts fit inside the previously glued assembly. Glue and clamp them. After the glue dries, install angle braces on the inside corners of the support assembly. Drill $5/32$" holes in the support assembly so you can mount it to the box. Place the bottom support inside the bottom edge of the box, and install $11/4$" deck screws.

3 Cut the bottom (F) to size. Drill $3/8$" drainage holes in (F) as shown. Drill $5/32$" holes around the edges and drive screws through them into the bottom support.

Install the Trim

1 Cut parts G, H, I, and J to size. Miter the ends as shown in **6–43** (the rear of parts I and the ends of G are not mitered). Now glue together the top and bottom molding assemblies and sand all the joints clean. Mark and drill the top and bottom

Window box

Materials List for Winsome Window Box

PART	FINISHED SIZE			MATL.	QTY.
	T	W	L		
A front	¾"	10"	36"	C	1
B back	¾"	10"	35¼"	C	1
C sides	¾"	10"	11⅝"	C	2
D supports	¾"	1½"	34½"	C	2
E supports	¾"	1½"	9"	C	2
F bottom	¾"	10½"	34½"	C	1
G trim	¾"	¾"	34½"	C	1
H spacers	¾"	1½"	10"	C	2
I trim	¾"	1½"	12¾"	C	4
J trim	¾"	1½"	37½"	C	2
K trim	⅜"	¾"	15¾"	C	4
L trim	⅜"	¾"	7"	C	8
M trim	⅜"	¾"	9"	C	4

Material Key: C = Cedar.
Supplies: Forty-six 1¼" deck screws; 4 angle braces; four ¼ x 5" galvanized lag screws with washers; waterproof glue; #17 x 1" brads.

molding (I, J) mounting holes in the box sides, and then set the moldings aside.

2 Cut trim pieces K, L, and M to size, mitering the ends. Glue the four trim assemblies together. Sand the sides that will show.

3 Apply glue to the back of the trim assemblies and press them in place. (Use masking tape to mark trim locations.) Secure the trim to the box with brads.

4 Now glue and screw the top and bottom molding assemblies in place on the box.

5 Take spacers (H) and screw them to the back of box where shown in the Side Section View in **6-44**.

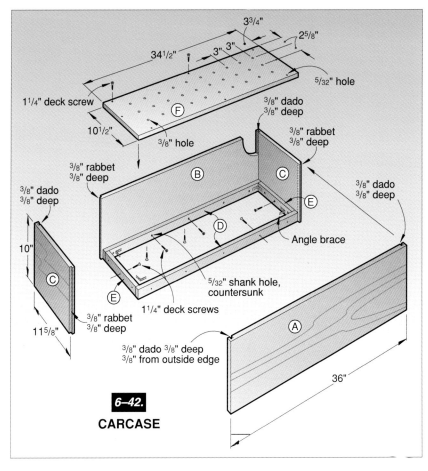

6-42.
CARCASE

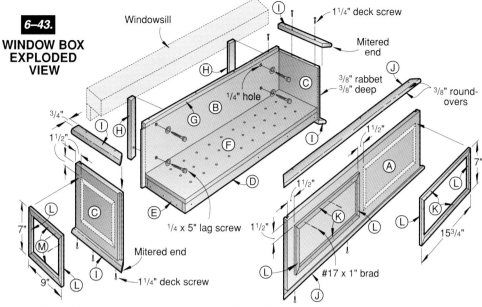

6–43.
WINDOW BOX EXPLODED VIEW

Windowsill

$1^{1}/_{4}$" deck screw

Mitered end

$3/_{8}$" rabbet
$3/_{8}$" deep

$3/_{8}$" round-overs

$1/_{4}$" hole

$3/_{4}$"

$1^{1}/_{2}$"

$1^{1}/_{2}$"

$1^{1}/_{2}$"

$1^{1}/_{2}$"

7"

$15^{3}/_{4}$"

#17 x 1" brad

7"

9"

$1/_{4}$ x 5" lag screw

Mitered end

$1^{1}/_{4}$" deck screw

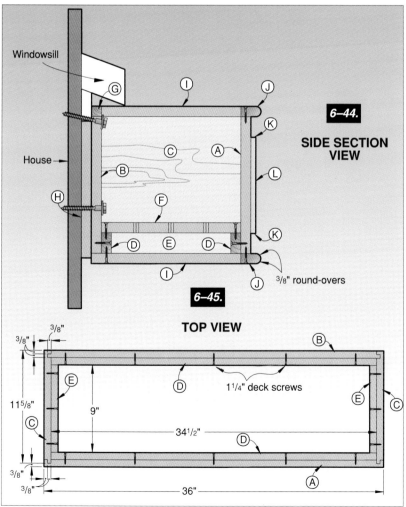

Windowsill

6–44.
SIDE SECTION VIEW

House

$3/_{8}$" round-overs

6–45.
TOP VIEW

$3/_{8}$"
$3/_{8}$"
$3/_{8}$"

$11^{5}/_{8}$"

9"

$34^{1}/_{2}$"

$1^{1}/_{4}$" deck screws

$3/_{8}$"
$3/_{8}$"

36"

6 Finish the planter as desired. To attach, drill $1/_{4}$" holes through the back of the box and spacers as shown. Insert lag screws with washers. Dry-fit the box to house the wall below the sill. Tap lag screws to mark hole positions, then drill $13/_{16}$" holes into the wall. With a wrench, secure the lag screws. Then, fill the box with your favorite growing things.

TRADITIONAL TRELLIS

Shaped much like a graceful, old-time fan, this elegant trellis is also a breeze to build. It's so easy, in fact, that you just may decide to build several of them for the flower garden.

➤ *Note: For best results, select stock that is knot-free and straight-grained. Cedar was used for the trellis shown here because of its availability, but you can use another weather-resistant wood. The trellis was made from one 6' length of cedar 2 x 6.*

Make the Arm Assembly

1 Plane or resaw a piece of stock to $1\frac{1}{8} \times 3\frac{1}{2} \times 72"$. Set your tablesaw's rip fence $\frac{1}{8}"$ from the inside edge of the blade, and rip seven arms (A).

2 Stack the arms face to face, and join them together with masking tape at several locations. Mark the centerpoints of the holes on the top arm of the stack where shown in **6-46**. Next, adjust the fence on your drill press, centering a $\frac{1}{4}"$ bit in the width of the stock as shown in Drilling the Arms (**6-47**). Drill these holes where marked; then switch to a $\frac{7}{16}"$ bit, and complete the drilling.

3 Cut the threaded brass rod into two $2\frac{5}{8}"$ lengths with a hacksaw.

4 Remove enough strips of masking tape at the bottom end of the stacked arms to enable you to spread glue. Use weatherproof glue.

5 Insert the threaded brass rods through the $\frac{1}{4}"$ holes, position the washers, and tighten the acorn nuts. Clamp the assembly, and remove excess glue with a damp rag. Let the assembly dry, then unclamp and sand the glued area smooth. Remove any remaining tape.

Make the Spreaders

1 Rip three 36" lengths of stock to $\frac{3}{8}"$ square. Set one aside as a blank for the top spreader (B), and

Traditional trellis

Materials List for Traditional Trellis

PART	FINISHED SIZE			MATL.	QTY.
	T	W	L		
A arms	$\frac{5}{16}"$	$1\frac{1}{8}"$	72"	C	7
B top spreader	$\frac{3}{8}"$	$\frac{3}{8}"$	36"	C	1
C* middle spreader	$\frac{3}{8}"$	$\frac{3}{8}"$	$18\frac{1}{4}"$	C	1
D* bottom spreader	$\frac{3}{8}"$	$\frac{3}{8}"$	$7\frac{9}{16}"$	C	1

*Cut part to final size during construction. Please read all instructions before cutting.
Material Key: C = Cedar.
Supplies: One $\frac{1}{4}"$ threaded brass rod 6" long; four $\frac{1}{4}"$ brass washers; four $\frac{1}{4}"$ brass acorn nuts; twenty-one #18 x $\frac{5}{8}"$ solid brass escutcheon pins; one $\frac{3}{4}$ x 36" electrical conduit; two $\frac{3}{4}"$ conduit straps; four #10 x 1" panhead sheet-metal screws.

crosscut the second to make blanks for the middle spreader (C) and bottom spreader (D). Use the third blank to make test cuts.

2 Tilt your tablesaw blade to 45°, and set the fence where shown on the Chamfer Detail in **6-46**. Make a test piece by nudging your fence until the blade just nicks the corner of a blank. Feed a few inches into the running blade, then carefully pull back. Rotate the blank to chamfer each of the sides. Test-fit the blank into the hole in the arm assembly. Ideally, you want a loosely sliding fit. When you are satisfied with the setup, chamfer all three spreaders, using a pushstick to complete the cuts.

Assemble the Trellis

1 Mark the center of each spreader, then insert them through the holes in the arm assembly. Fan the trellis arms, and center the top spreader in the middle arm. Drive a #18 × 5/8" solid brass escutcheon pin through each spreader. One way to make pilot holes is to snip the head off a pin and chuck it into your drill.

2 Use the block to space the trellis arms on the top spreader. (Refer to Using the Spacer Block [**6–48** and **6–49**] for directions.) Fasten each arm to the top spreader by repeating the drilling and nailing procedure explained in *Step 1*.

3 Attach the middle arm to the midpoint of the center spreader. Then, use the 3/4" dimension of the spacer block to gauge the position of the outermost arms, and nail them in place. Position the remaining arms by measurement or by eye, and

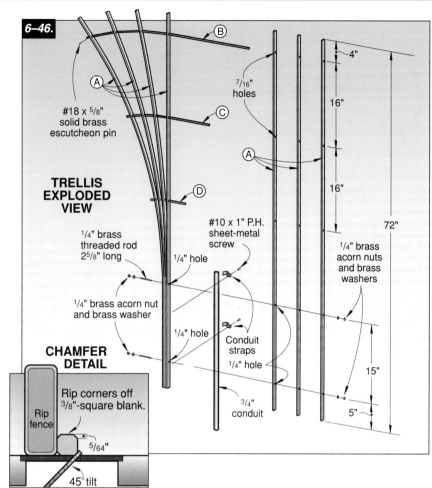

6–46.

TRELLIS EXPLODED VIEW

#18 × 5/8" solid brass escutcheon pin

1/4" brass threaded rod 2 5/8" long

1/4" brass acorn nut and brass washer

CHAMFER DETAIL

Rip corners off 3/8"-square blank.

Rip fence

5/64"

45° tilt

1/4" hole

1/4" hole

1/4" hole

7/16" holes

#10 × 1" P.H. sheet-metal screw

Conduit straps

3/4" conduit

4"

16"

16"

72"

1/4" brass acorn nuts and brass washers

15"

5"

fasten them. Repeat the process for the bottom spreader.

4 Apply finish to the trellis, if desired. Drive a 3/4 × 36"

length of electrical conduit 20" deep into the ground. Attach conduit straps where shown in **6–46**.

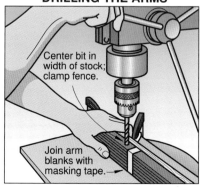

6–47.
DRILLING THE ARMS

Center bit in width of stock; clamp fence.

Join arm blanks with masking tape.

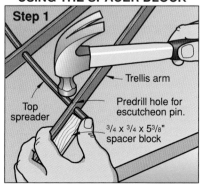

6–48.
USING THE SPACER BLOCK

Step 1

Trellis arm

Predrill hole for escutcheon pin.

Top spreader

3/4 × 3/4 × 5 3/8" spacer block

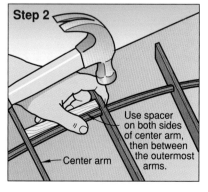

6–49.
USING THE SPACER BLOCK

Step 2

Use spacer on both sides of center arm, then between the outermost arms.

Center arm

7

Accents for the Home Front

So far, this book has presented outdoor projects that will ensure increased enjoyment of your deck, lawn, patio, or porch. This chapter includes projects with interesting details that will enhance your outdoor spaces.

Start with the high-visibility mailbox post and planter. It's sure to impress your postal carrier, as well as friends and neighbors. And it's adaptable for city or country use.

If you've noticed delivery people slowly driving up and down the street where you live looking for your house number, the neighborly welcome sign on *page 166* is meant for you. Its backlighted numerals really stand out after dusk, and the simple wiring system is easy to assemble. And talking about lights, the nifty candle lanterns on *page 171* are meant to add a warm, comfy glow to evenings spent

relaxing outdoors. For the little time it will take you to make them, they will create quite an impression.

This chapter contains two projects especially meant for winged visitors. On *page 174* you'll find a wonderfully designed birdbath that will not only please them, but looks great, too. And because birds always like to be fed—and it's great fun watching them—a suet feeder has been included on *page 178*. There's also a timely, just-for-fun decorative birdhouse on *page 181*. Finally, you'll find all you need to know about making birdhouses on *page 185* to get you started.

MAILBOX POST AND PLANTER

Create curbside appeal with a mailbox post and planter destined to be the envy of the neighborhood. Standing 65" tall and accented by flowers, this stylish design will show off your green thumb as well as your craftsmanship.

Make the Post Assembly Parts

➤*Note: Waterproof polyurethane glue was used for all the glue-ups in this project; see the Shop Tip on the following page for guidelines on its use. Also, where the project calls for medium-density overlay (MDO) plywood, use the type that has an amber face on both sides for best durability.*

1 From a 4 x 4 nominal (3½ x 3½" actual) cedar post, cut post (A) and crossarm (B) to the lengths listed in the Materials List.

Mailbox post and planter

Materials List for Mailbox Post and Planter

PART	FINISHED SIZE			MATL.	QTY.
	T	W	L		
POST ASSEMBLY					
A post	3½"	3½"	46"	C	1
B crossarm	3½"	3½"	35½"	C	1
C* bottom trim	1½"	2⅛"	7"	LC	4
D* top trim	1½"	2⅛"	5½"	LC	4
E* crossarm brackets	2½"	3½"	13¾"	C	2
F mailbox base	¾"	6⅛"	17½"	P	1
POST SUPPORT					
G sides	¾"	5"	27¼"	P	2
H front and back	¾"	3½"	27¼"	P	2
I* trim	¾"	5"	6½"	C	4
PLANTER BOX					
J ends	¾"	7¼"	10⅜"	P	2
K sides	¾"	7¼"	18¾"	P	2
L top	¾"	12⅛"	21¼"	P	1
M* mounting base	1¼"	4½"	18¾"	C	1
N* horizontal trim	⅜"	1½"	17¼"	C	4
O* vertical trim	⅜"	1½"	7¼"	C	4
SUPPORT POST					
P** post	3½"	3½"	48"	PT	1

*Parts initially cut oversized. See the instructions.
**Minimum post length is 36½". See text for installation requirements.
Materials Key: C = Cedar; LC = Laminated cedar; P = Plywood, type MDO; PT = Pressure-treated lumber.
Supplies: Waterproof polyurethane glue; spray adhesive; 1½", 2", and 3" deck screws; #6 x ⅝" panhead screws; #20 biscuits; 6d galvanized nails; weather-resistant hardening wood putty; post cap; standard-size mailbox; 9"-diameter pots (2); paintable silicone caulk; oil-based exterior primer; exterior latex paint; 8"-diameter tube form; concrete; gravel.

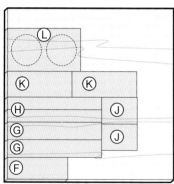

¾ x 48 x 48" MDO plywood

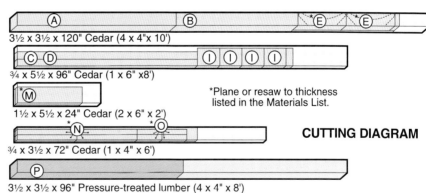

3½ x 3½ x 120" Cedar (4 x 4"x 10')

¾ x 5½ x 96" Cedar (1 x 6" x8')

1½ x 5½ x 24" Cedar (2 x 6" x 2')

*Plane or resaw to thickness listed in the Materials List.

¾ x 3½ x 72" Cedar (1 x 4" x 6')

CUTTING DIAGRAM

3½ x 3½ x 96" Pressure-treated lumber (4 x 4" x 8')

shop TIP

Waterproof polyurethane glue cures when exposed to moisture in the air and in the wood. For best results, apply the glue to only one of the two surfaces to be joined. Then spray a light mist of water on the nonglued surface, and join the parts together. Because the glue can cause skin and eye irritation, wear gloves and use eye protection.

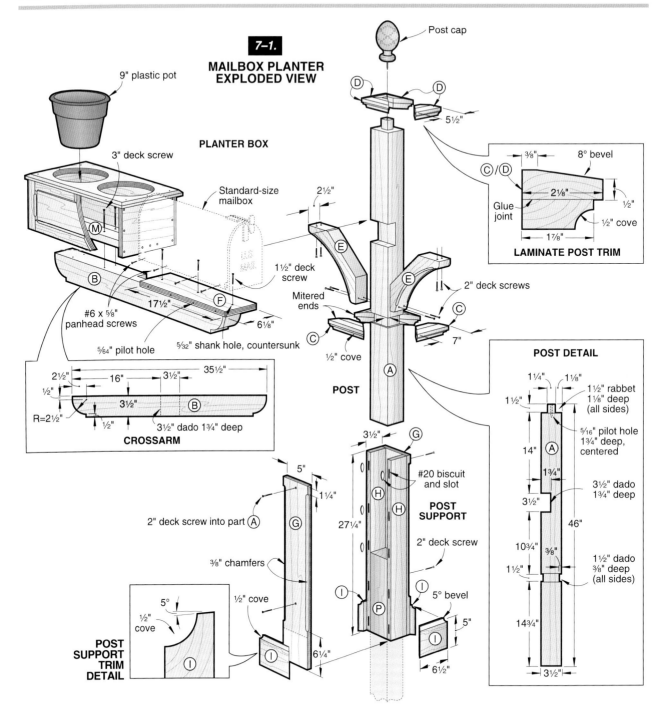

7–1.

MAILBOX PLANTER EXPLODED VIEW

9" plastic pot

Post cap

PLANTER BOX

3" deck screw

Standard-size mailbox

LAMINATE POST TRIM

8° bevel
⅜"
2⅛"
½"
½" cove
1⅞"
Glue joint
©/Ⓓ

2½"

Ⓜ

1½" deck screw

Ⓔ

Ⓔ

2" deck screws

Ⓑ

17½"

Ⓕ

6⅛"

Mitered ends

© 2" deck screws

#6 x ⅝" panhead screws

⁵⁄₆₄" pilot hole

⁵⁄₃₂" shank hole, countersunk

½" cove

© 7"

Ⓐ

POST

POST DETAIL

35½"
2½" 16" 3½"
½" 3½" Ⓑ
R=2½" ½" 3½" dado 1¾" deep
CROSSARM

1¼" 1⅛"
1½" 1½" rabbet 1⅛" deep (all sides)
⁵⁄₁₆" pilot hole 1¾" deep, centered
14" Ⓐ
1¾"
3½" dado 1¾" deep
3½"
46"
10¾" ⅜"
1½" 1½" dado ⅜" deep (all sides)
14¾"
3½"

3½" Ⓖ

5"
1¼"

#20 biscuit and slot

Ⓗ

Ⓗ

POST SUPPORT

27¼"

2" deck screw into part Ⓐ

Ⓖ

2" deck screw

⅜" chamfers

Ⓘ Ⓘ

Ⓟ

5° bevel

5"

½" cove

½" cove

POST SUPPORT TRIM DETAIL

5°
½" cove
Ⓘ

Ⓘ

6¼"

6½"

2 Cut the 3½" dadoes in the post and crossarm for the half-lap joint, where dimensioned in the Post Detail and Crossarm drawing in **7–1**. Also, cut the 1½" dadoes and 1½" rabbets around the post.

3 Drill the pilot hole centered in the top of the post for the post cap, where shown.

4 Mark the 2½" radius on the crossarm at both ends, where dimensioned in the Crossarm

drawing in **7–1**. Band-saw the contoured surface, and sand smooth.

5 To make the post bottom trim (C) and top trim (D), start by ripping two 52"-long strips from

Place the post on support blocks to make it easy to install the trim. Lightly spray the nonglued surfaces with water to accelerate curing of the glue.

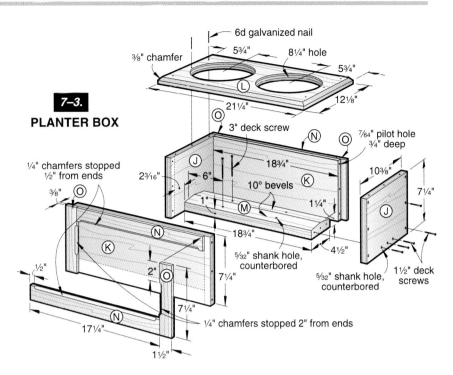

7–3.

PLANTER BOX

$\frac{3}{4}$" cedar. Make one strip $1\frac{7}{8}$" wide and the other $2\frac{1}{8}$" wide. Rout a $\frac{1}{2}$" cove on the $1\frac{7}{8}$"-wide strip, where shown on the Laminated Post Trim drawing in **7–1**. Glue (use waterproof polyurethane type) the top of the $1\frac{7}{8}$"-wide strip to the bottom of the $2\frac{1}{8}$"-wide strip, making their back edges flush. Clamp the strips together. After the glue dries, bevel-rip the blank to form the 8° bevel, where shown.

6 Miter-cut the bottom trim pieces (C) and top trim pieces (D) from the glued-up blank to fit the post. Glue, assemble, and secure the trim to the post with a band clamp, as shown in **7–2**.

7 Make the crossarm brackets (E) by first planing or ripping a piece of 4 x 4 cedar 30" long to

$2\frac{1}{2}$" thickness. Crosscut this piece to make two $3\frac{1}{2}$ x 14" blanks. Enlarge the Crossarm Bracket pattern (**7–6**) to full size, and make two photocopies of it. Adhere a pattern to each blank with spray adhesive. Then, cut the brackets to shape by bandsawing to the pattern lines, and drill the counterbored holes for mounting screws, where shown on the pattern. Also, rout a $\frac{1}{4}$" chamfer on the curved edges of the brackets, where shown.

8 From $\frac{3}{4}$" MDO plywood, cut the mailbox base (F) to size. The base fits inside the bottom of the mailbox. The bottom of the standard-size mailbox shown on *page 161* measures $\frac{3}{4}$ x $6\frac{1}{8}$ x $18\frac{1}{2}$". If your mailbox has a different size bottom, adjust the size of the base accordingly. Also, make the base 1" shorter in length

than the mailbox's bottom length to allow clearance for opening the mailbox door. Drill three countersunk shank holes in the base for attaching it to the crossarm with screws, where shown on the Exploded View drawing in **7–1**.

Make the Post Support

1 From $\frac{3}{4}$" MDO plywood, cut the post-support sides (G) and front and back pieces (H) to the sizes listed.

2 Using a biscuit joiner, cut slots for #20 biscuits in the post-support pieces, where shown on the Exploded View drawing (**7–1**). Glue and assemble the post support with biscuits. Clamp together and check for square. Then, rout a $\frac{3}{8}$" chamfer on the edges of the sides, where shown.

7–4.

Use the inner set of start/stop lines on your router fence when routing the stopped chamfers on the horizontal trim, and use the outer lines when routing the vertical trim.

3 From ¾"-thick cedar, cut a 5 x 28" blank for the trim (I). Rout a ½" cove on the top edge, where shown on the Exploded View drawing in **7–1**. Then, bevel-rip the blank to cut the 5° bevel along the top edge, where shown on the Post-Support Trim Detail in **7–1**, with the bevel sloping toward the cove.

4 Miter-cut the trim pieces from the blank to fit the post support. Glue and assemble the trim to the support, where shown on the Exploded View drawing in **7–1**, and secure with a band clamp.

Build the Planter Box

1 From ¾" MDO plywood, cut the planter box ends (J), sides (K), and top (L) to the sizes listed.

2 Using a jigsaw, cut two 8¼"-diameter holes in the top, where shown in **7–3** (*page 163*) to hold 9"-diameter pots. If you use a different size pot, adjust the hole size and spacing accordingly. Rout a ⅜" chamfer around the top, as shown.

3 Glue and clamp the ends (J) and sides (K) to form the box. After checking for square, drill pilot and counterbored shank holes for the screws through the ends and into the sides, and drive in the screws.

4 Make the mounting base (M) by first planing a 24"-long piece of 2 x 6 cedar to 1¼" thickness; then, trim it to the size listed. Bevel-rip the 10° bevels on the base. Drill four ⁵⁄₃₂" shank holes with counterbores in the base for the mounting screws.

5 Glue the base in the box. Drill three counterbored shank holes in the box ends for the screws, and drive in the screws.

6 Make the planter box's horizontal trim pieces (N) and vertical trim pieces (O) by first cutting a 3½ x 52" blank from ¾"-thick cedar. Plane the blank to ⅜" thickness. Rip two 1½"-wide strips from the blank. Now, cut the trim pieces to size from the strips.

7 On your router table, rout stopped ¼" chamfers on the trim pieces, where shown. To do this, mark two sets of start and stop lines on your router table fence for aligning the ends of the trim, as shown in **7–4**. To locate

7–5. **SUPPORT POST HOLE**

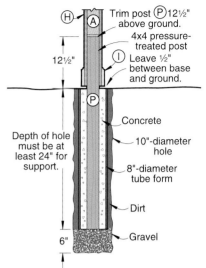

the marks, measure from the outside diameter of your chamfering bit at the table surface in both the infeed and outfeed directions. For the horizontal trim, measure ½" in each direction. For the vertical trim, measure 2" in each direction. Then, rout the chamfers on the trim, as shown.

8 Glue the trim to the box, where shown in **7–3**. Now, glue the top (L) to the box, making sure it is centered. Drive 6d galvanized nails through the top and into the box, where shown, and set the nailheads ¹⁄₁₆" below the surface.

Finish and Install the Mailbox Planter

1 Glue and clamp the crossarm (B) to the post (A). Then, position the assembly with the bottom of the post up, and glue and screw the crossarm brackets (E) to the post and crossarm, where shown on the Exploded View drawing in **7–1**.

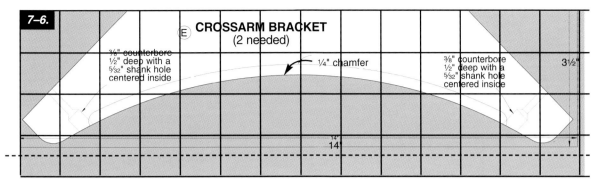

7–6.

(E) **CROSSARM BRACKET**
(2 needed)

⅜" counterbore
½" deep with a
5/32" shank hole
centered inside

¼" chamfer

⅜" counterbore
½" deep with a
5/32" shank hole
centered inside

3½"

14"

GRIDDED PATTERN 1 square =1"

2 Fill all counterbored screw holes, nail holes, and voids in plywood with a weather-resistant hardening wood putty. (Exterior wood putty was used for the mailbox planter shown on *page 161*.) Sand it flush when it is dry. Seal gaps in joints with paintable silicone caulk. Then, apply an exterior oil-based primer to all wood surfaces, including the inside surfaces of the planter box.

3 Mount the planter box and mailbox base (F) to the crossarm with screws, where shown on the Exploded View drawing in **7–1**. Leave a small gap between the back edge of the mailbox base and the post to allow for the rear thickness of the mailbox. (The gap for the mailbox planter shown on *page 161* is ⅛".) Thread the post cap onto the post.

4 Paint all exposed wood surfaces with an exterior latex paint of your choice.

5 Refer to the Shop Tip "Before You Dig" below for guidelines on locating and installing a mailbox. After determining a suitable location, install the 4 x 4 pressure-treated post (P) in the ground with concrete, as shown in **7–5**. Trim the post, where shown.

6 Finally, slide the post support (G/H/I) over the post, stopping ½" above the ground, and drive two deck screws through the support into the post, where shown on the Exploded View in **7–1**. Insert the mailbox post (A) into the support until the bottom post trim (C) contacts the post support. Secure the post in the support with two deck screws, where shown. Apply paint to the screwheads. Attach your mailbox to the base. Place two pots in the planter box openings and, when weather permits, plant some colorful flowers in the pots.

Before You Dig

Don't be too impatient to plant your new mailbox post. A quick call to your local postmaster could save you the aggravation of relocating the post (and possibly missing your mail delivery) if you put it in the wrong place. Requirements for locating a mailbox vary, depending on state and local regulations and roadside/curb conditions.

Generally, the U.S. Postal Service requires that mailboxes be installed with their bottoms 42 to 48" from the road surface and set back 6 to 8" from the front face of the curb. The mailbox shown on page 161 has a box height of approximately 44". If these specifications don't meet your local code, you can modify the length of the mailbox post or post support as appropriate.

Also, if you need to dig a new hole or make your existing hole deeper for proper post support, for your safety make sure that there are no underground utilities in the area. Many utility companies list a toll-free number in the Yellow Pages for information on locating underground utilities. If you have difficulty finding a number, call the North American One Call Referral System at 888/258-0808 for a number to call in your state.

NEIGHBORLY NUMBERS

With this project, no one—not even the pizza delivery man—will have trouble finding your house. By day, this sign offers a cheery welcome, and at night, its 4" backlighted numerals won't leave any question as to where you call home.

Neighborly numbers

Materials List for Neighborly Numbers

PART	FINISHED SIZE			MATL.	QTY.
	T	W	L		
A* signboard	1¹⁄₁₆"	3½"	16"	C	1
B sides	1¹⁄₁₆"	3½"	3½"	C	2
C cleats	1"	1"	3½"	C	2
D numerals	1¹⁄₁₆"	from pattern as required			

Length of signboard will vary, depending on the number of numerals required. Read text before cutting any material.
Material Key: C = Cedar.
Supplies: #8 x 1½" flathead wood screws; #8 x 2" flathead wood screws; #2 x ½" panhead screws; 12-volt license plate lights (NAPA #425-WD); 12.6-volt transformer 18-gauge lamp wires as needed; wire nuts; electrical tape; ⅜" dowel.

7–7.

CLEAT DETAIL

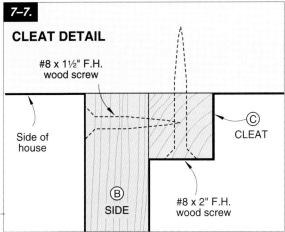

#8 x 1½" F.H. wood screw

Side of house

Ⓒ CLEAT

Ⓑ SIDE

#8 x 2" F.H. wood screw

7–8.

LIGHT DETAIL

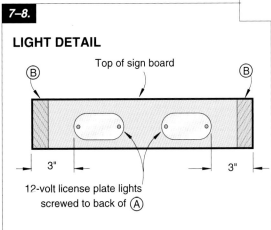

Top of sign board

Ⓑ   Ⓑ

3"   3"

12-volt license plate lights screwed to back of Ⓐ

7–9.

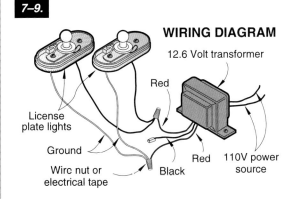

WIRING DIAGRAM

12.6 Volt transformer

Red

License plate lights

Ground

Wire nut or electrical tape

Black

Red

110V power source

Cut the Parts

1 From a 24" length of $1\frac{1}{16}$ x 6" cedar decking stock, rip $\frac{1}{2}$" off one edge, then reset the fence and rip a $3\frac{1}{2}$"-wide strip to square the edges. From this strip, crosscut one 16" length for the signboard (A), two $2\frac{1}{4}$" lengths for the sides (B), and two 1 x 1 x $3\frac{1}{2}$" pieces for the cleats (C). If your house has lap siding, crosscut one end of each side at an angle to offset the siding's slope.
➤ *Note: As shown on the previous page, the 16" signboard (A) holds four numerals. If you have more numerals in your street address, buy extra stock and add 4" to the length for each additional numeral (3" for numeral 1). Center the word Welcome on the signboard.*

2 Using carbon paper or a photocopier, make a full-size copy of the Welcome patterns and the numbers in **7–11** and **7–12**. Join the two Welcome patterns to complete the word, then cut around the outside, leaving a $\frac{1}{4}$" margin.

3 Scribe a faint line $\frac{7}{8}$" from the bottom on the face of the signboard, and $1\frac{3}{4}$" in from each end. Next, apply a light misting of spray adhesive to the back of the pattern. Then place the pattern on the board, aligning the bottom of the letters on the horizontal line, and centering them between the two vertical lines.

4 To recess the Welcome letters in the signboard, first angle the scrollsaw table to $2\frac{1}{2}°$ from perpendicular to make the bevel

text continues on page 170

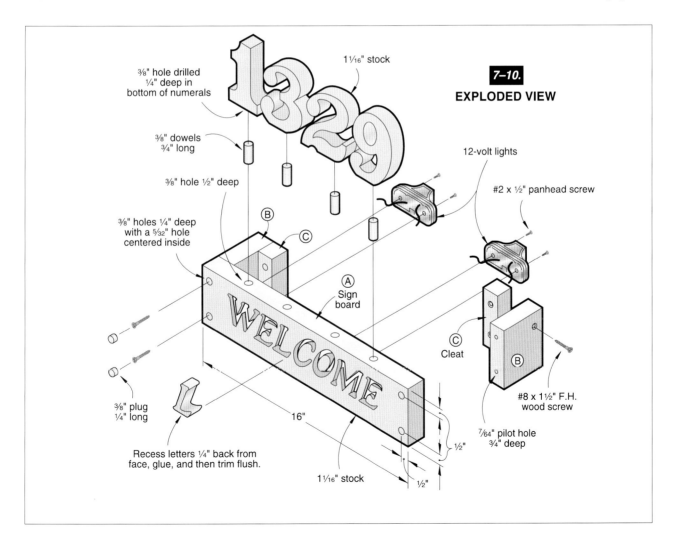

7–10.
EXPLODED VIEW

$\frac{3}{8}$" hole drilled $\frac{1}{4}$" deep in bottom of numerals

$1\frac{1}{16}$" stock

$\frac{3}{8}$" dowels $\frac{3}{4}$" long

$\frac{3}{8}$" hole $\frac{1}{2}$" deep

$\frac{3}{8}$" holes $\frac{1}{4}$" deep with a $\frac{5}{32}$" hole centered inside

12-volt lights

#2 x $\frac{1}{2}$" panhead screw

Ⓑ

Ⓒ

Ⓐ Sign board

Ⓒ Cleat

Ⓑ

$\frac{3}{8}$" plug $\frac{1}{4}$" long

16"

#8 x $1\frac{1}{2}$" F.H. wood screw

$\frac{7}{64}$" pilot hole $\frac{3}{4}$" deep

$\frac{1}{2}$"

Recess letters $\frac{1}{4}$" back from face, glue, and then trim flush.

$1\frac{1}{16}$" stock

$\frac{1}{2}$"

Drill a $\frac{1}{16}$" start hole.

Cut on dashed line for a 9.

Cut on dashed line for a 6.

7–11. HOUSE SIGN NUMBER PATTERNS

Drill a 1/16" start hole.

The number and letter patterns have been reduced to 80%. They must be enlarged to 125% for full size.

7–12. **HOUSE SIGN NUMBER PATTERNS (continued)**

cut. (Cutting on a bevel closes the saw kerf space when you push in the cutout.) Test by cutting a circle on a piece of $1\frac{1}{16}$" scrap, and then push the cutout into the piece to make certain it does not fall out. If it does fall out, tilt the table one more degree, and test again. (A #5 blade with $12\frac{1}{2}$ teeth per inch was used to recess the Welcome letters shown on *page 166*.)

5 You need to drill the start holes in the signboard at the same angle you'll be sawing the letters. To do this, place the board face up on your drill-press table. Next, put a $\frac{1}{8}$"-thick scrap under the piece, near the top edge, to tilt the word Welcome at an angle to the drill bit. Now, drill $\frac{1}{16}$" start holes, where shown on each letter. Before drilling the start hole for the inside line of the O letter, move the scrap to the bottom edge so it tilts the word Welcome in the opposite direction.

6 Thread your scrollsaw blade through the first start hole, and then saw around the letter. (Center the saw blade on the line.) When sawing, keep the letter on the downhill side of the blade to maintain the bevel. Cut around the remaining letters—except inside the O—the same way. When cutting out the inside of the letter O, keep the letter on the uphill side of the blade.

7 Rip and crosscut a 15" length (longer if you need more than four numerals) of the cedar stock to $4\frac{1}{2}$" width. Adhere the numeral

patterns to the face of the piece. (Run the grain horizontally through the letters to match the grain direction on the signboard.) Set your scrollsaw table perpendicular to the blade, and saw out each numeral. Sand the cut edges of the numerals to smooth the curves.

Assemble the Sign

1 Place the signboard face up on a flat surface and position $\frac{1}{4}$"-thick spacers under it at each end. Using water-resistant glue, stick each letter (except the O center) in its hole, pushing the letters through until they touch the surface underneath. After the glue dries, turn the board on its face, and glue the O center in its space, pushing it flush with the front face.

2 After the glue has dried, cut off the excess from the letters on the back side. (A tablesaw can be used.) Sand both front and back faces with 100-grit sandpaper. Mark, drill, and counterbore the four holes in the front face of the signboard, as detailed in **7–10** (*page 167*). Drill and countersink the holes in each side part (B) and the mounting cleats.

3 Arrange your numbers on the top edge of the signboard. Mark a vertical line on the back of the signboard to locate each dowel hole. Using these lines as guides, drill $\frac{3}{8}$" holes in the top edge of the signboard. Now, drill matching holes in the bottoms of the letters, as shown in **7–10**.

4 Glue and screw the sides to the back of the signboard. Using a $\frac{3}{8}$" plug cutter, make four cedar plugs. Glue them in the counterbored holes in the sign front.

5 Glue $\frac{3}{4}$" lengths of $\frac{3}{8}$" dowels in the holes in the numerals, then in holes in the top of the signboard. Align. After the glue dries, sand the numerals and plugs flush with the signboard's front.

Add the Lights

1 Mount the lights to the back of the signboard. (Use #2 x $\frac{1}{2}$" panhead screws, and chisel shallow grooves under the fixture to provide clearance for the wires.) Wire the two lights as shown on the wiring diagram in **7–9** (18-gauge lamp wire on the low-voltage side was used for the lights shown on *page 166*).

➤ *Note: To backlight the numerals, two 12-volt license-plate lights were attached upside down to the back of the signboard, and wired through a 12-volt transformer. You can wire a switch between the transformer and power supply, or use an existing light switch to control the sign light.*

2 Mount the two cleats to your house as shown on the Cleat Detail in **7–7**. Finally, complete the wiring.

PORCH-AND-PATIO CANDLE LANTERNS

Discover a clever method for cutting half-lap joints safely and accurately with this fun and practical project. You can mix and match three heights to suit your style.

➤ *Note: Buy glass before you make the lanterns so you can size the base rabbet. (One-eight-inch cord glass was used for the lanterns shown on this page.) To build the three different size lanterns, have your glass dealer cut four 3⁹⁄₁₆"-wide pieces each to 3¾", 4¾", and 5¾" in length.*

Cut the Stiles and Rails

1 Make the half-lap jig shown in **7–13** to cut the ends of the stiles (A) and rails (B).

2 Resaw and plane stock to ¼" thick for the stiles and rails. The stock thickness must equal the depth of the center dado in the half-lap jig for accurate joints. Rip the stock into ½"-wide strips. (You'll need about 21 feet of ¼ x ½" stock for the three lanterns shown on this page.)

3 Crosscut the stiles (A) and rails (B) to the lengths listed in the Materials List.

4 Install a ½" dado blade in your saw, and add an auxiliary fence. Locate the fence next

Candle lanterns

to the dado set. Now, lay a stile (A) into the dado in the half-lap jig. Place the jig face down on the saw table with the rabbeted edge against the auxiliary fence, trapping the stile against the table. Push the stile against the fence. Cut a half lap on one end of each stile, and both ends of each rail, where shown in **7–14** and as shown in **7–15**. Reset the fence, rotate the jig, and cut the half laps on the lower end of each stile.

Assemble the Sides

1 Referring to the Exploded View in (**7–16** on *page 173*), glue and assemble the four sides for each lantern, keeping each side square.

2 Cut a ⅛" groove ⅛" deep in each side assembly, where shown on the Exploded View in **7–16**.

Materials List for Candle Lanterns

PART	FINISHED SIZE			MATL.	QTY.
	T	W	L		
A* small lantern stiles	¼"	½"	4⅜"	M	8
A* medium lantern stiles	¼"	½"	5⅜"	M	8
A* large lantern stiles	¼"	½"	6⅜"	M	8
B* rails	¼"	½"	4¼"	M	24
C bases	⅜"	4"	4"	M	3
D* top trim	½"	1"	5⅛"	M	12

Parts initially cut oversized. See instructions.
Material Key: M = Mahogany.
Supplies: #8 x 1½" brass flathead wood screws; cord glass, four pieces each 3⁹⁄₁₆ x 3¾", 3⁹⁄₁₆ x 4¾", 3⁹⁄₁₆ x 5¾"; quick-set epoxy; 24-gauge x 4 x 10" copper.

3 Bevel both edges of each side to 45°. (A router table and a 45° chamfer bit can be used.)

Make the Bases

1 Cut the bases (C) to size. Cut the rabbets, where shown on the Exploded View (**7–16**) and Base Detail (**7–17**). Make the width of the rabbets ³⁄₁₆", plus the thickness of the glass.

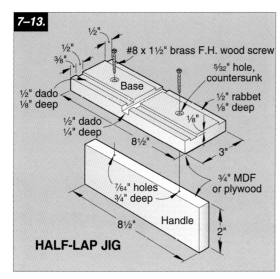

7–13.

½"
½"
⅜"
#8 x 1½" brass F.H. wood screw
5/32" hole, countersunk
Base
½" dado ⅛" deep
½" rabbet ⅛" deep
⅛"
½" dado ¼" deep
8½"
3"
¾" MDF or plywood
7/64" holes ¾" deep
8½"
Handle
2"
HALF-LAP JIG

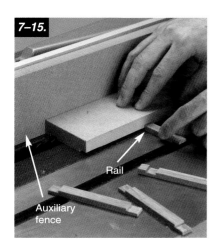

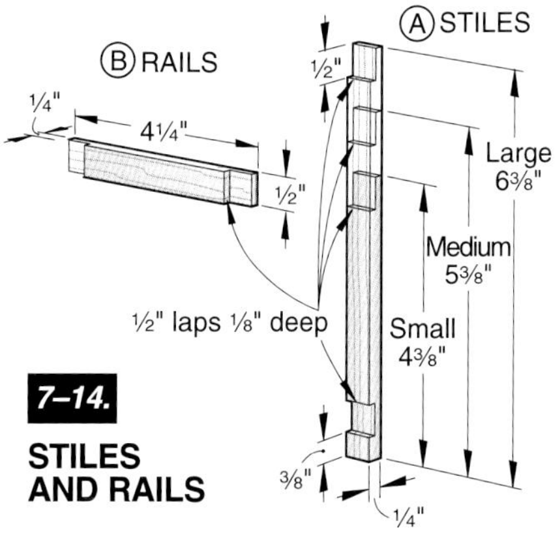

7–14.

STILES AND RAILS

Ⓑ RAILS
Ⓐ STILES
¼"
4¼"
½"
½"
½" laps ⅛" deep
½"
Large 6⅜"
Medium 5⅜"
Small 4⅜"
⅜"
¼"

7–15.

Rail
Auxiliary fence

Keep the end of the stile or rail pressed against the saw fence when you cut the half laps.

2 Drill four ¼" drainage holes in each base where shown on the Base Detail (**7–17**).

Glue Up the Lanterns and Make the Trim

1 Lay side by side four assembled lantern sides on the workbench with the grooved and mitered faces down. Put strips of masking tape across them at the top and the bottom. Carefully flip over the taped assemblies.

2 Apply glue to the sides' beveled edges. Place the tongue of the base (C) into the groove in one side (don't glue), and wrap

the other sides around the base, as shown in **7–18.** Similarly assemble the other two lanterns.

3 Cut three ½ x 1 x 24" pieces of stock for the top trim (D). Rout a ¼" roundover on one edge of each piece, as shown in *Step 1* of **7–19**.

4 Rabbet the stock with your tablesaw, as shown in *Step 2.*

5 Miter-cut the trim pieces (D) to length. Install the glass in the lantern, and dry-fit the trim pieces. The trim's ⅛" lip fits inside the glass. Glue and clamp the top trim frame together.

6 Cut out the copper iris motifs, using the pattern(s) in **7–20** and following the instructions in Cutting Copper.

shop TIP

Cutting Copper

For material, you'll need 24-gauge sheet copper, available at home centers or in hardware, crafts, and hobby stores. You'll also need a paper pattern, spray adhesive, ⅛" hardboard scrap, and the three-step process that follows.

❶ Cut the pattern. Rough-cut three pieces of ⅛" hardboard and two pieces of sheet copper to slightly larger than the paper pattern you wish to duplicate in copper. Using spray adhesive, make a sandwich blank, bonding together the five pieces, with the copper pieces separated by the wood. Adhere the pattern to the sandwich top. Now, drill any blade start-holes through the pattern for inside cuts, and scroll-saw the pattern to shape using a no. 2 blade (20 teeth per inch) at high speed.

➤ *Note: For quality control, avoid scrollsawing more than two pieces of copper in this manner at the same time.*

❷ Sand the burrs. Carefully pry apart the scrollsawn sandwich, wipe off the adhesive from the copper motif with paint thinner, and rinse with water.

Next, place the motif on a flat surface, and, with a sanding block and 220-grit sandpaper, sand the copper surface, removing any burrs along the edges of the piece.

❸ Apply the heat. Place a piece of scrap copper on scrapwood. Using a propane torch on a low setting, apply heat to the copper, keeping the nozzle about three inches from the surface. Move the flame back and forth to avoid scorching. What you want to achieve is a pinkish-orange coloration. Once you feel comfortable with the process, try heating the real copper motif.

7-16. **CANDLE LANTERNS EXPLODED VIEW**

¼" round-over

$5\frac{1}{8}$"

45° miters

Cord glass

$3\frac{9}{16}$"

24-gauge copper iris silhouette

$3\frac{3}{4}$" for small lantern
$4\frac{3}{4}$" for medium lantern
$5\frac{3}{4}$" for large lantern

45° miters

⅛" groove
⅛" deep

½"

$\frac{5}{16}$" rabbet
¼" deep

½"

½"
⅜"

4" 4"

⅛"

½"

$4\frac{1}{4}$"

7-17. **BASE DETAIL**

4"

$\frac{5}{16}$" rabbet
¼" deep

¼" drain holes

4"

⅝"

⅝"

$\frac{5}{16}$"

7-18.

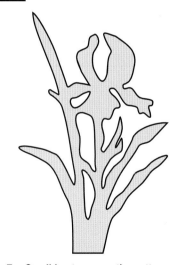

Wrap the sides around the base (C) and secure with strips of masking tape. Glue the miters, but don't glue the base into the grooves.

Finish the Parts and Install the Glass

1 Sand all the parts. Apply a clear, exterior finish.

2 Slide the glass into the base grooves, smooth side out. Epoxy a top trim assembly in place.

3 Apply a dab of quick-set epoxy to the back of each iris cutout. Now, position the iris cutouts on opposite sides of the lantern.

4 Set a votive candle at the base's center. A long fireplace match or a butane fire lighter makes lighting the wick easy.

7-19.

STEP 1

Fence

1"

½"

⅛"

¼" round-over bit

STEP 2

⅛" ⅜"

Fence

Tablesaw

¼" dado blade

7-20. **PATTERN FOR LANTERN**

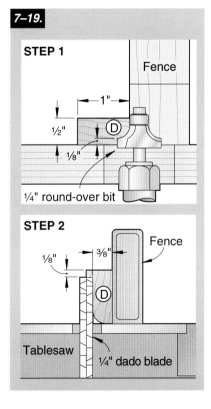

- For Small Lantern, use the pattern above at same size.
- For Medium Lantern, enlarge pattern above to 125%.
- For Large Lantern, enlarge pattern above to 160%.

Birdbath with colorful apple cutouts

CUTTING DIAGRAM

$1\frac{1}{2}$ x $3\frac{1}{2}$ x 96" (2 x 4) Cedar

$1\frac{1}{2}$ x $5\frac{1}{2}$ x 96" (2 x 6) Cedar   *Plane or resaw to thickness listed in the Materials List.

Materials List for Beauty of a Birdbath

PART	FINISHED SIZE			MATL.	QTY.
	T	W	L		
A bowl supports	$1\frac{1}{2}$"	3"	$11\frac{1}{16}$"	C	3
B feet	$1\frac{1}{2}$"	3"	$10\frac{1}{4}$"	C	3
C wide upright	$1\frac{1}{4}$"	$5\frac{1}{4}$"	18"	C	3
D thin uprights	$1\frac{1}{4}$"	$1\frac{1}{2}$"	18"	C	3

Material Key: C = Cedar.
Supplies: $\frac{5}{16}$ x $3\frac{1}{2}$" and $\frac{5}{16}$ x $4\frac{1}{2}$" lag bolts; $\frac{5}{16}$" flat washers; clear lacquer; red and green exterior enamel; clear exterior finish; silicone adhesive; $19\frac{3}{4}$"-diameter plastic flower-pot saucer.

7–21.
BIRDBATH EXPLODED VIEW

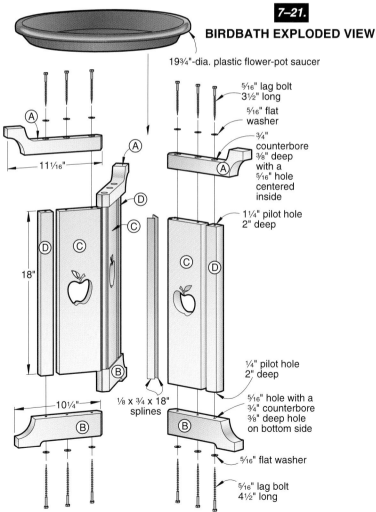

$19\frac{3}{4}$"-dia. plastic flower-pot saucer

$\frac{5}{16}$" lag bolt $3\frac{1}{2}$" long

$\frac{5}{16}$" flat washer

$\frac{3}{4}$" counterbore $\frac{3}{8}$" deep with a $\frac{5}{16}$" hole centered inside

$1\frac{1}{4}$" pilot hole 2" deep

$11\frac{1}{16}$"

18"

$10\frac{1}{4}$"

$\frac{1}{8}$ x $\frac{3}{4}$ x 18" splines

$\frac{1}{4}$" pilot hole 2" deep

$\frac{5}{16}$" hole with a $\frac{3}{4}$" counterbore $\frac{3}{8}$" deep hole on bottom side

$\frac{5}{16}$" flat washer

$\frac{5}{16}$" lag bolt $4\frac{1}{2}$" long

BEAUTY OF A BIRDBATH

This easy-to-build project is a real paradise for birds—and with its trio of attractive apple cutouts, it also brings a touch of Eden to your lawn or garden.

Saw the Parts

1 Cut all parts to the sizes shown in the Materials List. You can saw all of them from two pieces of western red cedar— a 2 x 4 and a 2 x 6, each 8' long. Cedar lumber is often knotty, so select boards that will allow you to avoid the worst of the knots.

7–22.

To saw the spline slots in the wide uprights, tilt the saw blade 30° from vertical. Position the rip fence to locate the slot correctly.

7–23.

A fence on the drill-press table helps center the counterbores and bolt holes in the bowl supports and feet.

7–24.

Work from the bottom upward when assembling the splined three-way joint.

2 Saw 30° bevels on both sides of one end of each bowl support (A) and foot (B). The bevels should meet at the middle of the end, as shown by the Top Section (Top View) drawing in **7–26** and the Exploded View drawing (**7–21**). To cut the bevels uniformly, tilt your tablesaw's blade 30° from vertical, then set up your miter gauge with an auxiliary fence. Position a stop block on the auxiliary fence to cut each set of parts.

3 Bevel-rip each wide upright (C) along both sides of one edge. The bevels should meet at the middle of the edge. After sawing the bevels, sand or hand-plane a slight flat at the point, shown in the Wide Upright drawing (**7–28**). This will create space for excess glue to squeeze into at assembly time.

4 Saw spline slots in the wide uprights where shown in the Wide Upright drawing (**7–28**). To accomplish this, leave the saw blade tilted to 30°, and attach an auxiliary fence to your saw's fence. Adjust the fence position and the blade elevation to cut the spline slots as dimensioned. Then, saw the slots, standing the workpiece on its beveled edge as shown in **7–22**.

5 Lay out the end profiles on the bowl supports (A) and feet (B), following the radii and dimensions shown on the Parts View drawings (**7–29**). Band-saw the pieces to shape, remaining

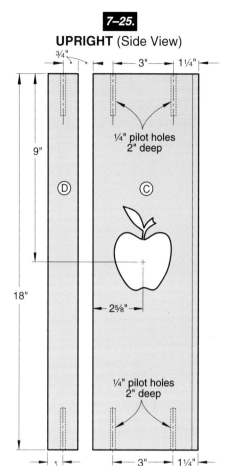

7–25.

UPRIGHT (Side View)

¾"

3"

1¼"

9"

18"

D

C

¼" pilot holes 2" deep

2⅝"

¼" pilot holes 2" deep

¾"

3"

1¼"

slightly outside the layout lines. Then, sand to the lines.

6 Saw three ⅛ x ¾ x 18" plywood or hardboard splines for the center joint.

Drill the Holes

1 Lay out the hole centerlines on the edges of parts A and B, following the dimensions in the Parts View drawings (**7–29**). Draw the lines on the edges that will be counterbored in the base.

2 At the center of the edge, bore a ¾" hole ⅜" deep at each centerline. (You can use a drill press and Forstner bit, positioning a fence to center the bit on the edge.)

3 After drilling the counterbores, change to a $5/16$" bit, and drill through the center of the counterbores, as shown in **7–23**. The fence you set for drilling the counterbores will help you drill the bolt holes accurately.

Add the Apples

1 Make three full-size copies of the pattern for the apple design (**7–27**).

2 Apply a copy of the pattern to each wide upright where shown. Rubber cement or spray

adhesive will hold it. (If you use spray adhesive, follow the manufacturer's instructions for temporary bonding.) Point the leaf away from the upright's beveled edge.

3 Drill a blade start-hole inside the apple, and scroll-saw along the pattern line. A #7 blade, .045 x .018" with 12 teeth per inch, works well for scroll-sawing the thick cedar. Sand as necessary.

4 Paint the sawn apple edge red and the leaf and stem green. Here's how to do this: First, brush clear lacquer onto the sawn edges and the surfaces around the apples, extending about 1" from the cutout. The lacquer helps keep

the paint from wicking into the wood grain, and masks the faces around the cutout for a tidier paint job.

After the lacquer dries, paint the leaf and stem green. Let that dry, then paint the apple red. To paint the cutouts, you can spray some aerosol enamel into a paper cup, and brush it on.

5 After the paint dries, sand the faces of the wide uprights to remove the lacquer.

6 Rout or sand $1/8$" roundovers on all parts. Do not round over the ends of the upright members (C, D). Finish-sand all parts.

shop TIP

Lock the birdbath's triple uprights together with three vertical splines. Cut them from $1/8$"-thick plywood or hardboard (not solid stock) for maximum durability, and assemble the joint with water-resistant glue.

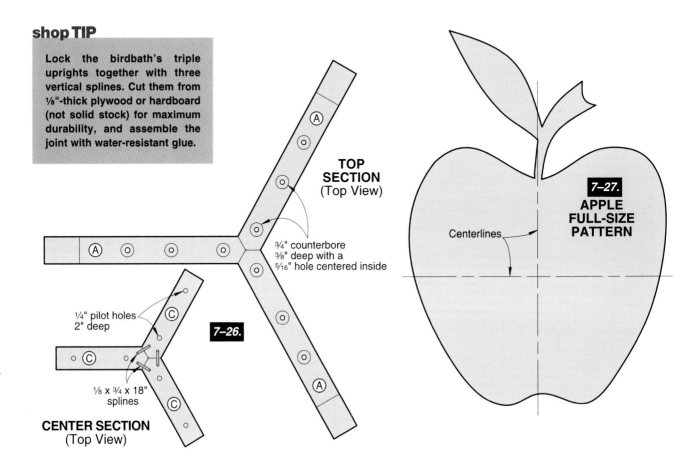

TOP SECTION (Top View)

$3/4$" counterbore $3/8$" deep with a $5/16$" hole centered inside

7–26.

$1/4$" pilot holes 2" deep

$1/8$ x $3/4$ x 18" splines

CENTER SECTION (Top View)

Centerlines

7–27.
APPLE FULL-SIZE PATTERN

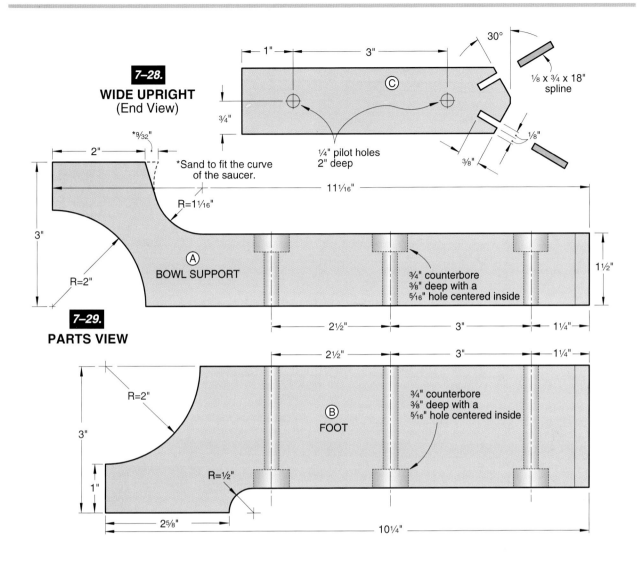

7–28.
WIDE UPRIGHT
(End View)

$\frac{1}{8}$ x $\frac{3}{4}$ x 18" spline

30°

$\frac{1}{4}$" pilot holes 2" deep

*Sand to fit the curve of the saucer.

$\Ⓐ$ BOWL SUPPORT

$\frac{3}{4}$" counterbore $\frac{3}{8}$" deep with a $\frac{5}{16}$" hole centered inside

7–29.
PARTS VIEW

$\Ⓑ$ FOOT

$\frac{3}{4}$" counterbore $\frac{3}{8}$" deep with a $\frac{5}{16}$" hole centered inside

Assemble the Birdbath

1 Dry-assemble the three wide uprights (C) and three splines. To fit the parts together, insert a spline into the right-hand bevel of each part C. Then, bring the parts together at the bottom, and working upward, push the three-way joint together, as shown in **7–24** *(page 175)*. Pull the joint firmly together with two band clamps to check the fit.

2 When you're satisfied that the parts fit together properly, undo the clamps, separate the parts, and reassemble with water-resistant glue. Clamp until dry.

3 Stand the assembled wide uprights on end, top end up. Place the three bowl supports on top of the assembly, centering each from side to side with their junction over the center of the upright assembly.

4 Hold the bowl supports in position, and mark the centers for pilot holes into the uprights. Inserting a pencil or one of the lag bolts through the holes in part A will mark the centers.

5 Drill $\frac{1}{4}$" pilot holes 2" deep. Attach the bowl supports to the wide uprights with $\frac{5}{16}$ x $3\frac{1}{2}$" lag bolts and washers. A socket wrench ($\frac{1}{2}$") makes driving the bolts into the counterbores easier.

6 Stand the assembly on its top, and drill pilot holes for the feet (B), following the same procedure. Attach the feet to the uprights with $\frac{5}{16}$ x $4\frac{1}{2}$" lag bolts and washers.

7 Slide the narrow uprights (D) into position, mark pilot hole centers in both ends, and drill the pilot holes. Bolt the uprights into place. Handscrew clamps will hold the narrow uprights while you drive in the bolts.

8 Sand the assembled birdbath base, and apply a clear, penetrating, exterior finish. After it dries, place the tray in the bowl supports. The birdbath shown on *page 174* was designed to hold a $19\frac{3}{4}$"-diameter plastic flower-pot saucer for a 24" pot.

You should be able to purchase a similar saucer at a garden-supply shop. You can secure the light-weight bowl to the bowl supports with a few dabs of silicone adhesive.

Suet feeder

SUET FEEDER

B irds flock to the high-energy nourishment provided by suet cakes. This good-looking feeder features a top that slides up the support cables, allowing you to replenish suet quickly and easily. Whether you build one for your-self or a dozen for gifts, you'll surely gain a flock of feathered friends.

Make the Top and Sides

1 Cut the top (A) to size. (Mahogany was used for the suet feeder shown here, but redwood, cedar, teak, or cypress also work.)

2 Raise your tablesaw blade $1\frac{1}{2}$" above the surface of the saw table. Angle the blade 25° from vertical and away from the rip fence. Position the fence $\frac{1}{4}$" away from the bottom edge of the blade.

3 Fit your tablesaw with a zero-clearance insert. Using a push block or fence saddle to keep your fingers safely away from the blade, bevel-rip both ends of the top (A). Now, bevel-rip the edges of the top piece. Cut the two sides (B) to 3 x 8". To house the $\frac{1}{2}$" hardware cloth (galvanized wire mesh), cut a pair of $\frac{1}{8}$" grooves $\frac{1}{4}$" deep on the inside face of each, where shown in **7–31**.

4 Mark the location, and cut a $\frac{3}{4}$" dado $\frac{1}{4}$" deep in each side (B) where dimensioned.

7–30.

SUET FEEDER EXPLODED VIEW

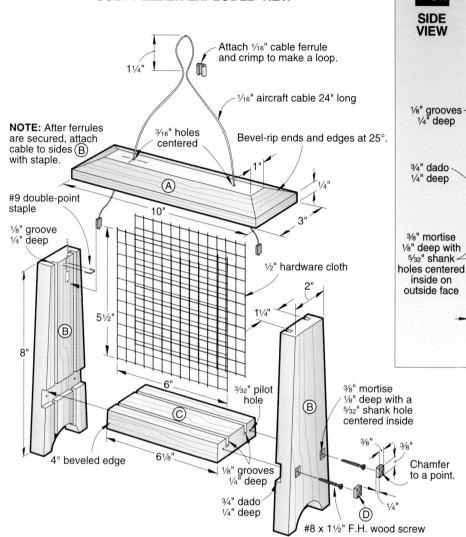

Attach $\frac{1}{16}$" cable ferrule and crimp to make a loop.

$1\frac{1}{4}$"

$\frac{1}{16}$" aircraft cable 24" long

NOTE: After ferrules are secured, attach cable to sides (B) with staple.

$\frac{3}{16}$" holes centered

Bevel-rip ends and edges at 25°.

1"

$\frac{1}{4}$"

(A)

#9 double-point staple

10"

3"

$\frac{1}{8}$" groove $\frac{1}{4}$" deep

$\frac{1}{2}$" hardware cloth

(B)

$5\frac{1}{2}$"

8"

2"

$1\frac{1}{4}$"

(B)

6"

$\frac{3}{32}$" pilot hole

(C)

$\frac{3}{8}$" mortise $\frac{1}{8}$" deep with a $\frac{5}{32}$" shank hole centered inside

4° beveled edge

$6\frac{1}{8}$"

$\frac{1}{8}$" grooves $\frac{1}{4}$" deep

$\frac{3}{4}$" dado $\frac{1}{4}$" deep

$\frac{3}{8}$" $\frac{3}{8}$"

Chamfer to a point.

$\frac{1}{4}$"

(D)

#8 x $1\frac{1}{2}$" F.H. wood screw

7–31.

SIDE VIEW

2"

$\frac{1}{4}$" $\frac{1}{8}$" $\frac{1}{8}$" $\frac{1}{4}$"

$\frac{1}{2}$" $1\frac{1}{4}$" $\frac{1}{2}$"

(B)

SIDE (inside face shown)

$\frac{1}{8}$" grooves $\frac{1}{4}$" deep

$\frac{3}{4}$" dado $\frac{1}{4}$" deep

$\frac{3}{16}$"

8"

$\frac{3}{8}$" mortise $\frac{1}{8}$" deep with $\frac{5}{32}$" shank holes centered inside on outside face

$\frac{3}{4}$"

$\frac{3}{8}$"

$1\frac{3}{4}$"

R = 1"

$\frac{5}{8}$"

$\frac{3}{4}$"

$\frac{3}{8}$"

3"

Materials List for Suet Feeder					
PART	**FINISHED SIZE**			**MATL.**	**QTY.**
	T	**W**	**L**		
A top	$\frac{3}{4}$"	3"	10"	C	1
B sides	$\frac{3}{4}$"	3"	8"	C	2
C* bottom	$\frac{3}{4}$"	$2\frac{3}{4}$"	$6\frac{1}{8}$"	C	1
D* plugs	$\frac{3}{8}$"	$\frac{3}{8}$"	$\frac{1}{4}$"	W	4

**Pieces cut initially oversize; see instructions.*
Materials Key: C = Choice (mahogany, redwood, cedar, teak, or cypress); W = walnut or other dark hardwood.
Supplies: $\frac{1}{2}$ x $5\frac{1}{2}$ x 6" hardware cloth (2 pieces); $\frac{1}{16}$" aircraft cable 24" long; $\frac{1}{16}$" cable ferrules (3); # 8 x $1\frac{1}{2}$" flathead wood screws (4); #9 double-point staples (2).

7–32.

With the pieces still separate, staple the ferruled ends of the cable to the inside face of the sides.

5 Locate and cut a pair of $\frac{3}{8}$"-square mortises $\frac{1}{8}$" deep on the outside face of each side (B), centering the mortises over the dado. (They can be cut with a mortising machine or formed by drilling a hole and squaring the sides with a chisel.) Now, drill a $\frac{5}{32}$" shank hole, centered in each mortise.

6 Mark the angled cuts along both edges of the sides (B) and the radiused bottom ends where dimensioned. Cut and sand to the marked lines to complete each side piece.

Add the Bottom and Prepare for Assembly

1 Cut the bottom (C) to size, bevel-ripping the edges at 4°. Take your time when ripping the edges—you want the beveled edges of C to be flush with the angled outside edges of B.

2 Cut two $\frac{1}{8}$" grooves $\frac{1}{4}$" deep on the top face of the bottom (C) to align with the previously cut grooves in the sides (B).

3 Clamp (but do not glue) the bottom (C) between the sides (B). Check for square. Center the top (A) on the assembly, and mark the hole locations for the cable on the bottom side of the top. The holes should be flush with the inside face of each side piece. Remove the top and drill the $\frac{3}{16}$" holes where marked.

4 With the sides (B) and bottom (C) still dry-clamped together, use a tin snips to cut two pieces of $\frac{1}{2}$" hardware cloth to fit snugly into the $\frac{1}{8}$" grooves. Next, using the shank holes in the mortises as guides, drill pilot holes $1\frac{1}{4}$" deep into the ends of the bottom.

5 Remove the clamp, and disassemble the sides (B) and bottom (C). Sand all four pieces.

Add the Cable and Assemble the Feeder

1 Cut a piece of $\frac{1}{16}$" aircraft cable to 24" in length. Loop the top center section where shown in **7–30** (*page 179*), and crimp a cable ferrule $1\frac{1}{4}$" from the top end of the loop. Slide the ends of the cable through the holes in the top (A). Then, crimp a ferrule onto each end of the cable where shown in **7–30**.

2 Staple just above the ferrules on the ends of the cable to secure the cable to the inside face of each side (B), as shown in **7–32**.

3 Cut a 10" length of $\frac{3}{8}$"-square dark stock. (Walnut was used for the Suet Feeder on *page 178*. You could also use mahogany and a black permanent marker to stain the stock after sanding the chamfers.) Sand chamfers to form a point on both ends. (This can be done with a disc sander.) Next, crosscut a $\frac{1}{4}$"-long plug (D) from each end of the stock. Repeat the process to form another set of plugs.

4 Fit the bottom (C) between the sides (B), aligning the grooves with those in the sides. Drive the screws through the previously drilled shank and pilot holes. Check for square. Glue one plug in each mortise to hide the screwhead. Apply a clear exterior penetrating-oil finish. Slide the two pieces of hardware cloth in place, insert a cake of suet, and hang it at an inviting location.

BIRDHOUSE GONE CUCKOO

It might seem a little cuckoo to build a clock that doesn't tell time, but in this case, it's a smart move, because the mock clock is actually a decorative birdhouse to add charm to your deck or patio.

Make the Birdhouse

1 Cut the parts to the sizes shown in the Materials List. Refer to the Parts View drawing (**7–33**), then saw the peaked gable on the back and front (A, D). For a neat job, lay out the cutting line on the front (D). Stack that part on top of the back (A), with the good side of each facing upward. Fasten them together temporarily with double-faced tape. Make sure the top edges and both side edges are flush before sawing the cutting lines on your tablesaw. Separate the pieces.

Mock clock birdhouse

4 Tilt your tablesaw blade to cut a 30° bevel. Saw a bevel along the top of each side, taking care to cut the low side of the bevel on the outside of each piece. Also bevel each roof piece (C), where shown on the Exploded View (**7–34**). On those, the long side of the bevel goes to the outside.

5 Chuck a $\frac{3}{8}$" roundover bit in your table-mounted router. Rout along both sides on the back edge of the bottom (E) to create a rounded edge.

6 Mark the position for the entry hole on the front. Then, with a drill press and holesaw, bore the entry hole. Drill the mounting hole in the back and the three ventilation holes on each side.

7 Using #17 x 1" brads and glue, attach the two sides (B) to the back (A). (If your birdhouse will go outside, use water-resistant glue.) The sides fasten onto the edges of the back. Then, nail and glue the front (D) to the sides. The front fits onto the edges of the sides. Set the nails and fill the holes.

8 Position the bottom (E) inside the assembly where shown. On each side, drill a $\frac{7}{64}$" pilot hole through the side (B) into the edge of the bottom. The bottom will pivot on screws in these holes to open for cleaning. Then drill a pilot hole centered on the front (D) into the bottom's edge.

Materials List for Birdhouse Gone Cuckoo

PART	FINISHED SIZE			MATL.	QTY.
	T	W	L		
A back	$\frac{1}{2}$"	5"	$14\frac{3}{8}$"	C	1
B sides	$\frac{1}{2}$"	$5\frac{1}{2}$"	$12\frac{1}{2}$"	C	2
C roofs	$\frac{1}{2}$"	5"	7"	C	2
D front	$\frac{1}{2}$"	6"	$8\frac{3}{4}$"	C	1
E bottom	$\frac{1}{2}$"	$4\frac{7}{8}$"	5"	C	1
F shutter	$\frac{1}{8}$"	$\frac{3}{4}$"	$1\frac{1}{2}$"	HB	2
G pendulum	$\frac{1}{8}$"	$2\frac{1}{4}$"	$4\frac{1}{2}$"	HB	1
H hands	$\frac{1}{8}$"	$1\frac{1}{2}$"	3"	HB	1

Materials Key: HB = Tempered hardboard, C = Cedar.
Supplies: Metal clock face with Arabic numeral, $4\frac{1}{4}$" diameter; #17 x 1" brads; slow-set epoxy.

2 Photocopy the full-size pattern for the lower portion of the back (**7–35**). Affix the pattern to the back (A) with rubber cement or spray adhesive, and then band-saw or scroll-saw the curved bottom.

3 Copy the pattern for the bottom portion of the side (**7–34**). Stack the two side pieces (B) for cutting, with the good sides out. Adhere the pattern to the top piece, then band-saw or scroll-saw the profile.

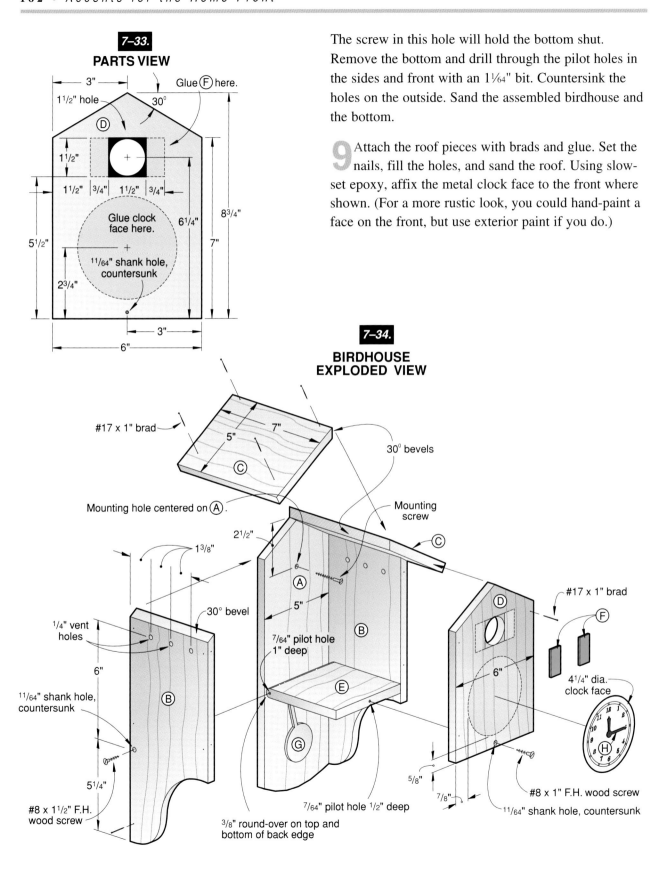

7–33.
PARTS VIEW

3"
Glue (F) here.
$1^1/2$" hole
30°
(D)
$1^1/2$"
$1^1/2$" | $3/4$" | $1^1/2$" | $3/4$"
Glue clock face here.
$5^1/2$"
$6^1/4$"
$8^3/4$"
7"
$^{11}/_{64}$" shank hole, countersunk
$2^3/4$"
3"
6"

The screw in this hole will hold the bottom shut. Remove the bottom and drill through the pilot holes in the sides and front with an $1^1/_{64}$" bit. Countersink the holes on the outside. Sand the assembled birdhouse and the bottom.

9 Attach the roof pieces with brads and glue. Set the nails, fill the holes, and sand the roof. Using slow-set epoxy, affix the metal clock face to the front where shown. (For a more rustic look, you could hand-paint a face on the front, but use exterior paint if you do.)

7–34.
BIRDHOUSE
EXPLODED VIEW

#17 x 1" brad
5"
7"
(C)
30° bevels
Mounting hole centered on (A).
Mounting screw
(C)
$2^1/2$"
$1^3/8$"
(A)
#17 x 1" brad
(F)
$1/4$" vent holes
30° bevel
5"
(B)
(D)
6"
6"
$7/64$" pilot hole 1" deep
$^{11}/_{64}$" shank hole, countersunk
(B)
(E)
$4^1/4$" dia. clock face
(G)
(H)
$5^1/4$"
$5/8$"
#8 x $1^1/2$" F.H. wood screw
$7/8$"
#8 x 1" F.H. wood screw
$7/64$" pilot hole $1/2$" deep
$3/8$" round-over on top and bottom of back edge
$^{11}/_{64}$" shank hole, countersunk

7-35.
BACK AND PENDULUM PATTERNS

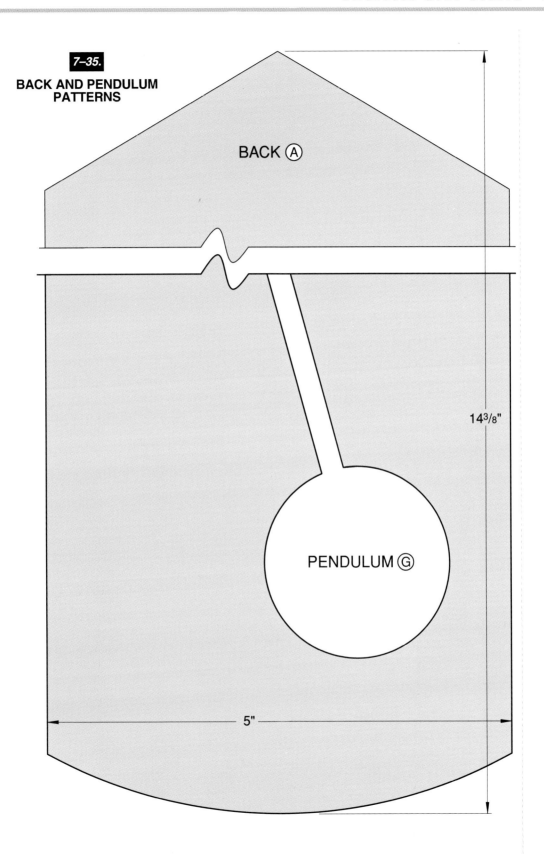

BACK Ⓐ

14³/₈"

PENDULUM Ⓖ

5"

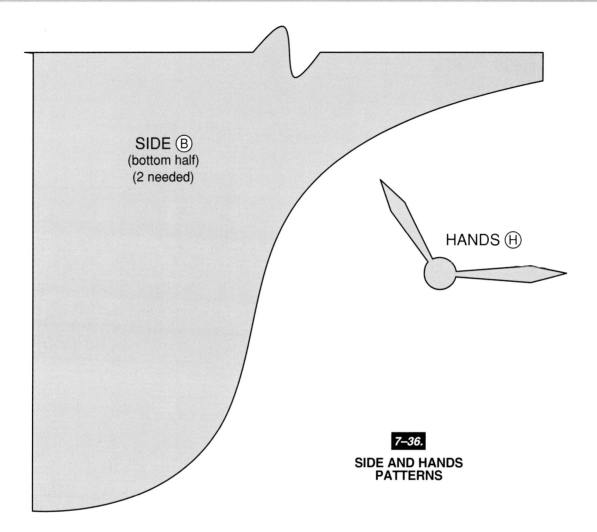

SIDE Ⓑ
(bottom half)
(2 needed)

HANDS Ⓗ

7–36.
SIDE AND HANDS
PATTERNS

10 Trace the patterns for the hands and pendulum (**7–35** and **7–36**) onto the ⅛" stock. (You can cut the hands, pendulum, and the shutters from tempered hardboard.) Scroll-saw the hands and pendulum. Paint them copper or gold. Paint one face and all edges of each shutter (F) green. Draw a square around the entry hole where shown, then paint black inside it.

11 Glue the hands, pendulum, and shutters into place. The pendulum should appear to pivot behind the top of the face. Apply two coats of an exterior finish to the birdhouse and the bottom. Install the bottom, and dab matching paint on the screwheads.

BUILDING FOR BIRDS

The same trees, shrubs, and flowering plants that make your yard beautiful and inviting for humans can also provide food and shelter for birds in your region. Here's how to accommodate the ones you want to attract.

You'll find few things in life as pleasant as watching and listening to the activity of song-birds. From dawn to dusk they display boundless energy as they nest, feed, and raise their families. But today's cities and suburbs usually lack the old-growth trees that provide nesting cavities for the dozens of songbird species that require them.

Luckily, it's easy and fun to

Twelve Important Do's and Don'ts

❶ *Don't build a house just for "birds." Build houses, nesting boxes, and other structures with specific types of birds in mind because each species has different size and entrance-hole requirements. See the chart for suggested dimensions and allowable entrance-hole sizes for songbird species. (A hole cut to the correct size keeps unwanted birds out. For instance, sparrows will only enter holes $1\frac{1}{4}$ and larger.) Drill all holes—entrance and ventilation—at a slight upward angle to prevent rain from blowing in.*

❷ *Wood is the preferred material for birdhouses. (Metal does not provide heat insulation.) But use only pine, cedar, redwood, or cypress—not treated wood or plywood—for functional, nontoxic birdhouses.*

❸ *Assemble cedar and redwood birdhouses with galvanized screws or concrete-coated or ring-shank nails. If you don't, the joints will eventually loosen. For pine houses, you can use standard fasteners.*

❹ *Always build the birdhouse so that the sides enclose the floor. This keeps rain from seeping into the sidewall/floor joint. To slow deterioration of the floor, recess it $\frac{1}{4}"$.*

❺ *Make the front edge of the birdhouse roof overhang at least 2". The overhang protects the entrance hole from rain and keeps predators from reaching in from above.*

❻ *So that you can clean out birdhouses semiannually (before and after nesting season), always build them with a hinged side or roof. Use rustproof hinges and either a screw closure or a pair of roofing nails and wire to discourage raiding by raccoons and other predators.*

❼ *Drill at least four $\frac{3}{8}"$-diameter drain holes in the bottom of a house (except on some special designs for bluebirds and wood duck nesting boxes). Drain holes allow rain and condensation to escape. Clear them every time you clean the house.*

❽ *For ventilation in all birdhouses (except duck boxes), drill at least two $\frac{5}{8}"$ holes near the top on both sides. Wood provides great insulation, so interiors can overheat unless hot air can escape.*

❾ *Never put a perch on a birdhouse. Perches encourage sparrows and European starlings, which compete with—and often kill—songbirds.*

❿ *Do not paint, stain, or apply preservative to the inside of a birdhouse. You may, however, coat the outside back of a birdhouse (the most prone to rot) with preservative, or paint the entire exterior with exterior-grade enamel.*

Firmly attach all houses to a support post, building, or tree. If you think that cats and/or raccoons will be a problem with a post mount, discourage them with sheet-metal shields tacked to the post. Or, smear the post with grease. Wren houses can swing suspended from an eave or tree limb from two points instead of just one.

⓫ *How high should you mount a birdhouse? Most songbirds nest within a range of 4 to 15 feet aboveground. Remember, though, that you need to reach it for cleaning. And remember to provide shade for at least part of the day.*

⓬ *To avoid territorial fights, space houses for songbirds at least 20 feet apart. Bluebirds are especially contentious, so space their houses 100 yards apart. Purple martins and wildfowl, such as wood ducks, don't defend their territories as fiercely as do other species.*

shop TIP

Many heavily blooming and fruit-bearing shrubs and trees are favorite feeding places for birds. To keep the birds from devouring your strawberries, raspberries, or cherries, plant a few mulberry, serviceberry, or elderberry bushes for them. Similarly, Virginia creeper may divert the birds from a crop of grapes.

Entrance-Hole Sizes and Hole Heights for Building for Birds

BIRD	ENTRANCE-HOLE SIZE	HEIGHT
Bluebird	1⅜ x 2¼" oval	7"
Wren	1" diameter	7"
Chickadee	1⅛" diameter	7"
House finch	2" diameter	4"
Nuthatch	1¼" diameter	6"
Warbler	1¼" diameter	7"
Titmouse	1¼" diameter	6"
Wood duck	3 x 4" oval	18"

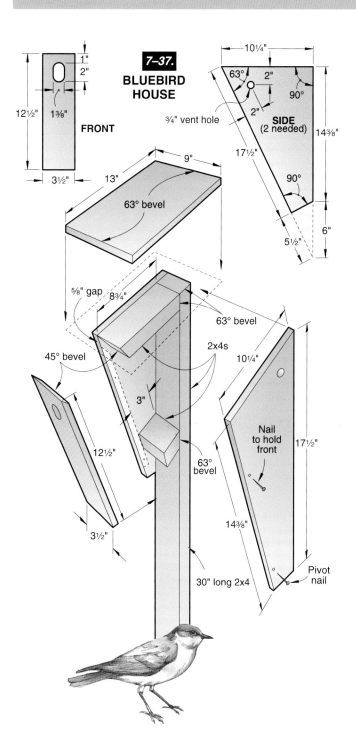

7–37. BLUEBIRD HOUSE

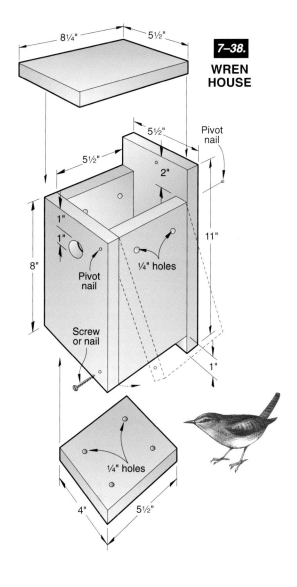

7–38. WREN HOUSE

simulate these natural nesting spots with birdhouses designed specifically for songbirds, not pesty house sparrows and starlings. You can even give nature

a hand by providing boxes for waterfowl. Illus. **7–40** shows a nest box suited for wood ducks.

For advice and guidelines on proper home building, follow the

construction pointers and "Twelve Important Do's and Don'ts." You'll guarantee yourself some of nature's finest entertainment.

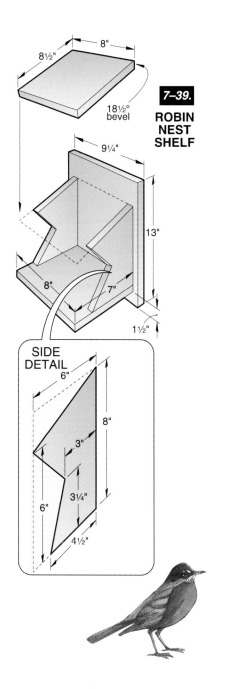

7-39.
ROBIN NEST SHELF

SIDE DETAIL

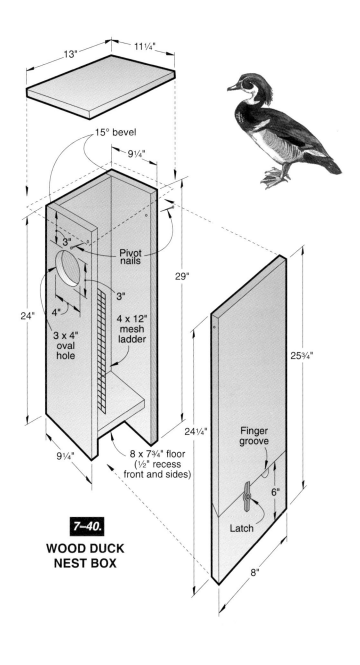

7-40.
WOOD DUCK NEST BOX

METRIC EQUIVALENTS CHART
Inches to Millimeters and Centimeters

MM=MILLIMETERS   CM=CENTIMETERS

INCHES	MM	CM	INCHES	CM	INCHES	CM
1/8	3	0.3	9	22.9	30	76.2
1/4	6	0.6	10	25.4	31	78.7
3/8	10	1.0	11	27.9	32	81.3
1/2	13	1.3	12	30.5	33	83.8
5/8	16	1.6	13	33.0	34	86.4
3/4	19	1.9	14	35.6	35	88.9
7/8	22	2.2	15	38.1	36	91.4
1	25	2.5	16	40.6	37	94.0
1 1/4	32	3.2	17	43.2	38	96.5
1 1/2	38	3.8	18	45.7	39	99.1
1 3/4	44	4.4	19	48.3	48	101.6
2	51	5.1	20	50.8	41	104.1
2 1/2	64	6.4	21	53.3	42	106.7
3	76	7.6	22	55.9	43	109.2
3 1/2	89	8.9	23	58.4	44	111.8
4	102	10.2	24	61.0	45	114.3
4 1/2	114	11.4	25	63.5	46	116.8
5	127	12.7	26	66.0	47	119.4
6	152	15.2	27	68.6	48	121.9

Index

Credits

Special thanks to the following people or companies for their contributions:

Dave Algren, of the Minnesota Dept. of Natural Resources

Nongame Wildlife Division, for project design in Chapter 7

David Ashe, for project design in Chapters 6 and 7

Marty Baldwin, for photographs in Chapters 3, 4, 5, 6, and 7

Kevin Boyle, for text in Chapters 5 and 6 and project designs in Chapters 5 and 7

Bob Calmer, for photographs in Chapter 4

James R. Downing, for project designs in Chapter 3, 4, 5, and 7

Kim Downing, for illustrations in Chapters 3, 4, and 7

Owen Duvall, for text in Chapters 5, 6, and 7

Randall Foshee, for illustrations in Chapter 4

Thomas Frazier, for text in Chapter 7

Chuck Hedlund, for text in Chapters 3, 5, and 6, and for project designs in Chapters 6 and 7

Hetherington Photography, for photographs in Chapters 2, 3, 4, 5, 6, and 7

Hopkins Associates, for photographs in Chapters 3, 4, 6, and 7

Lorna Johnson, for drawings in Chapters 3, 4, 5, 6, and 7

Larry Johnston, for text in Chapter 7

Marlen Kemmet, for producing material used in Chapters 3 and 4, supplying text for Chapters 5 and 7, and project design in Chapter 7

Roxanne LeMoine, for illustrations in Chapters 3, 5, 6, and 7

Jeff Mertz, for project designs in Chapters 3 and 5

Mike Mittermeier, for illustrations in Chapters 6 and 7

Donovan Nagel, for project design in Chapter 6

Paula Nelson, for project design in Chapter 6

Ode Design, for illustrations in Chapter 4, 6, and 7

Bruce Pierce, for project design in Chapter 5

Robert J. Settich, for text in Chapter 6

Peter J. Stephano, for text in Chapter 7

Jim Stevensen, for illustrations in Chapter 7

David Stone, for text in Chapter 6

Jan Svec, for text in Chapters 3 and 5

Jerry Tedrow, for project design in Chapter 5

Bill Zaun, for illustrations in Chapters 3 and 4

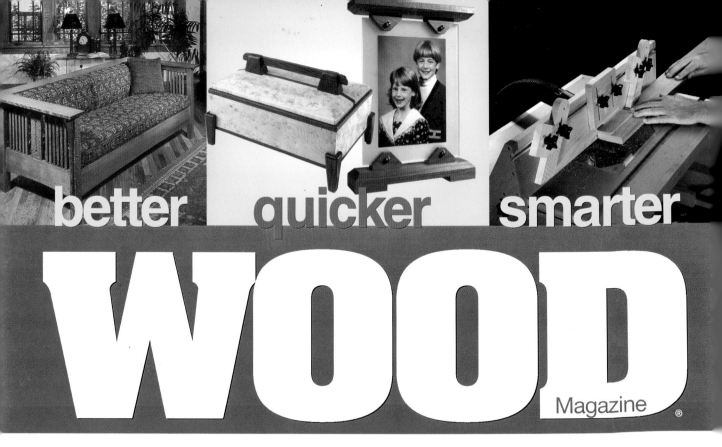

better   quicker   smarter

WOOD Magazine

Only WOOD Magazine delivers the
woodworking know-how you need, including ...

Over ... year

Tim

Ing

Ful

Am

Sp

...st deal on

Apply glue beads 1" ap...

Custom...
to width...

WOOD MAGAZINE
SHOP
TESTED
APPROVED

This seal is your assurance that we build
every project, verify every fact, and test every
reviewed tool in our workshop to guarantee
your success and complete satisfaction.

call 1-800-374-9663

or visit us online at
www.woodonline.com

chamfer

MADISON-JEFFERSON COUNTY PUBLIC LIBRARY